Finding Monte Cristo

Finding Monte Cristo
*Alexandre Dumas and
the French Atlantic World*

Eric Martone

McFarland & Company, Inc., Publishers
Jefferson, North Carolina

LIBRARY OF CONGRESS CATALOGUING-IN-PUBLICATION DATA

Names: Martone, Eric, author.
Title: Finding Monte Cristo : Alexandre Dumas and the French Atlantic world / Eric Martone.
Description: Jefferson, North Carolina : McFarland & Company, Inc., Publishers, 2018 | Includes bibliographical references and index.
Identifiers: LCCN 2018023997 | ISBN 9781476673202 (softcover : acid free paper) ∞
Subjects: LCSH: Dumas, Alexandre, 1802–1870—Influence. | France—Colonies—America—Intellectual life. | France—Colonies—Africa—Intellectual life. | France—Colonies—America—Race relations. | France—Colonies—Africa—Race relations. | France—Race relations.
Classification: LCC PQ2230 .M317 2018 | DDC 843/.7—dc23
LC record available at https://lccn.loc.gov/2018023997

BRITISH LIBRARY CATALOGUING DATA ARE AVAILABLE

ISBN (print) 978-1-4766-7320-2
ISBN (ebook) 978-1-4766-3339-8

© 2018 Eric Martone. All rights reserved

No part of this book may be reproduced or transmitted in any form or by any means, electronic or mechanical, including photocopying or recording, or by any information storage and retrieval system, without permission in writing from the publisher.

Front cover: Alexandre Dumas in an 1855 photograph; background map of the Atlantic Ocean, 1831 (iStock)

Printed in the United States of America

McFarland & Company, Inc., Publishers
 Box 611, Jefferson, North Carolina 28640
 www.mcfarlandpub.com

To my children,
Domenic and Gianna

Table of Contents

Acknowledgments	viii
Preface	1
Introduction	3
1. "Black Skin, White Masks" in Nineteenth-Century France: Alexandre Dumas and His Experiences as an Exotic Other, 1829–1870	13
2. A Hero of Assimilation: Alexandre Dumas and the French Caribbean, 1848–1930	50
3. Creating a Local Black Identity in a Global Context: Alexandre Dumas as an African American *Lieu de Mémoire*, 1840–1930	67
4. Forgetting Alexandre Dumas: *Négritude* and the French Caribbean and Africa in the Mid-Twentieth Century, 1930–1970	94
5. Alexandre Dumas *Métissé*: Celebrating Dumas as a Symbol of a Diverse France, 1946–2002	111
Chapter Notes	151
Bibliography	180
Index	201

Acknowledgments

I would like to thank the peer reviewers for their constructive feedback and many useful suggestions for revision that helped improve the final product.

I would also like to thank some of my former mentors, past students, and current colleagues at Mercy College for their support, including Michael Nolan at Western Connecticut State University, who guided me into the world of being a historian of modern France and to whom I owe much thanks; Benjamin Freud; Andrew Peiser; Mel Wermuth; and Howard Miller. In various ways, talking to them about European and French history, Dumas, or academia helped me improve my work and maintain a degree of sanity and/or encouraged me along the path toward the completion of this book.

Chapter 3 presents a slightly revised version of my article "Creating a Local Black Identity in a Global Context: The French Writer Alexandre Dumas as an African American *Lieu de Mémoire*," which appeared in the *Journal of Global History* 5, no. 3 (2010): 395–422, published by Cambridge University Press. It is reprinted with permission. I would like to thank the journal's editors for believing in my work and their willingness to work with me through several revisions at the start of my academic career. Further, some of the material in this book, particularly in Chapter 5, includes revised elements of my introduction to a collection I edited, *The Black Musketeer: Reevaluating Alexandre Dumas in the Francophone World*, which was published by Cambridge Scholars in 2011, and reappropriated in this book with permission. All images and photographs are my own unless otherwise indicated.

The research that went into some of the chapters of my doctoral dissertation at Stony Brook University inspired what ultimately became this book. At Stony Brook, I would particularly like to thank my advisor, Wolf

Acknowledgments

Schäfer, and dissertation committee member Larry Frohman for their help, guidance, and encouragement. Other members of the History Department I would like to acknowledge with my appreciation include Shirley Lim and Herman Lebovics, my initial advisor, who assisted me through my first year of doctoral studies and encouraged me to pursue a dissertation topic on Dumas and French identity. I would also like to thank E. Anthony Hurley of the Africana Studies Department for serving as a member of my dissertation committee. I am indebted to them for their willingness to involve themselves in my academic development at that stage, as it allowed me to ascend to my current professional career path and the realization of many longtime goals.

Over the course of its many incarnations, this project has received funding in the form of a Bernadotte E. Schmitt Grant from the American Historical Association and a faculty development grant from Mercy College. The Institute for European Studies at Indiana University, Bloomington, also financially supported work on an interdisciplinary secondary school unit, which is available on its website, based on some of the research that found its way into this book.

Finally, but certainly not least, I would to thank my wife, Nicole; our two children, Domenic and Gianna; and the rest of my family for their love and support.

Preface

Some children want to be movie stars or music icons when they grow up, while still others dream of becoming professional athletes. What I wanted was to be a professional historian. History has never relinquished its hold over my imagination, and for that I am grateful. While many factors and people around me (including many wonderful social studies teachers) helped direct my interests into the field of European history, my interest in French history in particular was nurtured by one individual: Alexandre Dumas. As a child, I remember being excited about such television events as the mini-series on Napoleon and Josephine starring Armand Assante and Jacqueline Bisset, or devouring historical fiction novels featuring the adventures of heroes like Horatio Hornblower and the Scarlet Pimpernel. But Dumas's works were my favorite. Figures and dramas from long ago were brought vividly to life, and the adventures of the musketeers—Athos, Porthos, Aramis, and d'Artagnan—and the Count of Monte Cristo thrilled me like no other books could. Not only did these characters become my heroes, but so did their creator and Dumas's France became a primary subject of my historical focus as I grew into adulthood. In many ways, then, the journey that culminated in this book was launched many decades ago when I was but a child.

Dumas, however, has inspired more individuals than just me. His nineteenth-century works have been continuously translated into different languages and many remain in print. Films and television series based on his work, like BBC America's popular series *The Musketeers* (2014–2016), continue to enthrall global audiences. Dumas is among the most famous literary figures in Western literature and one of the "great men" of France—as well as arguably the most famous person of black descent in the nineteenth-century Atlantic world—and it might be logical to conclude that he is studied widely. But surprisingly, scholars—especially those

Preface

writing in English—have generally not taken much notice of him. Studies exploring Dumas's status as a French national symbol have been particularly absent. Historians have the power to give voice to untold stories, and when I became a historian, voicing Dumas's story seemed a logical choice. Hopefully, this book is one significant step toward remedying this oversight in academic scholarship, helping to unveil Dumas's extremely significant and multifaceted legacy.

Although *Finding Monte Cristo* is academic in nature, it has been designed to be accessible to the general educated reader. Targeted toward diverse scholars, students, and the educated public, the book was written under the assumption that the reader does not have detailed knowledge about European and French history, French literature, or Dumas. Readers looking for a biography of Dumas, however, will be disappointed. While the book does provide some biographical details for those unfamiliar with Dumas and his life, its focus is on Dumas as a symbolic entity and as a reference point for French and francophone individuals within the Atlantic region in their ongoing efforts to re-conceptualize their place in the world and relationship with French culture. At the heart of these efforts has been the question of how to reconcile his dual racial identities within his context as a French symbol. In a figurative sense, then, the book is not about one Alexandre Dumas, but many. Each chapter focuses on a different, particular perception of Dumas and how/why these perceptions change over time. A major factor influencing these conceptions of Dumas is shifting concepts of global diversity.

I hope this book will make a significant addition to works on Dumas. Since limited scholarship exists linking Dumas to a broader notion of French Atlantic history, some of the material addressed in this book, such as a review of French social discourse leading to Dumas's interment in the Panthéon in Paris, Dumas's bid for election as a representative of Guadeloupe in the French government, and the way he became a figure within the African American cultural memory, are new to Dumas scholarship. By exploring his historical, cultural and social significance, particularly in relation to national identity and ethnic history, it provides a new dimension to our understanding of Dumas.

Introduction

Alexandre Dumas (1802–1870), the popular nineteenth-century French author of *The Three Musketeers* and *The Count of Monte Cristo*, has never been out of the public spotlight.[1] Dumas's books, still in print and the source of countless television and cinematic adaptations, have made him an enduring symbol of French culture. Born in Villers-Cotterêts in northern France in 1802, Dumas was the son of a French Revolutionary War general born on the French colony of St. Domingue (now Haiti) to an African slave and a Norman aristocrat.[2] After his father died in 1806, the young Dumas had only a modest upbringing and basic education. Among Dumas's early teachers was the venerable cleric Abbé Grégoire, first as a student in the latter's school and later through private lessons. France was a tumultuous place in Dumas's youth, as the Revolution gave way to Napoleon, who in turn was followed by the monarchy's restoration. After arriving in Paris from the French countryside as a young man with modest assets, Dumas moonlighted as a writer while working as a clerk to the duc d'Orléans, the future King Louis-Philippe (r. 1830–1848). Dumas, however, quickly established himself as a dramatist during the 1830s, leading the French Romantic movement. He subsequently became interested in composing novels during the 1840s. In keeping with customary practices in French theater, however, he often worked with collaborators. His literary output also included travel books, short stories, memoirs, poems, several journals, children's books, and even a cookbook. Dumas's vast body of work and seemingly enormous energy inspired nineteenth-century French historian Jules Michelet to declare him "a force of nature, like an inextinguishable volcano or a great American river."[3]

As a result of his celebrity, biographies of Dumas have flooded bookstores' shelves since his own lifetime. Therefore, one might have assumed that a film about a part of his life—notably his literary collaboration with

Introduction

the uncredited but duly financially compensated Auguste Maquet—would not have created an uproar. But in 2010, a new film entitled *L'autre Dumas* ("The Other Dumas"), inspired by a well-received stage play, received strong protests from several sectors within French society.[4] The major "revelation" in the film's plot—that Dumas's most beloved pieces of literature, signed by him alone, were in fact co-authored with another writer—was not the major problem.[5] Nor was it the film's exploration of who should be viewed as these works' "true" author and the nature of authorship. The problem was internationally-renowned French actor Gérard Depardieu, who played the role of Dumas in the film. The film's producers, seeking to better market the film within France and abroad, wanted to cast a star well known across the globe. Further, they wanted an actor whom they felt could embody Dumas's larger-than-life persona.[6] Depardieu, a larger-than-life and critically-acclaimed actor who had appeared in countless European and American films, seemed the perfect choice.[7]

The problem with Depardieu was that for some he had the wrong skin color. Dumas, as the grandson of a Caribbean slave and Norman noble, was of biracial descent. Mocked in France during his lifetime for his ancestry and "exotic" appearance, Dumas nevertheless rose to become a famous and prosperous figure. Contemporary France, whose social make-up has changed radically during the course of the twentieth and early twenty-first centuries, has found itself at a crossroads. While we often think of France as a "European" country, it is a trans-regional polity currently comprised of 18 administrative regions (as well as additional territorial collectivities), only 13 of which are located in Continental Europe; the rest are situated in the Caribbean, South America, and Africa.[8] With its overseas population and an increasing percentage of its Continental European population comprised of individuals with connections to its previous colonial empires in the Caribbean, Africa, and Asia, the French state has had to rethink its colonial past as well as its present to establish political and cultural cohesiveness.[9] Much of this rethinking has been encouraged by French citizens with connections to France's former colonial empire, as several civil groups representing French minorities have emerged in recent decades. Such groups were among those who most vehemently protested *L'autre Dumas*. For example, Patrick Lozès, then president of the *Conseil Représentatif des Associations Noires* in France, described the casting of Depardieu as "very shocking" and "insulting," adding that the film "puts in question the place of black and ethnically

Introduction

mixed actors in French cinema, for they cannot play any roles other than those of their type, whereas white actors, considered 'universal' actors, can play all sorts of characters irrespective of their appearance." He then asked rhetorically, "In 150 years' time could the role of Barack Obama be played in a film by a white actor with a fuzzy wig? Can Martin Luther King be played by a white?" Claude Ribbe, a French social activist and writer of French Caribbean descent, was especially intense in his condemnation of the film, arguing that it was "ridiculous" to conceive Depardieu as Dumas, an "Afro-descendant [and] son of a Haitian slave." He thus called for "all the descendants of slaves or indigenous populations" in France to rally against this "racist" offense and form of "colonial propaganda" he perceived as intended to obscure the legacy of one of the "heroes of diversity." Yet, the debate was not confined to intellectuals and activists. Former "Miss France," Sonia Rolland, of Rwandan descent, even weighed in on the matter, arguing that Dumas had "black African physical characteristics," but in the film was depicted in appearance as a typical white Frenchman, thereby demonstrating "debates about national identity."[10]

The film's producers seemingly meant no offense; they had never even considered a non-white actor for the role because to them Dumas was neither a colonial nor black figure. In its coverage of this controversy, the international press often erroneously reported that Depardieu darkened his face and donned an "Afro-wig" to play Dumas. While Depardieu wore a gray curly-haired wig, there was no intent on the part of the filmmakers to have Depardieu appear to be of black descent, which such articles implied. If this was true, that would mean the filmmakers believed Dumas should have been depicted as demonstrating characteristics stereotypical of individuals of black descent. However, when the controversy arose, the filmmakers merely fell on the rationale that Dumas was also three-quarters white and had attributes stereotypical of individuals of white descent to defend their choice. As the director remarked, Dumas "had blue eyes." Thus, the casting of an actor of black or mixed racial descent instead of Depardieu would have been "a historical error."[11] Therefore, it was not a case of filmmakers casting a white actor to portray Dumas as a figure of black descent, but whether the figure of Dumas should be depicted as "white" or "black." Such competing and contested views of Dumas reflect wider efforts to create "official" memories for the French people of the French state who themselves have competing memories as a result of the French state's steady progression to a global polity as a

Introduction

result of colonialism, which therefore served as a globalizing agent. What it means to be French has not been static, but rather in a constant state of revision during the past two centuries despite proclamations of cultural continuity.

These debates over whether Dumas should be depicted as "black" or "white" revealed another crucial problem: within the contemporary cultural and political discussions over French history in the public sphere, certain individuals (like Dumas) had become "heroes" to French citizens with connections to the former French colonial empire. The French tendency over the past century and a half since Dumas's death was to rationalize the writer's mixed racial ancestry by "white-washing" him, or perceiving his white ancestry as dominant and obscuring his colonial connections to make him a French symbol more in line with existing mainstream notions of French national identity. As we shall see, this image was often reinforced visually through illustrations of the writer in various editions of his work, advertisements, and elsewhere in the public sphere. By casting a white actor like Depardieu in the role, the film thus obscured Dumas's black, colonial heritage and denied France's contemporary minority groups of both a "hero of diversity" and a role in shaping French history and culture. National histories, which help shape the collective memory, tell the story of how the nation, a social construction, came to be by erasing the incongruities through which national identity was formed into a linear and seemingly inevitable progression, thereby fashioning modern national consciousness. As Étienne Balibar has argued, the "formation of the nation thus appears as the fulfillment of a 'project' stretching over centuries, in which there are different stages and moments of coming to self-awareness."[12] Nations' histories, or stories, are thus concerned with introducing and shaping characters and events to reflect some type of narrative leading to the endpoint of the present. In other words, history creates a story of how the present (or the endpoint) came to be. Groups not included or perceived in contributing to this developmental process are conceived as excluded from the present nation, or at least as its illegitimate heirs.

The broader context of the debate over whether Dumas should be portrayed as "black" or "white," then, was the ostracization of the contributions of individuals with colonial connections from French culture and the national memory. As Pierre-André Taguieff has suggested, twentieth- and twenty-first-century French racism, despite the French borrowing of certain American terms, did not actually emerge from a strict white-black

Introduction

historical divide as in the United States, but as a tension between "authentic/native" citizens and increasingly-numerous "ethnic outsiders," arriving mostly from former French colonies.[13] Therefore, comments in 1925 from Arthur Schomburg, a Puerto Rican historian of black descent, regarding the African American experience were equally applicable to France in 2010, with the substitution of a "native"/colonial French divide for the black/white American one: "By virtue of their being regarded as something 'exceptional' ... [earlier individuals of achievement who were of black descent were] unfairly disassociated from the group, and group credit lost accordingly.... [Consequently] the first true writing of Negro history is the rewriting of ... our common American history [to represent] historical truth."[14]

French historical memory thus became the battleground on which intellectuals from the former colonies in the Caribbean and Africa sought to define themselves and their places in French history, which cast people of color outside its narrative of development. In this battle, they were influenced by wider trends within the Atlantic word, forged by links dating from earlier colonialism and the slave trade. Among the first steps in this process, as Schomburg's earlier comment suggests, was the identification and celebration of "heroes" in the past—a phrase echoed in Ribbe's comments quoted earlier. Since history creates a story outlining the nation's development, and who constitutes membership within it, the rewriting of history is a crucial first step for the renegotiation of national identity. Reconciliation attempts within the French context thus sought in general to change the discourse of belonging to renegotiate membership and memory to lay the groundwork for an attempt to join the mainstream.[15] During the 1990s and 2000s, increasingly mobilized minority groups made reconciliation demands rooted in claims against colonialism as a system of domination and exploitation whose effects continued to cause socio-economic damage to the descendants of those who lived under the system. Such efforts were nevertheless "forward looking" because they conceived such recognition as a way to transform "the current conditions of deprivation suffered by the groups in question" through "broader projects of social transformation."[16] Such a history echoed Martinican intellectual Frantz Fanon's postwar views, which called for "a new history of man" written by the victors in conjunction with the vanquished to not only record Europe's accomplishments, "but also its crimes."[17] Emerging from this context, the campaign to portray Dumas as a symbol, or hero, of diversity

Introduction

was a campaign to rewrite the history of France and the broader French Atlantic world, which we can perceive as the francophone cultural region of Europe, Africa, and the Caribbean forged during colonialism and the slave trade.

Yet Dumas had not always been a "hero" among minority groups within France or individuals within France's colonies and overseas territories. Nor was their image of Dumas the only one circulating within the collective French consciousness in both the metropole, or the French mainland in Europe, and the French Atlantic world. Such groups have struggled in their quest to establish their own sense of self. Globalization generally refers to a process across national and other boundaries involving accelerated flows or intensified connections of capital, people, technology, information, etc. But it can also involve disconnections, marginalization, and dispossession. Dumas, as can be gleaned from his works and miscellaneous writings, including his portrayals of race and slavery, had ambivalent and contradictory feelings about his own identity. Dumas's black colonial heritage was a frequent source of alienation during his lifetime, as he faced various forms of racism in France. Nevertheless, he wrote that he retained a "strong emotion" for France "contrary to what one might expect."[18] I would suggest, however, that he expressed a sense of "homelessness," or unbelonging, through his identification with "Monte Cristo." His celebrated novel, *The Count of Monte Cristo*, was itself inspired by his Caribbean family history.[19] But throughout his life, Dumas incessantly, almost obsessively, named things after "Monte Cristo." As Dumas scholar Gilles Henry notes, it was his "personal signification of choice." As part of this "name fetish," he founded two journals entitled *Monte-Cristo* (in 1854 and 1867) and gave the name to one of his boats, a novel, a four-part play, and—perhaps most tellingly—the famous and idealistic château in which he lived.[20] Through his feelings of alienation and dislocation, which will be explored in more detail in Chapter 1, Dumas constantly strove to find a place where he could belong, an isolated figure in search for an identity within a larger collectivity. For him, "Monte Cristo" seemed to symbolize the goal of this quest.

Just as "Monte Cristo" proved to be an elusive reality for Dumas, it proved equally elusive to those struggling to overcome slavery and its legacies in the French Atlantic world. But in Dumas, they found someone within whom they could either emulate, identity with, or, in some cases, use as a model of how not to be. The "colonial psyche," resulting in the

Introduction

inferiorization of indigenous or local cultures of the colonized, prompted various responses from the colonized, including a subconscious internalization of the colonizer's attitude that resulted in an attempt to adopt the colonizer's culture (which usually met some form of rejection from the colonizer), an attempt to renegotiate the colonizer's national identity to include its overseas and colonial populations, and attempts to develop unique ethnic identities. In all situations, a feeling of dislocation (or "homelessness"), alienness—in other words, a sense of "otherness"—needed to be overcome.[21] In overcoming this sense of "otherness," they were in essence searching for "home," a place where they felt that they belonged and could be treated as equals. Other groups within the Atlantic world were also searching for their own figurative "Monte Cristo" and in so doing, they also often turned toward Dumas, among the most recognizable figures of black descent. Even in his own lifetime, Dumas increasingly became a symbolic element within a French Atlantic world shaped by the African slave trade and its consequences, becoming an integral component within its memorial traditions. These memorial traditions, however, were shaped within the context of the French Atlantic world's colonial and former colonial population's quest to find a sense of belonging, a sense of "home." Despite having never been to the Caribbean, Dumas's struggles to define his own identity foreshadowed those of twentieth-century Caribbean and American intellectuals searching for their figurative "Monte Cristo." Thus, as Caribbean writer Antonio Benitez-Rojo argued, "skin color ... represents ... the color imposed by the violence of conquest and colonization ... and resented for its uprootedness; it is ... a kind of no-man's land where the permanent battle for the Caribbean self's fragmented identity is fought."[22] The French metropolitan reception to Dumas's dark skin color and black features were reminders that he did not seem to belong to the French nation. His alienation fostered a quest of self-identity that encouraged him to explore his African and Caribbean roots. Dumas's ambivalent sense of self demonstrated Chris Bongie's assertion that Creole identity includes a sense of being "a fragment, a part of some greater whole from which it is in exile and to which it must be related—in an act of (never completed) completion that is ... a loss of the ... traditionally conceived, unified and unitary, identity."[23] As Benitez-Rojo has articulated it, "one never becomes a wholly Caribbean person; one is always something more or something less, one ... is always involved for both the near and the long term in search for Caribbeanness, and ... the

Introduction

illusion of having completed it."[24] In response to this quest, Caribbean theorists Jean Barnabé, Patrick Chamoiseau, and Raphaël Confiant, similar to intellectual Édouard Glissant and his conception of *métissage*, have spoken of the ideology of *créolité* as "the annihilation of the false universality of monolingualism and purity." They celebrate diversity and cultural mixings, which create a "kaleidoscopic," or mosaic, identity; Dumas, too, came to espouse a more cosmopolitan outlook to national identities.[25]

Together, we will trace the relationship between the French Atlantic world and Dumas both during his lifetime and after his death, analyzing political and intellectual discourse to examine the social memorializations of Dumas over time. In so doing, we will illuminate some prominent underlying global tensions and causes instigating these varying (re)conceptualizations of the writer relating to the reconciliation of his dual racial identities. Fluctuating portraits of Dumas suggest that we can perceive him not only as a historical figure, but also as a *lieu de mémoire*, which can be defined as "any significant entity, whether material or non-material in nature, which by dint of human will or the work of time has become a symbolic element of the memorial heritage of any community."[26] Since *lieux de mémoire* are in a state of flux, the Dumas of memory has had its own complex construction dating from Dumas's lifetime. Obviously, the two are linked—the Dumas of memory derives its reality from the Dumas of history, and the Dumas of history is reconstituted in retrospect by the Dumas of memory—but the constant re-imagining of Dumas over time has created a mythical one of memory selectively distinct from the historical one, imposing an intentionally anachronistic interpretation on the Dumas of the past to create one to meet the needs of different presents. Intellectuals from the late nineteenth century onward created their own imaginative vision of what Dumas had represented in order to employ it ideologically to support or counter the prevailing mainstream view(s) of French Atlantic history. Through the course of this book, we will explore Dumas's reception during his lifetime and immediately afterward in both the French metropole (Chapter 1) and overseas France (Chapter 2) as a result of his biraciality and French Caribbean colonial heritage; his nineteenth- and early twentieth-century reception among African Americans, including francophone African Americans, which influenced his interpretation within the French Atlantic world (Chapter 3); his reception among *Négritude* writers in the French Caribbean and Africa during the first half of the twentieth century (Chapter 4); and finally his reception among

Introduction

contemporary French intellectuals in both the French metropole and overseas departments and territories, which culminated in his interment in the Panthéon, a mausoleum for France's most honored citizens, in 2002 (Chapter 5). Such re-imaginings have perhaps realized Dumas's 1850s prophecy, "I shall not be of any great importance until after my death."[27]

As one of the most famous literary figures in Western literature, arguably the most famous person of black descent in the nineteenth-century Atlantic world, and one of the "great men" of France, it might be logical to conclude that Dumas is a widely studied subject. However, in 2002, Didier Decoin, the acting president of the *Société des Amis d'Alexandre Dumas*, expressed his hope that the writer's bicentennial would "renew the interest of readers" and scholars, since "not a single thesis" had been "dedicated to Dumas since 1904," thereby gaining him a place in school curricula.[28] While an overstatement, Dumas has not been a traditional, or long-standing, focus of much academic scholarship. While there are several French books about Dumas in print, many are of a popular nature. Only since 2002 did he begin to be studied widely in mainstream global academia. For example, there have been eight major academic collections of (predominantly French) scholarship published in Europe on Dumas from 1994 through 2017. Only one predates Dumas's interment in the Panthéon.[29] These academic works have been largely confined to the area of literary studies seeking to increase Dumas's critical prominence as a writer. Such scholarship, while significant and important to our understanding of Dumas, his work, and his influence, nevertheless largely ignores Dumas's biracial and colonial heritage, which includes the issues of slavery and his connections to the broader Atlantic world.[30] In general, studies exploring Dumas's status as a French national symbol have been woefully, and somewhat perplexingly, absent. This book, then, is an attempt to, in part, remedy this oversight and to help unveil Dumas's extremely significant and multifaceted legacy.

1

"Black Skin, White Masks" in Nineteenth-Century France

Alexandre Dumas and His Experiences as an Exotic Other, 1829–1870

In July 1847, over 600 of Paris's fashionable elite attended a housewarming party for Alexandre Dumas's still incomplete château in Port-Marly. The event was catered by the Pavillon Henri IV, the most chic restaurant in nearby Saint-Germain. Perfume smoked from incense burners as the crowd wined and dined at Dumas's expense. As host, Dumas, decorated with awards bestowed on him by French and foreign dignitaries, made his way through the crowd, entertaining his guests with his radiant smiles and colorful tales. The press reported that Dumas had ordered his architect, Hippolyte Durand, to build a château, a châtelet with two pavilions at the entrance, and a garden with several waterfalls. Although Durand objected on the grounds that the clayey soil would not support the château's foundation, Dumas, "no more discouraged than was Louis XIV" during the building of Versailles, ordered him to proceed, reportedly viewing money as no obstacle.[1] The writer Honoré de Balzac, who often criticized Dumas, attended the party and wrote that the château was "one of the most delicious follies ever built. It is the most royal chocolate-box in existence." He thought Dumas likely overpaid for the château, but even he had to admit his amazement. In a letter to a companion, he wrote: "If only you could see the place.... It is a charming villa ... for it looks on to the Terrace at Saint-Germain, and there is water!"[2]

Balzac was not the only one who was impressed. Journalist Léon Gozlan described the château as a "precious jewel" with "stone balconies, stained-glass windows, crosses, turrets and weathervanes." Although it was a pastiche of architectural styles, there was "an aura of the Renaissance about it" that gave it "a peculiar charm."[3] Another writer described it as a "beautiful building, half-château, half-villa" amidst "a wild garden ... [and] covered with exquisite traceries and sculptures copied from ... the Louvre."[4] The château also had several "poetic devices and emblems," including the arms of Dumas's noble grandfather and a frieze around the first floor of busts of great European dramatists, including Shakespeare, Byron, Goethe, and—naturally—Dumas. Finally, the entrance bore Dumas's motto, "I love who loves me."[5]

The château's grandeur extended into its interior, where the most celebrated attraction was the "Arab salon." Contemporaries described it as a "miracle [that] must be seen to be believed."[6] In 1846, while the château began construction, Dumas toured Spain and North Africa. Fascinated with Islamic art styles, he brought to France the Tunisian artist Hadj'-Younis and his son to decorate a salon in his château to reveal "all the splendors of the Arabian Nights."[7] Gozlan praised the Tunisian craftsmen who carried out a scheme of moldings, "the like of which is to be seen only on the Moorish ceilings of the Alhambra, an interlocking pattern of incised lines, the general effect of which is to produce the illusion of lace.... I was struck with admiration."[8]

Finally, the grounds included a small Gothic châtelet, surrounded by a moat. The exterior was carved with the titles of Dumas's works, enabling onlookers to "understand how the pen of M. Dumas can be the wand to build these fairy abodes." The châtelet contained a small study, in which Dumas worked. A spiral staircase led to a cell where, sometimes, he spent the night. There was a look-out platform from which he could watch his guests and a lever controlling a drawbridge to the island.[9]

The château, dubbed "Monte Cristo," blurred reality and fiction.[10] Contemporaries noted that its construction "was to realize a romance," for Dumas seemingly cast himself as the hero, Edmond Dantès, from his recent novel, *The Count of Monte Cristo*.[11] Although Dumas claimed a guest imposed the name on the château, he most likely chose it.[12] Like his novel's title character, Dumas staffed his château with African and Caribbean servants dressed in "native" garb. The château's elaborate and sensational nature emanated a sense of exoticness. As one account noted, Monte Cristo "rose from the earth as if by enchantment."[13] Adding a menagerie of exotic animals in a private zoo and aviary heightened the fantastic atmosphere. As the press reported, "blended with the sound of

1. "Black Skin, White Masks" in Nineteenth-Century France

falling waters—for an artificial torrent had been contrived, that tumbled over rocks as artificially arranged—was heard the chattering of monkeys, and the screaming of parrots, while huge barbaric dogs ... ranged through the groves."[14] Dumas enjoyed recounting how he acquired these animals, including a story about how he purchased a monkey and a macaw in Le Havre and carried them back to his hotel, "looking like a modern Robinson Crusoe" (Figure 1).[15] Consequently, Dumas described his estate as a

Figure 1: An illustration of Alexandre Dumas that accompanied his account of how he acquired a monkey and a macaw in Le Havre in the 1877 edition of his book *Adventures with My Pets*, published in Paris by Calmann-Lévy.

primordial "Garden of Eden in miniature," suggesting it was not only his estate, but a world unto itself that cast its visitors into an earlier, more primitive time, one of seemingly less "complexity" and greater equality. Dumas was the main figure within this world that seemed to exist out of the contemporary timeframe.[16] Illustrations of Monte Cristo focusing on the château (Figure 2) and châtelet (Figure 3) depicted the estate in a

Figure 2: Illustration of the Château de Monte Cristo featured in the February 28, 1848, edition of *L'Illustration* emphasizing its exotic and fantastic nature. Depictions of Alexandre Dumas's servants and animals seem to serve as guards to the gates of some "other" world (photograph akg-images/Gilles Mermet).

1. "Black Skin, White Masks" in Nineteenth-Century France

similar way, emphasizing its strange, fantasy nature by placing images of Dumas's servants and animals as guards to the gates of some "other" world. In crossing such gates, one crossed not only into a different space, but seemingly a different temporal dimension. Consequently, nineteenth-century socialite Comtesse Dash declared Dumas "an anachronism in this time."[17]

Figure 3: Another illustration of Monte Cristo featured in the February 28, 1848, edition of *L'Illustration* emphasizing its exotic and fantastic nature. This illustration depicts the chatêlet.

Finding Monte Cristo

In light of these observations and perceptions, we will explore in this chapter how Dumas and his contemporaries in metropolitan France reacted to his status as a biracial individual during his lifetime. These reactions were mediated through the lens of a worldview developing since the Age of Exploration.[18] Then, Europeans gained increasing geographic knowledge about the globe, encountering previously unknown peoples and cultures. Consequently, early globalization did not lead to a shrinking world, but rather a rapidly expanding one. Europeans' prior knowledge of the globe's territory and inhabitants had been limited since their contact with foreigners had been infrequent due to things like geography, poor transportation, and an agrarian economy. This new, "larger" world with an increasingly complex humanity was difficult for Europeans to grasp in its entirety; the globe thus seemed chaotic, or in a state of disorder. This intellectual challenge led to the formation of a defensive temporal geo-psychology (or worldview) that normalized European culture to protect its superiority. Social conceptions of time created notions of *progress* and the superiority of the present, suggesting that it is the culmination of a developing process. Non-Europeans were thus living in modernity's "child-hood," just as Europe had been more "primitive" in its past. "Others" thus became unmodern and non-contemporaneous.[19] Ernst Bloch expressed this worldview in 1932: "Not all people exist in the same Now. They do so only externally, through the fact that they can be seen today. But they are thereby not yet living at the same time with the others."[20] Traveling away from Europe was in essence a trip backward in time to a "primitive" era.[21] Joseph Marie de Gérando, for example, declared in his 1800 work on the "observation of savage peoples" that "the philosophical traveler, sailing to the ends of the earth, is in fact traveling in time; he is exploring the past; every step he makes is the passage of an age."[22]

While interpreting people from Africa and of black African descent within this worldview, Europeans ascribed certain physical and social characteristics with meanings of backwardness that rendered black Africans and individuals of black African descent as unmodern, seemingly justifying slavery and colonialism.[23] The French had encountered African peoples differing in appearance, customs, and religions, but they generally blended such diversity into a mono-cultural "African" with certain inherent traits in their efforts to understand global diversity. Such "spectacle-making" actions created an abstract character that constructed divisions attributable to unchangeable "essences" in black Africans' composition. In so

1. "Black Skin, White Masks" in Nineteenth-Century France

doing, Frenchmen were portrayed as superior and the norm from which the "exotic" African deviated.[24]

Early modern French travelers' accounts borrowed from each other, and ancient and medieval lore about Africa and blackness as symbolic of darkness and evil. Then prevalent climatic theories speculated that tropical temperatures made individuals unable to control their passions. A temperate (meaning European) climate was needed for "civilization." François de Paris, a French officer in Senegambia, wrote in 1682 that Africans spent days in idleness, excessive drinking, and fornication. Such ideas received attention during the Renaissance, when Jean Bodin argued that black Africans "can only restrain themselves with great difficulty, and once launched on debauchery, they maintain the most execrable voluptuousness. Hence the intimate relations between men and beasts that still give birth to monsters in Africa."[25] Eighteenth-century European intellectuals maintained negative appraisals of black Africans. As late as 1837, Frédéric de Portal wrote in a work about color symbolism that black, the "symbol of evil and falsity," represented "infernal love, egotism, hatred and all the passions of a degraded man."[26] Some intellectuals argued that blacks might eventually develop "civilization," but subsequent emphases on biology to explain social, cultural, and physical differences continued to place blacks as inferior. While some intellectuals also addressed slavery, they often fell short of calling for emancipation despite rhetoric about human equality. Further, eighteenth-century writers supporting abolition often put forth literary images of black Africans as "noble savages," creating exotic, tragic heroes.

Meanwhile, sugar, the Caribbean colonies' dominant crop, generated a large plantation economy, which became increasingly reliant on African slavery during the 1700s. Many French colonists, predominantly male, sired a rising number of multiracial individuals. Consequently, the circumstances surrounding Dumas's father's birth were not unique. Officials frequently tried to limit this group's growth and privileges to maintain a racial hierarchy. While slavery was mostly a colonial institution, the slave trade had links in the metropole, where many French elites in port cities profited from the enterprise. The slave trade linked France with Africa and the Caribbean, but also the Indian Ocean, where the colonies of Île de France (Mauritius) and Île de Bourbon (Réunion) existed. Despite such links, the horrific nature of slavery and the slave trade remained distant (and hence exotic) to most Frenchmen due to the nature of an external colonial empire. Further, relatively few people of black African descent, like Dumas, lived in eighteenth- and nineteenth-century metropolitan France, and during the Old Regime, many French courts had refused to uphold slavery in the metropole.[27]

Although the French Revolution abolished slavery, Napoleon Bonaparte reinstated it in the colonies. During the subsequent Bourbon Restoration (1814–1830), slavery continued while the slave trade remained illegal.[28] Colonial sugar producers enjoyed brief prosperity using more efficient production methods before foreign competition and lower-priced alternatives undercut them. The nineteenth-century Romantic Movement, of which Dumas was a leader, simultaneously ushered in new literature that shifted the intent of fictitious representations of black Africans and slavery. Rather than draw attention to abolitionism, Romantics used slavery and the slave trade as exotic literary backdrops, crafting popular adventure novels that often stereotyped Africans as lazy, ignorant, feeble-minded, and drunk to entertain middle-class readers.

French contemporaries thus interpreted Dumas within this cultural lens. During Dumas's nineteenth century, Paris witnessed popular exhibits of the "other" world beyond Europe that used methods of coordination and arrangement to superimpose a framework of meaning over its innumerable races, territories, and commodities based on the non-contemporaneity of the colonized. The arrangement created an effect of structure that did not exist in the real world, creating a culture in miniature that could be controlled and organized for European onlookers to comprehend.[29] People from other countries served during this era as the "ultimate exhibit," falling under the French gaze as exotic Others.[30] Although Claude Schopp, the French Dumas scholar *extrordinaire*, has declared Monte Cristo not a house, "but a monument to his glory," the château ultimately formulated an elaborate, exotic exhibit.[31] Amidst a large property with nothing else around it, the château was physically separated from the outside (European) world, and its specific components—like the Arab room, garden, aviary, zoo, and staff dressed in "native" costumes—demonstrated traces of the real presented within a framework that produced a fantastical effect of reality to satisfy French onlookers' fantasies. Dumas was at the center of this non-contemporaneous menagerie, becoming the ultimate exhibit on display associated with the exotic non–European world. By turning Dumas into an object due to their "intellectual curiosity," French society exerted a type of voyeuristic power over his being—gazing,

1. "Black Skin, White Masks" in Nineteenth-Century France

staring, and watching his every move—that Othered him, casting him as an outsider. While Dumas considered Monte Cristo among his great achievements, it ultimately underscored French public perceptions of him that associated him with the exotic non–European world that ostracized him from being regarded as truly "French." This social and cultural ostracization plagued him in life, profoundly impacting his work. With Monte Cristo's construction, Dumas unintentionally succumbed to the Othering of him held by many of his contemporaries, perpetuating his inferior status by building a grand and exotic stage on which he was the main "display." Within the context of this acquiescence, Monte Cristo marked Dumas's greatest failure. Consequently, despite his successes, the way in which Dumas was treated in France profoundly impacted how he perceived himself and his relationship to the Atlantic world.

Newspaper articles, memoirs, anecdotes, and Dumas's reflections thus allude to the difficulty he faced gaining acceptance as "French" because of his Caribbean ancestry. Dumas's detractors often accentuated his Africanness to demean his work and popularity, depicting him as backward or primitive; in other words, un–French. Dumas's dark skin and "African" features dominated perceptions of his identity more than anything else, including class.[32] Therefore, French views of Dumas reveal the complex conflations between French civil and national identity. A "nation-state" consists of two concepts that are not always mutually inclusive. "Nation" usually refers to a socially-constructed community perceiving itself as bonded because of distinct features like religion, language, and history, and is a cultural and/or ethnic entity. "State" usually refers to a geopolitical entity comprised of a fixed territory presided by a central government. A "nation-state" refers to the fusing of the two (often in complex and contradictory ways) into a sovereign state deriving its legitimacy from serving a body of citizens united by factors that define a cultural nation. French revolutionaries generally perceived society as comprised of a community of politically-conscious and equal citizens, but their efforts to form this community often revolved around cultural unity. These efforts' lasting legacy was the notion that "political inclusion has entailed cultural assimilation." Political opposition, non-assimilation, or failure to meet criteria for being culturally French could make one a "foreigner."[33]

Assimilation, however, is incompatible with Romantic conceptions of national belonging that took root in Dumas's France. Nineteenth-century Romantic conceptions of the nation-state perceived "natural" ethnocultural boundaries as existing "prior to and determinative of national and (ideally) state boundaries."[34] During the 1800s, intellectuals thus considered "race" a component of national identity. Invented "blood" ties allowed nations to create identities for themselves. Following this current, the French viewed themselves as Gauls and Franks. "Modernity" thus required the cultivation of pure races or ethnic groups. The Romantic historian, and Dumas's friend, Jules Michelet, for example, expressed the nation as a family, with France as the "mother" and the members of the nation as her children.[35]

The frequent result of these complex and contradictory views was that Dumas was often regarded as a French citizen within the state's legal framework, but a member of the "African" race due to his appearance and character. Consequently, Dumas could be a French citizen, but he remained an outsider to the French cultural nation. Dumas was often rejected as being fully "French" and his "exoticness" helped link him in the popular French imaginary to the Caribbean and African colonies. As journalist Hippolyte Romand noted in an 1834 article, Dumas was a *"nègre* in origin and French by birth," thereby implying that while being born in France to French citizens may have in turn made him a citizen, he was not a full member of the French cultural nation.[36] Such reactions, revealing the asymmetry between the French cultural and political nations, became more complex and illuminate the gap between the laws holding sway over French people's lives and the representations holding sway over their imaginary, particularly in reference to individuals with "colonial" connections.

Dumas, often reminded of his "inferior" background and non-acceptance into the French cultural nation, faced an external social perception that did not conform to his internal self-image; the result was a conflicted sense of self. As French society increasingly associated him with black individuals and slaves in the colonies, Dumas perceived himself, to some extent, as how others perceived him. French social norms simultaneously became a part of his individual personality and he consequently shared many French social prejudices toward individuals of black African descent. Consequently, Dumas developed a conflicted identity, unable to reconcile the seemingly incompatible selves of his being. In many ways, such sentiments reflect the notion of double consciousness expressed by African American intellectual W.E.B. DuBois, which will be addressed in Chapter 3.

1. "Black Skin, White Masks" in Nineteenth-Century France

Dumas As a Symbol of Non-Contemporaneity

While Monte Cristo unintentionally served as the ultimate exhibit of Dumas as a representative of the "non-contemporaneous world," he had long become an object on display. Among his era's most famous individuals, Dumas can be viewed as a modern "celebrity." Théophile Gautier recounted in his *Histoire du Romantisme* the 1831 premier of Dumas's masterpiece *Antony*: "The theater was truly in a state of delirium; the audience applauded, sobbed, wept, shouted. The realistic passion of the piece enflamed every heart." After the play, backstage "a crowd of delirious young Romantics mobbed Dumas, and in their enthusiasm tore to pieces the green coat he was wearing" as souvenirs.[37] Similarly, journalist Hippolyte de Villemessant confirmed that wherever Dumas went, "everyone turned his gaze on the celebrated romancer, whose tall figure dominated the assembly and who, smiling on friends known and unknown, could only make his way to his seat through a veritable fusillade of greetings and handshakes." When Dumas spoke, "the most famous personages stopped to listen; when he entered a room [everyone else was] ... eclipsed in the glory of this one man." Dumas was thus dubbed "the king of Paris ... the god of every class of society."[38] The *Revue et Gazette Musicale de Paris* similarly published a piece describing Dumas's sudden rise to fame, but also this newfound stardom's drawbacks. It asserted that "no physical change had occurred; nonetheless he was not the same man; he no longer belonged to himself; for the price of applause and honors he had sold himself to the public." Consequently, Dumas "was now a slave of caprice, fashion, even of cabals. He could feel his name torn from him as a fruit from its branch."[39]

Complicating Dumas's celebrity, however, was his brown skin, which signified his identity. Those encountering Dumas consequently regarded him as exotic in the sense that he was intriguingly unusual or different from other members of French society; this difference bred a certain type of excitement or curiosity. Dumas was also perceived as exotic in the sense that he was of foreign origin or character and therefore not a native Frenchman. Because of his celebrity, contemporaries often commented on their encounters with Dumas and usually noted his "African" physical appearance, which they found intriguingly different from the metropolitan majority. Accounts typically focused on three attributes: his skin color, hair, and lips. General Thiébault, who had served under Dumas's father, described the writer in 1834 as a young man "with skin like a *métis*, frizzy and thick hair like a *nègre*, [and] African lips." In 1837, writer Jules Lecomte also described Dumas as having a "brown" face and "frizzy hair." He argued that Dumas's "physical appearance" was "unusual ... and infinitely recalls the characteristics of *nègres*." Another writer, Benjamin Pifteau, described Dumas as "exotic" in appearance with "a broad face, long limbs, frizzy hair, a prominent jaw-line, and bronze skin." Journalist Hippolyte de Villemessant similarly declared that Dumas "had the frizzy hair and the thick lips of the *nègre*."[40] The daughter of Orientalist Charles Schoebel, Dumas's friend, later recalled her childhood fascination with Dumas's appearance: "I would plunge my small hands through the bushy mane that crowned Dumas's head. It was amusing to me to slip my fingers through this almost tropical mess," the frizziness of which was a "souvenir of Africa."[41]

Some contemporaries demonstrated animosity toward Dumas or made him the butt of jokes due to his black ancestry, reflecting long-standing stereotypes. Chief among them was Balzac. In 1844, he infamously expressed his contempt for the *"nègre"* Dumas after the former's poorly-selling serial novel *Les Paysans* was replaced with the latter's *La Reine Margot*.[42] Actress Mlle Mars, who performed in Dumas's early plays, demanded that the windows be opened after he left a room because she claimed he left an offensive *nègre* smell.[43] Paul Verlaine notoriously labeled an older Dumas "Uncle Tom" in a poem he wrote after risqué photos of the writer with his mistress, American actress Adah Menken, appeared in 1866. Dumas and Adah were compared to the white girl, Eva, and old black slave, Tom, in American abolitionist Harriet Beecher Stowe's novel, *Uncle Tom's Cabin*.[44] Even Dumas's friends could harbor racist attitudes. Victor Hugo, for one, drew a "portrait" of Dumas comprised of a scribbled circle, large frizzy hair, oversized lips, and a large nose.[45] During Paris's 1832 cholera epidemic, Dumas's maid informed him in a panic that a man who had died nearby was "already as black as a nigger!"[46] Dumas's son also reportedly joked that his father, short on funds, was "so conceited that he climbs the seat of his carriage in order to pretend that he has a Negro."[47] Even Charles Nodier, one of Dumas's mentors, said to him in jest, "you Negroes are all the same; you love glass beads and toys."[48]

Therefore, Dumas's appearance connected him in many French minds to black and multiracial individuals in the Caribbean colonies and to black Africans. By extension, this association linked him to the more primitive,

1. "Black Skin, White Masks" in Nineteenth-Century France

or backward, spaces beyond continental Europe. Such perceptions cast Dumas as foreign in origin and outside the French cultural nation. On one occasion, Dumas decided to attend a costume party as an "Albanian." Since his costume included a turban headdress, some guests thought Dumas was an "exotic" African Moor because of his ancestry. The actress Madame Malibran, set to perform in Shakespeare's *Othello*, interpreted his costume in this manner. Based on her suggestion, Zucchelli, the actor portraying Othello, wore a headdress like Dumas's.[49] The French press continued to publish caricatures emphasizing Dumas's "African" features (i.e., skin color, hair, and lips) to form a grotesque monster. Among the celebrated cartoonist Cham's most famous Dumas caricatures is one depicting the writer as an African cannibal, stirring a pot of historical figures in reference to Dumas's works (Figure 4). Such images were typical.[50]

Figure 4: This caricature of Alexandre Dumas from popular nineteenth-century illustrator Cham that appeared in *Le Charivari* on March 31, 1858, was typical of those that appeared in newspapers during Dumas's lifetime. Such caricatures emphasize Dumas's hair, skin color, and lips, which were generally perceived as representative of his black ancestry (Wikipedia Commons).

The illustrator Daumier also painted an exotic portrait of Dumas emphasizing his black Caribbean features and ancestry (Figure 5).[51]

A famous instance where Dumas's appearance prompted his association with the Caribbean colonies occurred during the French Revolution of 1830, which replaced the Bourbon dynasty with a cadet branch of the royal family.[52] Before the 1790s, depictions of African slavery often expressed sympathy for its victims. The Haitian Revolution and 1804 massacre of French whites on Haiti altered this view.[53] Tales of violence from the former colony became a form of sensationalist literature.[54] These accounts were still popular in 1830, when Dumas offered to get American Revolutionary War hero General Lafayette, then based at Paris's Hôtel de Ville, gunpowder from Soissons to repel further attacks from the ousted Bourbon king's supporters. The royalist Vicomte de Linières, head of the fort with the powder, refused Dumas's demands. Dumas, who then raised his pistol and threatened to fire, claimed that a "door opened and a woman burst into the room in a paroxysm of terror. 'Oh! My love, yield! yield!' she cried; 'it is a second revolt of the negroes!' ... And, saying this, she gazed at me with terrified eyes." Dumas asked the vicomte to send his wife away, but she continued to plead with her husband to yield in remembrance of her parents, "both massacred at Saint-Domingo!" It was at that point, Dumas wrote, that he had finally understood what she meant, for "she had taken me for negro, from my

Figure 5: A portrait of Alexandre Dumas from the 1860s commonly attributed to nineteenth-century illustrator Honoré Daumier, taken from an early twentieth-century art magazine.

1. "Black Skin, White Masks" in Nineteenth-Century France

fuzzy hair and complexion, burnt deep brown by three days' exposure to the sun [while fighting]." Dumas claimed that her terror stemmed from her colonial experiences, where she was "a daughter of M. and Madame de Saint-Janvier, who had been mercilessly killed under her very eyes during a revolt."[55] However, she was not the only one to connect Dumas to the colonies. Théophile Gautier noted in 1848 that "Dumas is Creole."[56] Further, Dumas's friend, writer Alfred de Musset, drew an 1834 caricature of him entitled "Antony-Louverture" that presented Dumas as a mixture of his character Antony and Haitian Revolutionary leader Toussaint L'Ouverture. The drawing mimicked a famous profile of L'Ouverture and the sculptor Dantan cast a bust of Dumas similar to Musset's caricature (Figures 6 and 7).[57]

 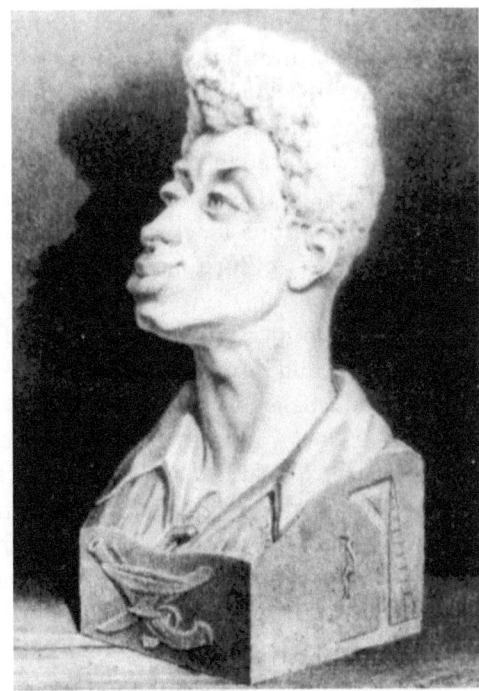

Left: Figure 6: A frequently reproduced nineteenth-century French illustration of Toussaint L'Ouverture (1743–1803), a leader of Haiti's revolutionary forces, by Nicolas-Eustache Maurin, printed in the 1830s by François-Séraphin Delpech (Wikipedia Commons). *Right:* Figure 7: A bust similar to an 1834 well-known cartoon by writer Alfred de Musset depicting Alexandre Dumas with the traits of Haitian Revolutionary leader Toussaint L'Ouverture appeared in *Le Charivari* on October 6, 1835.

Finding Monte Cristo

Among the most revealing evidence that ordinary Frenchmen perceived Dumas as foreign in origin and outside the familial French nation comes from Dumas himself, who recounted an episode in *Adventures with My Pets* in which he took an anonymous ride with an "amusing" cabriolet driver. The two happened to discuss the department of Aisne (where Dumas was born) and the driver listed famous men from there. However, he did not mention Dumas. Dumas asked him why not. The driver replied that he did not include Dumas because it was impossible for him to originate from the French department because Dumas "is a *nègre*!" As a result, he had to be from the Congo or Senegal.[58]

Dumas's *bon vivant* lifestyle was also perceived as contrary to prevailing, normative French middle-class sentiments of morality and thus indicative of his blackness, or foreignness, thereby casting him outside the French cultural nation. Many reports focused on Dumas's alleged spending habits, style of dress, late-night carousing, lack of work ethic, and extreme fondness for food and women as signs of "Africanness." One periodical argued that "he displayed the Ethiopian's fondness for bright colors and dress-eccentricities."[59] An 1871 obituary declared that Dumas reflected his black ancestry in being a man without restraint, acquiring "scores of fortunes" that he ran through "by his unbridled luxury and dissipation."[60] Another similarly claimed that Dumas's "purse was open at both ends, yawning to be filled at one and running empty at the other. Gold burned a hole in his pocket, and he hated to be hot."[61] Yet another article described his works as being written "with a carelessness, recklessness, and audacious pursuit of excitement." Dumas was criticized for using "scarcely any revision," which was attributed to his lack of reflective faculties. One 1871 article bluntly ascribed Dumas's excesses to his "Africanness," adding that he was sexually promiscuous, for "matrimony is an institution of which Dumas never comprehended the necessity or even the propriety."[62] While eating with Dumas, one interviewer noted that he had never seen anyone "eat so much like an animal" and felt as if he were "the guest of honor at one of La Fontaine's feasts of the animals."[63]

While exaggerated, Dumas's public excesses were to an extent characteristic of the Romantic Movement, whose adherents idolized English poet Lord Byron and often "copied his dandyism, his rages and ... his ... attitude of sensual license."[64] Nevertheless, black Africans served Europeans as a mirror to project their insecurities about themselves and their

1. "Black Skin, White Masks" in Nineteenth-Century France

world. According to Michel Foucault, the increasingly dominant bourgeoisie justified its group's superiority during the nineteenth century through moral restraint and control of their sexuality.[65] The struggle to obtain self-discipline, piety, sexual restraint, and other virtues created tensions that needed a release. As William Cohen has argued, "Europeans became obsessed with their own animality; they sought to flee the lowly condition imposed upon them by careful cultivation of soul and body." Consequently, Europeans transferred their suppressed fantasies onto black Africans.[66] Early modern French intellectuals had believed that black Africans possessed oversized sex organs and were highly susceptible to lust and sexual desires. This perception persisted, as nineteenth-century anthropologist Paul Broca supported this view.[67] Dumas was, therefore, subject to existing myths about men of African extraction. He recounted that early in his career he had already gained the sexual reputation "of being quite an Othello" in reference to Shakespeare's "black ram." Some contemporaries, like Vicomtesse de Saint-Mars, commented on Dumas as a sexual object, praising his "nice legs" and "beautiful blue eyes."[68]

During the 1830s, partially due to these associations, Dumas's literary reputation in the realm of French literature declined. Critics increasingly focused on his work's "immorality" and "childlike" lack of depth to argue that he had "all serious artists against him."[69] From 1829 to 1830, Dumas was critically and publicly perceived as the creator, or, along with Hugo as the co-creator, of the Romantic Movement in the theater. Dumas began to lose this position as the decade progressed. In contrast, Hugo's critical reputation soared at Dumas's expense. As critic Sainte-Beuve wrote, after 1832, Hugo was considered the greater writer "by several lengths." While Dumas had some talent, there was "something about that talent which one could almost describe as physical." Therefore, Dumas's work was perceived as a carnal overflow of his "tropical" vitality rather than thought-out, serious pieces.[70] Such perceptions only expanded during the 1840s, when Dumas was at the height of his fame. At that time, Dumas shifted his literary focus from plays to novels. The newspaper editor Émile de Girardin pioneered the idea of publishing novels in installments in 1836 to gain a competitive edge. Other newspapers began publishing serial novels as subscribers increasingly bought papers based on whose novel was being published in installments. Such new practices made fiction writing lucrative for the first time. Dumas had works commissioned at various papers, often simultaneously. The need to produce large quantities of work quickly prompted his use of collaborators, a common practice from the theater that he adopted for his novels.

In general, the forms of French racism Dumas encountered reflected deeply entrenched French racial perceptions rather than malicious attacks on Dumas's character or attempts to prevent him from rising in society. Dumas's novels' successes and his prolific output, however, provoked an intentionally racial attack intended to slander him. Jean-Baptiste Jacquot complained to the *Société des gens de lettres*, a French literary governing board, that Dumas and his collaborators had monopolized the publishing market. After his complaint was ignored, Jacquot (as Eugène de Mirecourt) published a pamphlet, *Fabrique de romans, Maison Alexandre Dumas et compagnie* (1845), declaring Dumas a *"nègre"* who wrote none of the works attributed to him. Instead, he presided over a writing-factory comprised of lesser-knowns who produced works for him to ascribe his name. The pamphlet used the French word *nègre*'s double meaning as a black slave from the colonies and a ghostwriter to attack Dumas professionally and personally. Mirecourt went through each of Dumas's works to unveil the "true" author, arguing that Dumas devoted "himself with magnificent sangfroid to the trade of piracy on the ocean of letters," who "boldly lands his prizes in all the bazaars of journalism and the bookshops." Further, Dumas hired "intellectual deserters and translators" at wages that lower them "to the condition of *nègres* working under the whip of a mulatto!"[71]

During the nineteenth century, like modern celebrities, false information about Dumas in the press was common.[72] Rumors had surrounded the composition of Dumas's works, which seemed too numerous for one individual. One popular anecdote was that Dumas's black servant wrote his novels for him.[73] During the 1840s, Charles Robin sarcastically summarized Dumas's detractors' opinions. He noted that "some people maintained that Dumas bought up complete manuscript novels from literary hacks ... [while] others would tell you, with an air of total conviction, that he kept ... poor devils shut up in his basement, scribbling away from morning to night." Further, there were those "who were sure all Dumas's novels were simply translations of obscure old English or German works."[74] There were, nevertheless, three scandals that gave some credence to Mirecourt's charges that Dumas placed his name on others' works. The first involved the authorship of *Le Tour de Nesle*. In 1832, publisher Félix Harel asked Dumas to revise a play by Frédéric Gaillardet. Dumas did not seek credit, but the publisher wanted to capitalize on Dumas's fame. As a compromise,

1. "Black Skin, White Masks" in Nineteenth-Century France

Gaillerdet's name was accompanied by a mysterious asterisk. Gaillardet, however, was unaware of Harel's dealings with Dumas and became furious. After the play's success, Dumas did not hesitate to mention his role at every opportunity. Gaillardet challenged Dumas to a duel and the affair became regular gossip among Parisian high society.[75] Next, Dumas had a falling out with his most fruitful collaborator, Auguste Maquet, a history professor with literary ambitions. Maquet eventually brought legal action against Dumas for additional royalties. Recognized as a participant in the creation of the works in which they had collaborated, Maquet was nevertheless awarded no additional revenue.[76] Finally, there is one well-known instance where Dumas signed a work in which he had no role in its composition. A collaborator, Paul Meurice, needed revenue to be a suitable match for his intended bride's family. He persuaded Dumas to sign *Les Deux Diane* and publish it for him, since a work by Dumas was more lucrative than one by Meurice.[77]

Much ado has been made in traditional scholarship and biographies about Dumas's extensive use of collaborators, but this was common practice among the era's French dramatists and was in itself not unique or scandalous.[78] Nor was it a guarded secret. In his non-fiction works, Dumas discussed his collaborators. The press and his contemporaries were aware of whom his collaborators were.[79] Dumas also assisted others as an anonymous collaborator.[80] However, Dumas's use of collaborators had started to attract negative attention by the 1830s because he was perceived as using it to create works for commercial gain rather than for art's sake.[81] For example, Antoine Fontenay, Dumas's associate, noted in his diary: "Went to see *Térésa* at the Opéra-Comique—It is a great success.... The play is announced as by Dumas. There is another author as well, but he has had to agree that his name shall not appear." A few days later, at a party, Fontenay encountered Dumas, who "had with him M. Anicet Bourgeois ... [his collaborator] on *Térésa*. They are busy with four other plays, all written in the same [capitalist] way. For shame!"[82]

Since it was no secret that Dumas wrote with collaborators, the "scandal" was that white Frenchmen were laboring "under the whip of a mulatto," thereby upsetting the social hierarchy. Since the Enlightenment, *nègre* was used as a euphemism for a black slave. It thus had a pejorative connotation. *Noir*, or "black," was considered the more humanizing term (although being "black" was still associated with slavery).[83] Consequently, calling Dumas a *nègre* was to mock him as a slave and colonial subject. In examining what was at stake in Mirecourt's pamphlet, it is important to take into account the era's "scientific" viewpoint as demonstrated in *L'Esprit des bêtes* (1847): "The animal is the mirror of man as man is the mirror of God.... Man invents, the animal imitates."[84] Therefore, denying Dumas's role in his works' creation was to argue that Dumas was an imitator, an "animal," primitive and backward to white Frenchmen due to his black ancestry.

Mirecourt's pamphlet also mocked Dumas's appearance, ancestry, and behavior to indicate his difference from other French people and similarity to inferior "savages": "Dumas's physique is well known: he has the stature of a drum-major, Herculean limbs at full stretch, protruding lips, an African nose, kinky hair, and a bronze face. His origin is written all over him; but it reveals itself even more in his character. Scratch the surface of Dumas and you will find the savage. There are elements of both the *nègre* and the marquis in him. However, the marquis is only skin deep. Remove some of the makeup, tear off the loose costume ... [and under] the civilized surface, the *nègre* soon bears his teeth at you. The marquis plays his role in public, while the *nègre* betrays himself in private."[85] Mirecourt further indicated Dumas's backward, primitive nature in his pamphlet: "His garments inconvenience him, he strips and works in picturesque undress of our first ancestors. He stretches out on the floor like a dog from the New World; he lunches on potatoes taken burning hot from the ashes of the hearth and devours them without removing the skins—*nègre*! ... Like the chiefs of Amerindian tribes, whom explorers persuade with baubles, Dumas loves everything that glistens, everything that shimmers. He has ribbons from various orders ... he pins his decorations on his chest. The toys seduce him ... —*nègre*!"[86] Thus, some detractors perceived Dumas, as a copier of others, as being primitive, backward, or even sub-human. As one paper claimed, Dumas, the "great leviathan," was in fact "a very shallow *monster* after all." As a "monster," his claim to nobility was mocked through his association with slaves in the colonies: "Who has not heard of the great leviathan of literature—the *St. Domingan* Marquis de la Pailleterie."[87] In another example, Victor Pavie declared that Dumas was foremost an African characterized "by the heat of his blood and the spontaneity of his nature" forged under the "rays of the black African sun." Consequently, Dumas was "a dramatic plagiarist, a compiler, not without verve, of Schiller, Shakespeare, [and] Goethe."[88]

The pamphlet's attack's personal and racist nature, however, proved

1. "Black Skin, White Masks" in Nineteenth-Century France

too much for some of Dumas's detractors. His nemesis, Balzac, conceded that it was "disgustingly stupid" even if he thought it was "the truth coarsely presented."[89] The pamphlet caused a sensation among Parisian society because of the personal attack against Dumas, who won public admiration by seemingly taking it in stride.[90] Nevertheless, it is difficult to imagine that the attack did not wound Dumas emotionally. Maquet, then Dumas's collaborator, supported him in a public letter detailing their arrangement as fair and honorable.[91] Dumas successfully pled his case before the *Société des gens de lettres*, which concluded that Mirecourt had defamed Dumas "in his origin, in his person, in his character, and in his private life."[92]

After subsequently receiving a brief prison sentence for slander, the embittered Mirecourt continued to disparage Dumas. In 1856, he published Dumas's biography, again calling Dumas a plagiarist and repeating his view about the "true" authors of Dumas's works, often citing his own pamphlet.[93] As Mirecourt argued, "Dumas *invents* nothing. His unique talent consists of the manner in which he arranges" others' work. Dumas "builds his framework with the material of others; nothing, absolutely nothing" is his own.[94] Continuing this racial attack on Dumas, illustrations in the biography depicted Dumas as an extremely dark individual (Figure 8).

Mirecourt's attacks did, however, reveal a broader concern. Contemporaries were uncertain how to classify and make sense of Dumas due to his biracial ancestry, just as earlier Europeans had difficulty interpreting global diversity. Consequently,

Figure 8: A portrait of Alexandre Dumas from Eugène de Mirecourt's 1856 biography of Dumas depicting the writer with dark skin and features.

debates about Dumas's exoticism in terms of both appearance and character within the context of French national belonging were not unanimously one-sided. Those who attempted to present Dumas as part of the French nation had to reconcile Dumas's Africanness with his Frenchness. Some described the "racial wars" fought within him. For example, Hippolyte de Villemessant declared that the French "race" had triumphed, for "the *nègre* had been beaten by civilized man; the impulsiveness of African blood had been tempered by the elegance of European civilization." Consequently, "what was repulsive in him had been transfigured by the clarity of his intelligence and his blossoming success." Therefore, Dumas was not foreign, but French.[95] Dumas's detractors, however, argued the reverse. Victor Pavie, for example, declared that "the refinements of an exuberant civilization have not been able to tame" Dumas's black blood.[96] Similarly, as the cartoonist Nadar noted, "the indications of the exotic race" in Dumas invited comparisons to human evolution.[97]

Dumas's Negative Self-Image and Perceptions of Race

Dumas's background and the atmosphere of the era in which he lived thus shaped his character. While he commonly identified himself as "Alexandre Dumas," his full name was "Alexandre Dumas Davy de la Pailleterie."[98] This formal name reflected his colonial and metropolitan heritage. "Davy de la Pailleterie" was the surname of his paternal grandfather, a noble from Normandy, while "Dumas" was that of his paternal grandmother, a black slave from the Caribbean colony of Saint Domingue. Dumas followed the surname preference of his father, Thomas-Alexandre, a Republican general in the French Revolution who abandoned his father's noble surname in favor of his mother's.[99] Dumas thus held a degree of disdain for his formal name, using it only for legal and official purposes.[100] He did assume his grandfather's noble title, which a commission had authorized his right to use, on at least one occasion, much to the mockery of his detractors, who argued that he had no right to it since he and/or his father were illegitimate.[101] This issue of Dumas's paternal grandparents' marriage was consequently a source of contention for him. Although Dumas mentions vaguely in his writings that his father was a "man of color," he never states explicitly that his grandmother was either black or a slave.[102]

1. "Black Skin, White Masks" in Nineteenth-Century France

In 1847, Dumas began writing his memoirs. His personal history proved a thorny subject for him because of his background, both in terms of his family's origins and his experiences growing up in the French countryside. The first volume largely details his father's exploits, described as a "Hercules of a mulatto," who despite being "a true son of the Colonies" was also "a son of France."[103] Dumas emphasizes his father's colonial, rather than racial, heritage by describing him as "American," "Creole," and even a "Cowboy."[104] Likely aware of the developing notion of "races," Dumas sought to insert additional details of refinement to prove that although a "*mulâtre*," his father was a member of the higher-regarded Amerindian (rather than African) race. Consequently, Dumas insists that his father had a "dark" complexion and a "well-shaped nose ... of the kind only found in the blending of Indian and Caucasian races." Despite his "powerful shoulders," he also possessed "the hands and feet of a woman. These feet were the envy of his mistresses.... [However,] the calf of his leg was the same width as my mother's waist."[105] This observation sought to counter current "scientific" thought, which posed that blacks had small calves and big feet.[106]

Dumas also revealed in his memoirs that as a boy he had the "charming nickname" of Berlick. In the account, when Dumas's mother was seven months pregnant, she allegedly attended the Whitsuntide festival in Villers-Cotterêts and came across a puppet show. This show, which Dumas's mother watched in horror, contained a devil character named Berlick. The devil puppet, black with a red tongue and tail, spoke "with a sort of growl." She grabbed her neighbor and cried: "Oh! My dear ... I shall give birth to a Berlick!" Despite all reassurances, she "remained convinced that she would bring forth a black-faced child with a red tail." She dreamt that her son jumped "inside her womb as only a demon could" and imagined that when he kicked, "she could feel the claws" of his feet. When Dumas was born, his face was dark due to being choked by his umbilical cord. When the midwife uttered a cry, Dumas's mother feared her suspicions were correct. At that moment, Dumas cried, but the cord, tight around his neck, caused it to sound like a growl. The doctor "hastened to reassure her" by setting Dumas's neck free, after which he assumed his natural state.[107] As a child, Dumas was blond, light-skinned, and blue-eyed (after puberty, his hair changed in color and took on a frizzy texture, and his skin became darker).[108] Some scholars have attempted to assess how this Berlick anecdote and name impacted Dumas's self-image.[109] However, this anecdote has also been used to demonstrate that Dumas's mother bore feelings of racial prejudice against her son.[110] Yet, pregnant women commonly have unusual dreams and fantasies.[111] As Dumas biographer Daniel Zimmerman has noted, Dumas's mother's fear/fantasy about having a dark-skinned child "is curious."[112] She loved her biracial husband and had given birth twice before.[113] Marie-Alexandrine-Aimée, the eldest of these two (the younger one having died), was dark in appearance; Thomas-Alexandre's letter to a friend announcing his son's birth described his daughter's "little black fingers."[114]

Dumas's alienation from the familial French nation due to his perceived exotic appearance and traits, discussed earlier in this chapter, impacted him long after he had reached adulthood and manifested itself in various ways. First, Dumas came to develop a negative self-image. Like most Frenchmen, Dumas viewed his "African" traits as signs of primitiveness and non-belonging.[115] In his memoirs, Dumas discusses his failed attempt to win the heart of actress Marie Dorval, who chose to be with his literary friend and rival, Alfred de Vigny. Dumas doubted that he ever had a chance, for, as he wrote, "Vigny is a poet of immense talent ... [and] a true gentleman. That is better than me, for I am a *mulâtre*." In another example, Dumas describes himself as "never ... good-looking" because he "had large brown eyes, with a dark complexion." Further, he notes that his hair is "frizzy" and when it becomes too long, it forms "a grotesque aureole round my head."[116] Dumas also describes his "impulsive character," reflective of what he perceives as his lack of intellectual capacity.[117]

Wherever Dumas went, people recognized him due to reproductions of his image. As Dumas declared, "my face ... is familiar at the very Antipodes." Due to his reputation for being free with money and having a taste for fine things, Dumas wrote that "every shopkeeper in the world, having read ... that it is my custom to squander my money, no sooner sees me walking up to his shop than he takes the virtuous resolution of selling whatever he has to sell three times more dear ... than to the general run of his victims." He attributed such popular recognition to the fact the he had been represented frequently "by my good friends [the famous cartoonists] Cham and Nadar. Can it be, then, that the two traitors were deceiving me all the while, and, instead of drawing my caricature, were giving the world my portrait?"[118] Such a comment suggested Dumas's belief that perhaps he actually looked like the grotesque caricatures that appeared in the press, noted earlier in this chapter, exaggerating his features perceived as indicating his black ancestry.

1. "Black Skin, White Masks" in Nineteenth-Century France

Another way Dumas's alienation from the French nation manifested itself was in his often expressed feelings of isolation and non-belonging. He once confessed, "For those who can appreciate her charms, solitude is the most loving of mistresses."[119] Dumas sometimes retaliated by exalting his black heritage, which inspired a popular anecdote in which a party guest asked Dumas about his opinion on blacks, for "if I am not mistaken, you have something of the negro blood in your veins." Dumas replied, "You are not mistaken at all, monsieur. My father was a mulatto, my grandfather was a negro, and my great-grandfather a monkey. You see, Monsieur, my pedigree begins where yours ends!"[120] In this anecdote of dubious authenticity, however, Dumas contradicts his own ancestry, switching his paternal black grandmother and his white grandfather.[121]

Dumas further reacted to his treatment as an Other by putting on different masks, or faces, to hide feelings of loneliness or isolation.[122] Contemporaries noted that Dumas often appeared "content with everything and everything in the world."[123] His larger-than-life public persona led one biographer to dub him the "Barnum of literature" in reference to Connecticut showman P.T. Barnum. The literary Goncourt brothers described Dumas in the 1860s as "a sort of giant with grey Negroid hair.... There is something about him of a fairground showman or a bagman in the *Arabian Nights*."[124] Yet, nineteenth-century African American poet Paul Laurence Dunbar's "We Wear the Mask"—which captures many of the sentiments expressed in twentieth-century French Caribbean intellectual Frantz Fanon's *Black Skin, White Masks*—conveys this false smile hiding an inner turmoil as related to the black experience. The poem reads:

> We wear the mask that grins and lies,
> It hides our cheeks and shades our eyes,—
> This debt we pay to human guile;
> With torn and bleeding hearts we smile,
> And mouth with myriad subtleties.
> Why should the world be over-wise,
> In counting all our tears and sighs?
> Nay, let them only see us, while
> We wear the mask.
> We smile, but, O great Christ, our cries
> To thee from tortured souls arise.
> We sing, but oh the clay is vile
> Beneath our feet, and long the mile;
> But let the world dream otherwise,
> We wear the mask![125]

Finding Monte Cristo

Comments from Dumas and his contemporaries suggest that Dunbar's poem can relate to Dumas. Vicomtesse de Saint-Mars, for example, observed that Dumas wore different "faces" in public and private. One "face" was the Dumas that was "exited, sentimental, passionate, living outside of this world" and in the sanctuary of his imagination, in his own "Monte Cristo."[126] Dumas noted that in his career he often wore a "mask on my mask" to appear as he felt the public wanted him to appear.[127] Since society gossiped about his "African" or "tropical" characteristics, Dumas, likely sub-consciously, catered to their expectations. As we have seen, his festivities at Monte Cristo ultimately accommodated this image. Consequently, Dumas's *Mohicans of Paris* includes an appropriate line of dialogue: "I say ... that you're parading faults you haven't got to hide the good qualities you have."[128]

Although Dumas was assigned characteristics stereotypical of Africans (i.e., lazy, lustful, prone to debauchery, and incapable of complex thought), the "face" that Dumas portrayed in private was often the opposite of this public image. His attorney against suits filed after his theater's bankruptcy in the 1840s described him as the victim "of preconceived ideas and rash judgments," vicious rumors by people who have never met him, and public acceptance of "thousands of more-or-less genuine anecdotes ... [that] take on reality to society." The private Dumas did not frolic in luxury, carouse all day and night, and squander his money. In fact, he was extremely un–"African." Dumas turned toward work as a means of escaping his loneliness. In describing Dumas's work habits, his attorney noted that he "works incessantly.... In the morning, the day, the evening, his imagination, always ready, pours out these thousands of treasures that make up his work."[129] Other contemporaries similarly asserted that Dumas followed such a schedule. One noted that Dumas "gets out of bed and ... writes a couple of pages; he calls for some hot water and while his man is bringing it he writes another twenty lines. He is told that breakfast is ready ... and he goes on writing." Later, when Dumas's guests were "taking coffee and cigars," Dumas would escape "to go back to his writing. He leaves the house to shop, to pay a few social calls; he gets home and continues where he has left off. He writes before meals and after meals; he goes to the theatre, has a late night supper and returns to go on writing."[130] Victor Hugo's son also recorded that Dumas had several couches around his home so that if he was tired he could collapse for a nap wherever he might be.[131] In contrast to Dumas's lavish public image, he dressed

1. "Black Skin, White Masks" in Nineteenth-Century France

modestly at home. One associate recalled that Dumas "dressed lightly, even in winter, with pants covering his feet, bare-headed, his arms bare ... moving constantly over his sheets of paper like an ox over his furrow." The Goncourt brothers also noted that at private parties Dumas "is the sober ... athlete of the serial novel," who "drinks no wine, takes no coffee, and does not smoke."[132]

A third effect of Dumas's alienation was the development of feelings of inadequacy and a need for constant professional recognition. A result of growing up as a biracial individual in nineteenth-century France was that Dumas "needed ... to feel self-confident, to know at every moment that he was as good as, and better than, [his detractors]." Therefore, he had to prove to his "own satisfaction" that he was "worth as much as, and more than, other men."[133] Such insecurity and need for recognition revealed itself in Dumas's quest for admission into the French Academy. During the 1830s and 1840s, Dumas vigorously campaigned to get himself admitted, repeatedly wondering why his efforts went unrewarded. In 1840, at which point there were three Academy vacancies, Dumas wrote to a friend: "What the devil! They must be calling for candidates in the streets of Paris by now—and the three serious candidates should be Hugo, myself, and de Vigny."[134] After Hugo entered the Academy, Dumas felt confident in his eventual succession to a seat and perceived the event as the transitioning of the institution "to the new young."[135] He continued to petition associates with any influence to put in a good word for him.[136] For example, Dumas wrote to his friend (and Academy member) Charles Nodier: "Do you think I should stand a chance now? Here's Hugo in, and his friends are all, more or less, mine.... If you think there is anything in my suggestion, do, please ... say, in my name, to your honorable fellow-members how much I should like to take a seat among them.... Mention your good opinion of me."[137] Dumas would ultimately never be elected to the French Academy. While Dumas's racial background likely contributed to the conservative Academy's refusals to admit him, his own *bon vivant* actions (sexual affairs, illegitimate children, debts, jokes) and the gossip about him (heading a "writing factory," commercialization of literature) seem to have been equal, if not stronger, deterrents.[138] The Academy took itself seriously and Dumas was perceived as the epitome of an "unserious" man of letters. Contemporary Delphine de Girardin summarized this position: "Is being famous such an obstacle, then? ... Why is it the famous find it so difficult to get elected? Is it a crime to have a right to recognition? ...

Finding Monte Cristo

Balzac and Alexandre Dumas write fifteen to eighteen volumes a year, and that, it seems, cannot be forgiven them. But these novels are excellent! That is no excuse; there are too many of them. But they are terrifically successful! That makes matters worse. Let a man write just one short, mediocre book which nobody reads, and then we'll think seriously about him."[139] In consolation, Dumas compared himself to Molière, who also never gained admittance into the Academy.[140] Such insecurity and need for recognition compelled Dumas to feel that he was "the brother of all 'outsiders,' no matter what the reason for their alienation from the social norm, whether colour, race, birth, illegitimacy or physical disability."[141]

Dumas's frequent association with the Caribbean colonies because of his appearance convinced him, to some extent, that he was "Caribbean" even though he had been born and raised in Villers-Cotterêts and had never even visited the Caribbean. For example, in his account of his actions in the French Revolution of 1830, Dumas noted that he had a "faintly Creole accent."[142] As biographer Jean Lacouture has noted, this is a "strange notation" compounded by Dumas's assertion in his memoirs that he had a "tropical" temperament, which distinguished him from others in French society.[143] How would Dumas have acquired a Creole accent? His father, who had left Saint-Domingue as a youth may have had a slight accent, but he died when Dumas was a toddler and therefore his influence would have been marginal. Dumas was raised in provincial France by his metropolitan mother and her family and educated by local priests. Further, while contemporaries were quick to describe Dumas's "exotic" physical features, they do not mention an accent. Therefore, it seems likely that Dumas did not have a Creole accent. However, his perception that he did suggests that he came to believe that he was somehow different from "native" Frenchmen as a result of the way he was treated. Therefore, in many ways, Dumas proved philosopher Jean-Paul Sartre's assertion, "I *am* as the Other sees me."[144]

Due to these feelings and growing sense of needing to find a "home," or sense of belonging, Dumas periodically expressed feelings of solidarity with other individuals of black African descent and the Atlantic world. He had commented that throughout his life, he "always had the strongest wish to visit Africa."[145] He was particularly sentimental about his Caribbean heritage in 1838 following his mother's death, which, he wrote, "awakens the old and eternal pain over the death of my father." That year, Dumas wrote a letter to his "compatriots" in Haiti, his father's birthplace,

1. "Black Skin, White Masks" in Nineteenth-Century France

about raising funds through subscription to erect in France a statue in his father's honor. He perceived the project as a pan-African endeavor. Dumas proposed "a subscription of one franc available to men of color only, from whichever part of the world in which they reside." This subscription would be supplemented by funds from the French king, French princes, and the Haitian government. Dumas estimated the statue's cost at around 20,000 to 25,000 francs; however, if 40,000 francs or more happened to be raised, two statues should be cast, one for France and one for Port-au-Prince. Further, he would escort the second statue to the Caribbean. Dumas cited his father's bravery, depicting him as evidence that the Haitians had "something to teach old Europe, so proud of its antiquity and its civilization," and that the Haitians and people of the French Caribbean "have furnished their share to the glory of France."[146] Also in 1838, Dumas wrote a letter to Cyrille Bissette, a biracial abolitionist from Martinique. Dumas was angered over the pro-slavery *Revue coloniale*'s false claim that his poetry was to appear in its pages. Dumas hoped Bissette would correct this error in his abolitionist journal, for "all my sympathies are instinctively and nationally for the opponents of the principles that these gentlemen defend." It was his intention to make this position clearly known "not only in France, but everywhere I can count my brothers in race and friends of color."[147] Such actions (and his successes) increased Dumas's popularity in Haiti and the French Caribbean. *The Count of Monte Cristo* was so revered that a celebrated Haitian writer was named Dantès Bellegarde.[148] Consequently, many Haitians, like ex-deputy and writer Demesvar Delorme, opened correspondence with Dumas. In 1869, shortly before his death, Dumas wrote to Delorme: "You honor America and this land of Haiti ... the cradle of my ancestors."[149]

At the same time, Dumas possessed similar attitudes toward black African individuals as his white peers, making him not only a victim of racism, but also a participant in its perpetuation. Such attitudes are reflected in his writings describing his black servants, which he had for most of his life. Even when he was a child in Villers-Cotterêts, his family had a black servant named Hippolyte, whom Dumas remembered as a great storyteller.[150] During his career, Dumas had two black servants whom he wrote about frequently: Alexis and Paul. As a boy, Alexis was presented to Dumas by a mistress as a surprise hidden in a flower basket (Figure 9). After removing the flowers, Dumas "caught sight of something black with two great white eyes, crouching at the bottom." He reached in and pulled

Finding Monte Cristo

Figure 9: An illustration accompanying Dumas's account of how he acquired his servant Alexis in the 1877 edition of his book *Adventures with My Pets*, published in Paris by Calmann-Lévy.

the boy out, upon which Alexis gave "a radiant smile with his two great starry eyes and his thirty-two teeth as white as snow." Dumas was informed that Alexis had been a Caribbean slave and that he spoke Creole. Dumas referred to Alexis as his "*protégé*," and despite mocking Creole as a "unique" Caribbean language almost identical to those of Europe, he noted

1. "Black Skin, White Masks" in Nineteenth-Century France

that he and Alexis "had always gone on, bye the bye, in our conversation, speaking Creole."[151] Thus, Dumas and his black servant had a common bond in their Caribbean origin and Dumas became fond of Alexis, hoping to serve as a type of mentor. The "problem," however, was that Alexis was too "black" for Dumas's efforts to be successful, which served as the source of humor in Dumas's accounts, earning the servant the nickname "Soulouque."[152]

A side product of this relationship, however, was Dumas's early attempts to incorporate Creole into French literature. Accounts of the Haitian Revolution contained some of the earliest written passages of Creole, which were included as part of the insurgents' dialogue. Some scholars have credited Dumas's contemporary, Prosper Mérimée, with pioneering the incorporation of colonial "local color," or dialect, into French literature. However, it is important to note that Dumas had initiated a similar process of attempting to incorporate Creole, or local colonial dialects, into French literature at the same time. In addition to providing Creole lines to Alexis among his accounts of his servant, Dumas incorporated a song, "Moi resté dans un p'tit la caze," in *Georges* (1843) that is written in a mix of French and Creole. Dumas's use of Creole is arguably more significant than Mérimée's, because unlike Mérimée, Dumas was a descendant of francophone Caribbean slaves who likely spoke a form of Creole.[153] Dumas addressed the issues of race and slavery in some of his fictional work, the most significant of which is his novel *Georges* (1843), set in the French colonies during 1810 to 1824 and featuring an elite hero of biracial descent who struggles to achieve equality among his white peers. Not a huge success by Dumas's standards, the novel explored many themes developed more fully in the subsequent *The Count of Monte Cristo* (serialized in newspapers from 1844 to 1845 and published in book form from 1845 to 1846). A more complete analysis of *Georges* will occur in Chapter 5.

Nevertheless, Dumas's conflicting attitudes toward Alexis can be observed from the fact that the servant is included in an account entitled *Adventures with My Pets* (1867), a collection of anecdotes published in journals from 1855 to 1865. Alexis was intended to entertain Dumas's white middle-class audience by virtue of his ignorance, his misplaced arrogance, and his affectations, which Dumas related with "benevolent mockery."[154] As Dumas tells it, in 1848, after the French abolition of slavery, Alexis asked him to be released from his post to join the navy. Once in the navy, Alexis feels that he is a sailor only in his "spare time," serving the Republic only after having finished serving his commander.[155] Consequently, Alexis joins the Garde Mobile, thinking it will be easy to get a medal. Without seeing any action (and hence without winning any shiny medals), Alexis returns to Dumas to request his old position. After Dumas refuses, the former servant joins the army. In Corsica, he writes to Dumas to request that his former master use his influence to get him released and to rehire him. Alexis complains that "there's nothing for a fellow to do—except the girls.... But ... everybody is a relation of everybody else in the place, and if you don't marry the wench afterward, they're sure to murder you." Alexis argues that since he is not an "efficient soldier," the officers will willingly release him.[156] After Dumas takes Alexis back under the condition that he will receive only room and board, the servant often dresses in his master's clothes. Alexis rationalizes that since Dumas works all day, and he is the one who goes out to run errands and "go after the ladies," he would put the clothes to better use.[157] However, Alexis decides to rejoin the army. Dumas gives him the wages that he would have received and tells him that the offer of room and board was a ruse to make him save money in spite of himself. Nevertheless, once Alexis has the money, he "was to be seen at all hours on the Boulevards, where he became known to all and sundry as the Black Prince."[158] In these anecdotes, then, Dumas, as a representative of French culture, tries to mold Alexis into a proper French individual. However, the servant's "African" nature prevents him from being truly "French," accentuating how different and backward blacks truly are. In other words, the anecdotes reveal a view that might best be summarized as one can take the African out of Africa, but one cannot take Africa out of the African. It is within the confines of this maxim that the humor unfolded. Alexis is shown to be wise-cracking, capricious, extravagant, lazy, vain, and lustful: all "African" traits that Dumas was ironically criticized as possessing.

Dumas's other servant Pierre, originally named Eau-de-Benjoin, was a "black-skinned" Abyssinian servant who accompanied Dumas during his 1840s travels in Spain and North Africa. Paul later died of fever in 1847 and was buried in the gardens at the Château de Monte Cristo.[159] In his accounts, Dumas describes Paul as lazy, untrustworthy, and impulsive. Dumas relates his acquisition of Paul, with slight variations in the details, in his account of his travels in Spain and later in *Adventures with My Pets*. As a boy, Eau-de-Benjoin became a servant to an English master, who purchased him in Gondar for a bottle of rum. During his years of service,

1. "Black Skin, White Masks" in Nineteenth-Century France

Eau-de-Benjoin travels across Europe and learns many languages. One day, his master commits suicide and Eau-de-Benjoin finds himself without a post or savings. Although he was paid well and "could have saved a good deal … thrift was not in his nature. A true son of the equator, loving everything that glittered, he squandered all he had on trash—or on rum." With "his candid eyes, ingenuous smile, and flashing teeth," he finds a new post with a French colonel, who takes him to North Africa. Eau-de-Benjoin is baptized and changes his name to Pierre. When his French master retires, Pierre is dismissed since the officer's pension will not allow him to keep a servant. A friend recommends Pierre to Dumas "as an invaluable valet." Dumas is hesitant to take on a new black servant because of Alexis's "laziness," but he takes Pierre on anyway. Once employed, Pierre changes his name after Dumas's gardener, also named Pierre, "took it very hard that my new man, and a Negro at that, should bear the same name. His seniority in my service, and his white skin, made him flatly refuse to change his own." Consequently, Pierre becomes Paul at Dumas's suggestion. The problem with Paul, however, is that he is lazy and too fond of rum. One day, Dumas finds Paul "dead drunk" and dismisses him. After he is sober, Paul goes into a rage reflective of his "tropical temperament" in which he screams that he will not lose this position too. Dumas keeps Paul in his employment after the servant promises not to drink so much, but "naturally" Paul breaks this promise.[160] While in Spain and North Africa, Paul moves "slow and torpid" like a "serpent."[161] Dumas once notices that Paul was working with unusual diligence; such an "outburst of energy" indicated that the servant hoped "to be pardoned for some lapse." Throughout their travels, Paul constantly eats and drinks, after which he takes naps on top of the luggage. When the mule makes a false step, the balance is disturbed and Paul slides to the ground, only to bounce back on top again. Dumas thus suggests that Paul "must be made of rubber. He is certainly the right color."[162]

As these anecdotes show, Dumas's attitude toward race was ambiguous. He was criticized as possessing many of the same characteristics he reproached in his black servants. However, Dumas does tell Alexis that if he is a good soldier, "everyone will swear that you are white."[163] Such a statement reflected Dumas's perception that race was socially constructed and that "whiteness" demonstrated positive attributes while blackness was something negative; social or cultural success could ultimately bleach one of blackness. In his anecdotes, Paul is described as showing "no sign whatever of the low brow, flat nose, and thick lips of the natives of the Congo or Mozambique." As an Abyssinian, he had a more "elegant shape" reflective of the "Arab ... race" despite his black skin.[164] Such impressions suggest that Dumas identified himself, or at least viewed himself as having more in common with, white French individuals. This is not to say that he was not proud of his Caribbean, or Creole, roots. To Dumas, however, his Frenchness harnessed such origins to make him a type of super Frenchman.

Consequently, a final way in which Dumas's alienation from the French nation impacted him was his espousal of a cosmopolitan outlook toward national identities. Dumas glorified *métissage*, or mixing, to produce the best of two "races," or ethnicities, in individuals to create a common human family. Such beliefs were likely influenced in part by his childhood teacher, Abbé Grégoire. Grégoire's Christian beliefs supported the vision of uniting humanity under the Church. Dumas recalled Grégoire in his memoirs as "not only a good priest," but also "an excellent friend of my father." Although never overtly religious, he attended Grégoire's school in Villers-Cotterêts and held the priest in high esteem as an "upright, worthy, and saintly man." The likely impact of Grégoire's association with General Dumas and Dumas—among the most celebrated French individuals of mixed racial descent during the Age of Revolutions—on Dumas has not been explored in scholarship. These ideas likely combined with those of some intellectuals at the time who supported the abolition of slavery. Around the same time that Dumas was Grégoire's pupil, French Revolutionary abolitionists had corresponded with Haitian officials to express ideas on how to bring them fully into European culture and Christianity, which they perceived as the way through which they could achieve social progress. Their vision for the elimination of racial prejudice called for the homogenization of races and cultures. They encouraged the "crossing of the races" in Haiti to create one race and one (European) culture: a "universal human family." Consequently, the divisions wrought by slavery could be healed, as "relations of blood can establish habitual relations" between the races. Furthermore, the new mixed race would be better than either had been on its own. Drawing from conclusions made from plant and animal cross-breeding, they argued that "all the physiologists attest that the crossed races are together more robust."[165] However, the belief in the hybrid's superiority was hotly contested, particularly during the nineteenth century.[166]

1. "Black Skin, White Masks" in Nineteenth-Century France

While Dumas's anecdotes in his memoirs about his beloved teacher jokingly relate that the only subject he learned from Grégoire was Latin, it seems that Grégoire's religious ideas and intellectuals' notions of hybridity impacted Dumas's thinking. Dumas devotes substantial space in his memoirs for Grégoire, whom he admired as a surrogate father. In fact, when Dumas leaves as a young man for Paris, the scene that unfolds in his memoirs between him and Grégoire parallels that between d'Artagnan and d'Artagnan the elder in Chapter 1 of his earlier *The Three Musketeers* (in which the elder gives his son three pieces of advice). Whether this scene actually happened or not is irrelevant: if "true," then Dumas paralleled the father-son scene in *The Three Musketeers* after his relationship with Grégoire; if "false," Dumas decided when writing his memoirs to create a scene similar to that in *The Three Musketeers* to foster notions of a similar relationship.[167] Adolescent identities are developed in conjunction with aspects of our social environment, including adult figures around us whom we revere. It seems probable that Grégoire, involved in Dumas's life at this time and interested in the Christian notion that "all men are brothers," influenced Dumas, who, as a man of mixed race, would also have been drawn to aspects of ideas about hybrids' superiority.

Examples abound in Dumas's work praising racial mixing and human harmony, suggesting shades of these influences.[168] Three examples can demonstrate this view. The first is from *The Woman with the Velvet Necklace*. The character Antonia, who is of Italo-German descent, was an amazing beauty, reflecting the best of both races:

> [W]ith the fine texture of skin, characteristic of the women of the North, she had the dead white color of the women of the South; thus her fine, thick flaxen hair, flying about in the slightest breeze like a golden vapor, shaded eyes and eyebrows of a velvety black. Strangely enough, the harmonious commingling of the two races was especially noticeable in her voice. So, when Antonia spoke German, the soft accents of the beautiful [Italian] language ... softened the harshness of the German accent, whereas ... when she spoke Italian, the somewhat too flexible [Italian] tongue ... assumed a firmness imparted to it the virile strength of the tongue of Schiller and Goethe. Nor was this fusion to be remarked on the physical side only. Antonia was mentally a marvelous and rare example of what the sun of Italy and the fogs of Germany can perform in the way of combining.[169]

Another example can be found in *The Last Vendée; or, The She-Wolves of Machecoul*. The "she-wolves," Mary and Bertha, are the twin daughters of the French Marquis de Souday and Eva, a poor English girl whom the noble met while in exile during the French Revolution. Dumas describes the girls as pure, or angelic, and blessed because of their mixed ancestry. Consequently, he writes: "their fair and rosy faces and curling hair were so like those of the cherubs that surrounded the Madonna over the high altar at Grand-Lieu before it was destroyed.... [T]he purity of race in their paternal ancestors had done marvels when strengthened with the vigorous Saxon blood of the plebeian mother."[170] *Gaul and France*, Dumas's history of ancient and medieval France, provides another example. He presents the French nation as an ongoing mixture of "races," thereby expanding on the nineteenth-century belief that France was composed of two distinct races (Gauls and Franks).[171] Dumas therefore demonstrated a more "cosmopolitan" outlook toward national identities than many of his contemporaries.[172]

Conclusion

The ideological construction of socio-temporal difference formed in the Age of Exploration dominated the West's cultural, social, political, and economic interactions with other peoples and cultures across the globe during the modern age. Dumas became the victim of a staring gaze wherever he went that could not be attributed exclusively to his literary fame. Both before and after Dumas became the "king of Paris," contemporaries noted his physical characteristics, like his thick lips, frizzy hair, and dark complexion, which made him appear physically and culturally distinct from the majority of white Frenchmen. In effect, these differences alienated Dumas from being fully French. Perceptions of Dumas as an exotic, or a curiosity, established him as the Other rather than a Frenchman, thereby ostracizing him from European space.

While Dumas identified himself foremost as French, his friends, associates, and the French public could not conceptually separate Dumas from the colonies and viewed him as an exotic Other. Therefore, French articulations of citizenship and nationhood made Dumas a French citizen while simultaneously casting him as an outsider to the French nation. Dumas's blackness, or sense of alienation on the basis of his physical attributes resulting from his black ancestry, created a conflicted sense of self that ultimately forced Dumas, consciously or not, to cultivate a public image as an exotic Other despite efforts to find a sense of belonging, of equality. This image further isolated him from French society and strengthened

1. "Black Skin, White Masks" in Nineteenth-Century France

public connections between him and the non–European world. Cultivated through fancy dress, exotic servants, travel narratives, and Monte Cristo, Dumas made himself an exotic exhibit of non-contemporaneity for the French gaze. Consequently, Dumas can be viewed as a tragic figure, functioning in a French society that compelled him to act "black" to maintain his status as a backward figure despite his cultural accomplishments to maintain the familial conception of an organic French national identity.

In light of how Dumas was perceived in metropolitan France because of his colonial Caribbean origins and mixed racial identity, one naturally wonders if Dumas would have been more accepted in the French Caribbean. In 1848, a revolution overthrew the government of King Louis-Philippe (itself established by a revolution in 1830) and formed the Second Republic. Dumas, his dream of a republic seemingly realized, dove into his opportunity to enter politics. He ran for various parliamentary seats in the French Chamber, but his widest support came not from the metropole, but from the French Caribbean.

2

A Hero of Assimilation
Alexandre Dumas and the French Caribbean, 1848–1930

Perhaps unsurprisingly, given his ancestral history, Dumas emerged as a significant figure during his lifetime in the French Caribbean. But he also, somewhat reluctantly, became an active participant in the mid-nineteenth-century French Caribbean political scene, then at the margins of an increasingly global French society. As early as 1831, Dumas had revealed his political ambitions, for in his view, "the man of letters was but the prelude to the politician."[1] Yet, Dumas had hoped to realize these ambitions in continental France. After the Revolution of 1848 and the creation of the Second Republic, Dumas seized the opportunity to enter the political arena in an attempt to win a legislative seat as a deputy within the French parliament. Under the usual circumstances, a celebrity like Dumas would have gained the largest degree of support from his home department. However, Dumas's left-wing republican reputation made him ill-suited to find success in the conservative department of Aisne. Dumas consequently ran for seats wherever he could muster local support, as candidate eligibility did not include rigid residency requirements. He set his hopes on winning in Yonne. There, however, he was heckled during speeches with taunts of being a "marquis," a "*nègre*," and a "*mulâtre*."[2] Dumas did not help his cause when, on at least one occasion, he set aside making a traditional speech in favor of providing a detailed account of his writing labors and earnings for the past twenty years, and how they had ultimately benefited financially 1,458 individuals.[3] Not many people, it seems, took Dumas seriously as a politician and many associated him with the "exotic," continuing the exhibitic perceptions discussed in Chapter 1 that linked him to a non-contemporaneous, colonial world. For example, Dumas once met with a M. du Chaffault, whose

2. A Hero of Assimilation

support Dumas believed could help him in the elections. After dinner—which Dumas put on Chaffault's tab—Chaffault noted in his journal, "I returned alone to Sens, my heart full of joy at having seen and heard a man of genius.... I still preserve the accounts I paid, which recall to me my two days passed in fairyland with 'Monte Cristo.'"[4] Predictably, Dumas made a poor showing in the elections. In light of the heckling he received and the "fairyland" aura that he exuded, it seems plausible that Dumas's black ancestry played a role, if not a decisive factor, in his electoral failure.[5] In Paris, where the total votes cast within the various districts ranged from about 8,000 to 24,000 votes in the 1848 elections, Dumas received no higher than the 1,681 votes he received in April. In June, Dumas received only 641 votes. In the April 1848 election in Seine-et-Oise, for example, Dumas did not even finish among the top 10 candidates. In Yonne, during the June 1848 election, Dumas finished fifth, with 3,458 votes, losing to Ramport-Lechin, a doctor, who received 18,969 votes.[6]

In 1848, the French government also abolished slavery, paving the way for the people of Martinique, Guadeloupe, and Guiana to become French citizens with parliamentary representation, municipal self-government, and protective social legislation. In response to the failure of his political ambitions in metropolitan France, Dumas supposedly made the oft-quoted, but dubious, remark that he should have run as an overseas representative in the Caribbean: "I will send them a lock of my hair so they will see that I am one of them."[7] In fact, Dumas was nominated and did run as a candidate on the French Caribbean island of Guadeloupe, although it seems that he did not take an overly active role in his candidature. As a result, his electoral efforts in overseas France have been ignored in academic scholarship. Nevertheless, his candidature in Guadeloupe sheds light on the emerging Dumas of myth in the French Caribbean, the growing role of the overseas departments and collective territories within France, and notions of French identity at the margins of an expanding French Atlantic world.

Bissette versus Schoelcher: The Battle Over Guadeloupe

Dumas's candidature in Guadeloupe was an episode of the much larger "*combat fratricide*" played out in the colonies between the partisans

Finding Monte Cristo

of the biracial Martinican abolitionist Cyrille Bissette and the partisans of the metropolitan abolitionist Victor Schoelcher that the local Caribbean press compared to the late medieval Italian conflict between the supporters of the pope (the Guelphs) and the supporters of the Holy Roman Emperor (the Ghibellines) over the investiture dispute.[8] As we saw in Chapter 1, Dumas had associated with Bissette in Paris and had written him a letter expressing his opposition to slavery and a sense of solidarity with "my brothers in race and friends of color."[9] Bissette, known for his fiery writings in defense of the rights of individuals of biracial descent and the abolition of slavery, was born in Fort-Royal (Fort-de-France) circa 1795 to a descendant of the Tacher de la Pagerie family, the same landholding family as Napoleon Bonaparte's first wife, Josephine. Bissette rose in prominence following the anonymous 1823 publication of his pamphlet that demanded "in the name of justice and of humanity" that King Louis XVIII's government eliminate special laws governing free people of color "and that they be granted legislation that accords with the present state of civilization."[10] After his conviction on charges of inciting the *gens de couleur* to revolt, Bissette was branded and deported from Martinique. He was released from prison two years after his arrival in the metropole. The "Bissette Affair" renewed white Creole fears about the threat to social power in the colonies posed by rising numbers of free *gens de couleur* and led to a renewal in the execution of discriminatory laws. In the metropole, the affair spurred outrage that eventually led to the new Colonial Charter of 1833. The Charter's "recognition" of the *gens de couleur* and their rights as French citizens, however, was applied unevenly throughout the French Caribbean. The tax and/or property requirements for enfranchisement were the highest in Martinique and Guadeloupe, where higher numbers of *gens of couleur* existed. Bissette criticized the laws as "the old regime, only legalized, with all its odious caste prejudice" and as an example of how the government had failed to live up to its promises of equality and liberty.[11]

As an informal representative of his class, Bissette published pamphlets and petitions attacking injustices against *gens de couleur*, only later including all individuals of black African descent. He came to call for the immediate abolition of slavery without slaveholder compensation, followed by free education for former slaves, and new work contract laws. In 1834, Bissette founded *La Revue des Colonies*, likely "the first periodical published by Negroes in France."[12] It is in this journal that Dumas

2. A Hero of Assimilation

published his letter discussed in Chapter 1 and earlier in this chapter expressing his sympathy for the abolition of slavery and solidarity with his "brothers in race and color." The *Revue*, in part, attempted to foster an "indigenous" literature through the publication of works like francophone Louisiana-born Victor Séjour's story "The Mulatto," the first published piece of African American fiction, and sought to supplement its local French focus with a global view that interpreted events within the context of race relations elsewhere.[13] At the heart of Bissette's consistent vision for the colonies, however, was union with "France" and the firm belief that racial conflict in the colonies was the fault of officials who "misinterpreted" its wishes. Therefore, he believed in a France symbolized by the Republic, which was demonstrative of equality, and a conservative France symbolized by the old regime, which supported slavery. As Bissette wrote, "we, children of France, do not ... indulge in ideas that are hostile toward her ... [for] France is too dear to us, its beneficial effects too precious and its protection too necessary.... [Yet] those who govern over us ... falsely interpret the wishes of France ... [and thus do not express faithfully] the intentions of the *mère-patrie*."[14]

Bissette's feud with the abolitionist Victor Schoelcher, whom posterity has dubbed the "Abraham Lincoln of France," was both long and bitter.[15] Their rivalry began in the early 1840s when Bissette published two refutations of Schoelcher's books about his travels and assessments of the French Caribbean, *Des colonies françaises: Abolition immédiate de l'esclavage* (1842) and *Colonies étrangères et Haïti: Résultats de l'Émancipation anglaise* (1842–1843). Schoelcher's books presented a negative assessment of blacks and *gens de couleur*'s civilizational acclivity and created a particularly disapproving view of the ambiguous role played by *gens de couleur* in the colonies. Bissette's criticism of Schoelcher revolved around two broad arguments. The first was that Schoelcher, whose research for the book was undertaken while hosted by white Creoles, created a distorted portrait of the French Caribbean that largely regurgitated white landholders' views. As Bissette summarized, "what I am refuting are the errors in which the author has all too readily fallen, treating as friends of the blacks the same people who have shown themselves to be their greatest enemies."[16] As a result, Schoelcher presented a history "copied from the pamphlets and memoirs of ... Saint-Domingue colonists who were among the most ardent opponents of blacks and *hommes de couleur*, and who were their torturers ... in the same way that ... Schoelcher's hosts still are."[17]

Finding Monte Cristo

Bissette's second argument alluded to the view that the experience of racial prejudice was something that had to be lived in order to be understood. In an 1846 letter to playwright Étienne Arago, Bissette had already questioned Schoelcher's "right and privilege to discuss our interests" on the basis that he was neither descended from slaves nor a victim of racial prejudice. As a result, an individual unacquainted with slavery or racial prejudice was poorly qualified to make the sort of patronizing claims Schoelcher made after only a short stay in the Caribbean. As Bissette explained, "it is a phenomenal error on his part to assume that a few months of traveling" makes him "a fountain of knowledge ... capable of writing about colonial customs and all other similar issues in big large volumes destined to become a standard point of reference." Unlike Abbé Grégoire and others, who were "true friends of our cause," Bissette perceived Schoelcher as having the pretension of offering himself as a "savior" who compelled "in a relentless and obsessive way, our gratitude."[18]

The rivalry between Bissette and Schoelcher intensified in 1848 to 1851 over the election campaigns during the short-lived Second Republic and formal abolition of French colonial slavery. The coup of Louis-Napoleon Bonaparte (the future Napoleon III) in December 1851, which ultimately ended the Republic and birthed the Second French Empire, resulted in the abolition of direct colonial parliamentary representation, thereby ending the Bissette-Schoelcher feud. In 1848, however, Schoelcher had presided over the government's Commission for the Abolition of Slavery, and, perhaps unsurprisingly given the bad blood between them, Bissette was denied a seat on the commission. The abolition of slavery and the expansion of universal male suffrage nevertheless opened new political opportunities for Bissette. In 1848, he was elected as one of the deputies for Martinique in the French Assembly. He was forced to resign, however, when his election was challenged on the grounds that no person still in bankruptcy could hold office in France. The following year, Bissette satisfied his creditors and was named to the Assembly, where he (along with Schoelcher) represented Martinique until 1851. Bissette had returned to the French Caribbean after decades in exile to form the "party of order and conciliation" to face Schoelcher and his allies. The Caribbean quickly became a battleground between the partisans of Bissette and those of Schoelcher, the former stronger in Martinique, the latter in Guadeloupe. Since Schoelcher was affiliated with the liberal left, Bissette allied himself with the right, which had opposed many of the principles for which

2. A Hero of Assimilation

Bissette had petitioned throughout his life, and made controversial alliances with white plantation owners.[19]

During the political mudslinging, Schoelcher predictably wrote a book slandering Bissette, who subsequently published a refutation noting that Schoelcher "nursed a deadly hatred for me: he swore ... to pursue me by all imaginable means, to harm me whenever and wherever he could. My friends become his enemies."[20] As a result, Dumas, as one of Bissette's most famous associates, was soon to become one of Schoelcher's bitterest adversaries. A tentative 1849 electoral race was forming in Guadeloupe between Bissette's partisans and Schoelcher and his biracial running mate Martinican François-Auguste Perrinon, who had written against slavery in St. Martin and had been charged with enforcing slavery's abolition in Martinique.[21] Dumas was thus a recognizable name that Bissette hoped to deploy in an attempt to defeat Schoelcher and his allies.[22]

Dumas, arguably the most famous celebrity of black descent in the nineteenth-century Atlantic world, came to be perceived in the second half of the nineteenth century as one who controversially failed to combat the injustice of slavery. This was particularly the case among African American intellectuals, which will be discussed in Chapter 3. However, within his lifetime, Dumas possessed a stronger anti-slavery reputation within France than he did afterward because of his anti-slavery position in works like his play, *Charles VII at the Homes of His Great Vassals* (1831), which featured a slave as the protagonist. As a result, Dumas was a suitable candidate for Bissette's faction. Although Dumas was influenced to an extent by his former teacher and abolitionist Abbé Grégoire, as well as his own ancestral background, he expressed his opposition to slavery largely on the basis of his republican and egalitarian (and somewhat left-wing) political views.

Dumas and the 1848 Elections in Guadeloupe

L'Avenir, a daily journal in Guadeloupe, first suggested in 1848 that the electoral committee of Pointe-à-Pitre, which favored Bissette's political faction, might endorse Dumas as a candidate. The journal's pages naturally noted the writer's political ambitions and that he was Bissette's associate. However, this alone was not sufficient to endorse Dumas as a candidate.

Finding Monte Cristo

As a result, it reported several perceived benefits in nominating Dumas, including "his connections in Paris, his talent and his celebrity, his personal ambition, his conservative principles, and above all, a necessary antagonism between himself and Schoelcher and Perrinon." Even if Dumas turned out to be something of a "dark horse" in the elections, endearing himself "only to a significant minority," the journal nevertheless reasoned that Dumas could rally enough attention to "disturb the sleep" of Schoelcher's partisans.[23] At that time, however, *L'Avenir*'s suggestion ultimately fell on deaf ears.

In the August 1848 and June 1849 elections in Guadeloupe, Schoelcher and his allies gained decisive victories. In 1849, for example, Perrinon and Schoelcher won more than 28,000 votes. In comparison, Bissette and his ally, Mondésir Richard, a biracial abolitionist from Guadeloupe, won slightly more than 8,000 votes. However, the June 1849 selections, the first in which former slaves had been allowed to vote, were marred by the violent suppression of protest groups on Marie-Galante. These groups, comprised mostly of Guadeloupe's black majority, believed white plantation owners had manipulated voting. Such electoral disorder prompted the results' invalidation. It was following this action that in January 1850, the electoral committee of Pointe-à-Pitre, as the "party of order and conciliation" opposed to the "montagnards" Schoelcher and Perrinon, reconvened to select candidates to represent them.[24] *L'Avenir* reported on January 6 that Abbé Charbonneau and local favorite Mondésir Richard received the committee's nominations. However, that evening, Richard gracefully—and surprisingly—declined the nomination. Instead, he resurrected the possibility of Dumas's candidature, publicly pleading his "fellow citizens to transfer to my friend Alexandre Dumas the votes that you would have given me." Borrowing from *L'Avenir*'s arguments the previous year, Richard similarly argued that Dumas, as "one of the glories of the population of color," would bring to Guadeloupe "the benefits of his celebrity, his immense talent, [and] his contacts all over the world."[25]

Three days later, *L'Avenir* naturally jumped on Richard's suggestion, featuring an article elaborating on its previously-reported reasons for supporting Dumas's candidature. Dumas's name was again noted for carrying with it "a true prestige" known across the globe. As a result, he would draw attention to Guadeloupe. The journal implied that the Caribbean territories were historically excluded from "France," severed from "civilization," and long ignored in the governmental decision-making process.

2. A Hero of Assimilation

Since Dumas was at heart Caribbean, despite his birth in the metropole and external "appearance of old Europe," he could help create a link that would help integrate Guadeloupe with "France," in an assimilationist manner similar to that articulated by Bissette earlier in this chapter. As the journal exclaimed, "How his fertile genius could be put to the use of our island! And how he could easily discover here treasures more extraordinary, more real, than that ... of Monte-Cristo." With Dumas as one of its representatives, Guadeloupe, and the French Caribbean in general, would "obtain finally the celebrity they lack" and Dumas's "friendship" would provide it with "numerous contacts with the press and with political men." Further, Dumas was well-suited to represent Guadeloupe since his Creole ancestry rendered his literary fame a credit to the people of the French Caribbean as a whole and individuals of black descent in particular. As *L'Avenir* noted, "it is the brilliant glint that the name of Alexandre Dumas casts on the entire colonial population and above all on the population of African origin." Dumas was therefore depicted as an *homme de couleur* with colonial Caribbean connections, his black ancestry emphasized in part to better resonate with the island's black majority. As "one of us," Dumas had the authority to serve as their representative in France. Yet, he also served as a foil to the white candidates seeking office. As a result, awarding Dumas a seat along with Bissette, the two "men who ... bring honor to *our* population, genius, intelligence and courage, work, love of country, and humanity as representatives of islands in the Caribbean," would add greater representation of French diversity "together with the whites in the legislative assembly."[26] While Dumas's nomination thus sparked a flurry of press coverage overseas, it made barely a ripple in the metropole, which possessed a degree of disinterest in seemingly mundane political events that seemed to be occurring a world away. When the metropolitan press eventually received news regarding Dumas's candidature, it made only passing references to the campaign in its newspapers.[27]

On January 8, the electoral committee of Basse-Terre formally endorsed Dumas's nomination as a member of "the party of order, conciliation, and true liberty," thereby expanding his political stature across the island. In making its nomination, the committee declared that Dumas was "a vast intelligence, a noble choir in the Metropole for the cause of order, and who shows triumph in the colony against the efforts of anarchy."[28] Of all the reasons previously given to support his candidature, the most significant remained the notion that Dumas could help strengthen the links between Guadeloupe and the metropole, making it a more integrated component of a more broadly conceived French cultural society.

Dumas's expanding political support did, however, spark some opposition in Guadeloupe. Even some members of Bissette's faction disapproved of Dumas. Most of what opposition existed to his candidature revolved around his unfamiliarity with the Caribbean, his perceived lack of contributing to the abolition of slavery, his dubious status as a "Creole," and his perceived lack of commitment to the conservative political principles of some of the Bissette faction's key allies. Nevertheless, *L'Avenir* continued to vocally support Dumas's candidacy, emphasizing its "surprise" at such opposition in light of "all that Alexandre Dumas has done, all that he has written, to combat social prejudices." In the newspaper's opinion, Dumas was the only man with enough clout in France and Europe to defend Guadeloupe's interests successfully; hopefully, the writer would forgive these public doubts.[29]

Such opposition to Dumas's candidature, however, foreshadowed his fate in the election. On January 16, *L'Avenir* reported that Bissette's faction had "succumbed to the montagnard and socialist party."[30] Schoelcher and Perrinon received a combined total of more than 30,000 votes to decisively beat Dumas (2,985 votes) and Charbonneau (3,009 votes).[31] Schoelcher would subsequently obtain a mythic reputation among early Caribbean elites as "the spiritual son of the Abbé Grégoire," a status that connected him to the esteemed French Revolutionary abolitionist and intellectual.[32] Nevertheless, in Guadeloupe, Dumas won the greatest percentage of total votes cast in any electoral race in which he ran and he won almost as many votes as the more politically seasoned Bissette had won previously in Guadeloupe in 1849.

Due to the state of the global communication networks between the Caribbean and the metropole, news of the results did not reach the metropolitan press until a month later. *L'Ordre*, for example, published a report on February 17 that it had received preliminary "news of the election in Guadeloupe of Alexandre Dumas as representative of the people.... It is all but certain that Schoelcher and Perrinon were elected by a vast majority thanks to the conflict that exists in the conservative party." The journal decided to subsequently turn its focus to the potential for electoral turmoil in the Caribbean, expressing its hope that these elections, unlike the

2. A Hero of Assimilation

previous ones, would not be "sullied ... by scenes of murder and indecency."[33] Definitive results of the (peaceful) election were forthcoming. Consequently, on February 25 and 26, *L'Ordre* published brief reports indicating the accuracy of the preliminary reports.[34]

Dumas's election campaign in Guadeloupe, although unsuccessful, nevertheless highlighted significant issues regarding identity in the French Caribbean during the nineteenth and early twentieth centuries. First, Bissette and his supporters, mostly Caribbean elites of biracial descent, perceived themselves as "French," despite their black ancestry and Creole origins, and were eager to be accepted as such by the metropole. Dumas thus became a beacon of light for such French Caribbean intellectuals.

Psychologists have identified three general stages in the development of an ethnic, or minority, identity. The development of a Caribbean identity within a larger French cultural collective has generally followed these stages. The first two stages are applicable to what we will discuss in this chapter and Chapter 4. In the first stage, which we can call the unexamined identity stage, identity issues related to the ethnic group have not been examined since the members of the "group" have not defined themselves as such but rather perceive themselves as part of the larger culture. In addition, members of the group may believe negative stereotypes about their ethnic group, and, as a result, often develop feelings of inadequacy. Eventually, an ethnic identity search emerges as a result of experiencing prejudice within the larger culture because of perceived differences that members of the group possess; the possession and recognition of these differences help constitute the "group." Members within the group subsequently enter a second stage spending time learning about and documenting an ethnic heritage.[35]

While experiencing the first stage of this broad process, French Caribbean individuals, particularly elites highly educated in French culture and who often spent time in the metropole, did not generally perceive themselves as "black," "Caribbean," or as an "Other." Rather, they were dark-skinned Frenchmen. They viewed "blacks" as "Africans" and shared Western views regarding Africans' primitiveness. Dumas was understandably a hero to such individuals who felt that it was easiest for colonized "Frenchmen" to disavow their "backwardness," reflected in their dark skin, to believe in their ability to become modern, and thereby achieve Frenchness. In many ways, Dumas shared similar views. As journalist Philibert

Finding Monte Cristo

Audebrand wrote in 1888, Dumas, despite his "face of an African," made "fast to see himself one of the children of the [French] Revolution."[36]

The psychological effects of racism, however, left a lasting legacy in the French Caribbean. Among the most influential mid-twentieth-century Caribbean intellectuals, Frantz Fanon, for one, suggested how it was "normal for the Antillean [Caribbean] to be a Negrophobe," particularly the higher educated ones, for "through his collective unconscious, the Antillean has assimilated all the archetypes of the European."[37] The colonized's assimilation of the French language implied in his/her mind the right to be included as an integral component of "France."[38] Assimilation thus bred the feeling that one was not really black (an outsider) but really French (an insider). As a result, over the course of the next century, Caribbean individuals would continue to be raised to believe in their "ancestors the Gauls," and to adopt "a white man's attitude" so that they did not perceive themselves "as Negro … [because] the Negro lives in Africa." Therefore, as Fanon argued, the Caribbean told himself that he was a dark-skinned Frenchmen and tended "to reject his black, uncivilized family at the level of imagination."[39] Nevertheless, despite being "white through the collective unconscious, through a large part of the personal unconscious, and through virtually the entire process of individuation," his skin color was still black.[40] Since Caribbean individuals were socio-culturally conditioned to the Western association of black skin with impurity, they came to despise themselves subconsciously because of an internalized inferiority, or in other words, abnormalize themselves into "a neurotic situation."[41] Fanon subsequently described this psychological condition as the "colonial complex" and we can perceive it as a reaction to the construction of a mentally dislocated identity defined in opposition to an Other when one is the Other.[42] Therefore, while modernity normalized European identities through relations to a "backward" other, "backward" others who assumed a European identity through colonialism and its legacies abnormalized themselves to a point of neurosis.

The refusal to accept the fact of one's blackness as a result of being raised within the colonial system, forced such individuals to resolve the tensions between the contempt for one's own black skin (and non-contemporaneity) by thinking of oneself in some sense as white (and contemporaneous with Europeans) thereby denying (or minimizing) one's black ancestry. Many within the French Caribbean positioned themselves in relation to metropolitan culture and perceived the French model as the

2. A Hero of Assimilation

only means to attain social status. Consequently, they largely subordinated any sense of a unique indigenous identity to larger French imitation.[43] Discourse that symbolized France as the "mother country" and Romantic nationalist currents depicting the nation as a family, echoing the views of Bissette and the proponents of Dumas's candidature in Guadeloupe, inspired the image of Caribbean individuals as displaced children longing to be reunited with their estranged parent. In order to rationalize feelings of alienation with feelings of (be)longing, Caribbean intellectuals created the myth of two Frances: the ideal France, a loving "mother" who adored all her "children" and therefore exemplified French universalism, and those French colonial officials at the grassroots level who "betrayed" the true France.

During the campaign in Guadeloupe, Dumas was repeatedly presented as a member of the French Caribbean, or "one of us," a person of black descent. Such claims were not simply political ploys to generate a sense of identification with a larger Caribbean public to garner votes. The need to ascertain this claim implied that it was a "revelation." One would never have known that Dumas was of Caribbean origin because he was a fully assimilated Frenchman. In other words, although he had dark skin, Dumas was regarded as not really "black," or "African," but "white," or "French," and his Caribbean family roots had no negative bearing on his status. The Caribbean emphasis on Dumas's black ancestry in the process of connecting him to the Caribbean paradoxically sought to prove how un-black he was in the metropole and therefore implied a reassurance that they too could attain Frenchness regardless of their dark skin. In other words, Dumas's Africanity was intended to emphasize how he had overcome his stigma, or "defect." Dumas, whose political supporters made vague claims that he did much to help his "countrymen" across the Atlantic, emerged as the Caribbean individual who made good in the metropole, and who could continue to use his celebrity to help bring ignored Guadeloupe to the metropole's attention, thereby bringing the two closer together and breaching perceived sociotemporal boundaries. White and black, French and colonial, Dumas physically embodied the "French Caribbean Dream," or union between overseas and metropolitan France and acceptance as "French" popular at the time. Dumas could therefore help overcome the "distance," or estrangement between the people of Guadeloupe—and the Caribbean in general—and their French "mother."

Finding Monte Cristo

Dumas as a French Caribbean Icon

The Dumas presented in the election campaign in Guadeloupe thus set the contours for nineteenth- and early twentieth-century perceptions of Dumas in the French Caribbean. During the nineteenth century, French Caribbean writers, in keeping with the colonial complex, followed metropolitan literary styles to express solidarity with the metropole and membership with the "modern" world. Even to the former French colony of Haiti, which became independent in 1804, France remained the cultural "center of attraction for Haitian writers." For such literary figures, Dumas was a role model. Therefore, as Lilyan Kesteloot has noted, nineteenth-century French Caribbean writers sought integration into the cultural stream of French literature and thus "blindly copied its masters, [men like] ... Alexandre Dumas."[44] Dumas held a place of prominence among all other "French" writers because of his Caribbean family origins and metropolitan success. Such a view, echoing the perceptions of Dumas outlined during his electoral campaign in Guadeloupe, suggested that cultural union with France was essential in finding a home, or place of belonging, and completing a French Caribbean sense of self. In an essay, early twentieth-century Haitian writer René Depestre, for one, recalled that in his youth his mother made him "speak French at the house.... She repeated unceasingly that our future was in French." As a result, Depestre recalled, "I was obsessed by France, thanks to my mother, who made me read ... Alexandre Dumas ... to instinctively develop my culture."[45]

During much of the nineteenth century, French Caribbean writers who visited Paris predictably sought to meet Dumas, who served as a mentor to many of them and sporadically expressed sentiments of solidarity on the basis of their common Caribbean origin.[46] Such expressions only fueled Dumas's reputation among Caribbean intellectuals who sought to culturally integrate the Caribbean with the metropole. For example, the Haitian writer and politician Demesvar Delorme was forced into exile due to political strife in the 1860s, the same decade in which he corresponded with Dumas, whose style inspired his 1873 novel *Francesca*.[47] In a December 1869 response to one of Delorme's letters, Dumas praised the writer's use of history to "present in a new light the men who have contributed most to inspire peoples with love of liberty ... and virtue." As a celebrated "child of the Caribbean," Delorme honored "the cradle of my [Dumas's] ancestors." Dumas expressed further hope that Delorme would help restore stability in Haiti

2. A Hero of Assimilation

so that it could join the great family of nations and expressed confidence that Delorme would leave a revered legacy in the field of letters and in Haitian history. In closing, Dumas wrote, "I embrace you as if I was your father, my dear Delorme, and in you I fraternize in heart with your compatriots, my own people."[48] Such expressions underscored Dumas's legacy within the French Caribbean during the nineteenth century as a Caribbean writer in spirit who symbolized the integration of French Caribbean writers with France's literary elites, creating a more global French culture.

Dumas, therefore, experienced a growing mythification in the French Atlantic world, particularly in the Caribbean. As early as 1856, some French periodicals had asserted that since "Dumas belongs to the African race of Haiti.... Haiti follows with affection all of the movements of MM. Alexandre Dumas."[49] Such comments reflected the popularity of both Dumas and his son. *La Fraternité*, a weekly journal published in Paris in the 1890s to serve "the interests of Haiti and the black race," often printed articles on Dumas and his family to appropriate them as "Caribbean" celebrities and to perpetuate a similar conception of Dumas as had existed during his campaign in Guadeloupe.[50] The journal, therefore, sought to emphasize Dumas's and his son, Dumas *fils*'s, black and French Caribbean ancestry as well as their pride in it. For example, an article in the May 9, 1894, issue of *La Fraternité* declared that "the three Dumases" (General Thomas-Alexandre Dumas, Alexandre Dumas, and Alexandre Dumas *fils*) had assisted in "the success of this crusade against slavery, this double injury to humanity and to God." Further, the article noted that although Dumas *fils* had "white skin," his father, Dumas, had demonstrated "African traits" and his grandfather, General Dumas, was "a very dark mulatto." However, Dumas *fils* had "no reason for wishing to conceal" this "origin so honorable" and consequently he "has never repudiated his black great-grandmother."[51] Another issue in June 1895 featured an article that further elaborated on the Dumas family's connections with Jérémie in Haiti, the "picturesque" home of the father of "the immortal romancer" Dumas.[52] The journal's articles also supported hybridity, posing the claim that the mixture of the "African" and French race "yields admirable results." Additional articles in *La Fraternité* argued that participation in French culture made such individuals part of the modern world, giving them a place of belonging. Such articles thus questioned whether it was right to maintain the "odious prejudice of color" where "the armies of civilization advance."[53] Many articles consequently focused on the "rising number" of "Negro" members within the culturally prestigious French Academy. Thus, in 1891, *La Fraternité* announced proudly that the Academy had "a descendant of a negro," although "not a very dark one," in the person of Dumas *fils*.⁵⁴ In 1894, he was joined by Cuban-born French "mulatto" writer José-Maria de Heredia. As intellectuals of France, the two, which had equals "in neither Europe nor America," demonstrated a "sentiment of solidarity of race" across the Atlantic world as well as hope to French Caribbean elites of gaining acceptance. Consequently, "negroes are as capable as whites of writing, painting, making music, of managing their affairs, and of governing."⁵⁵

The hold that Dumas and his family exerted on the Haitian and larger French Caribbean imagination remained long into the twentieth century. When American travel writer Blair Niles recounted in 1926 her voyage to Haiti, she heard tales about how Dumas's family had settled there. She even encountered an intoxicated Haitian gendarme reading a Dumas novel. The gendarme "boasted" that Dumas was "his cousin."⁵⁶ Tradition, or perhaps more accurately, legend, gave Dumas many "cousins" in Haiti. Perhaps the most famous was Baron de Vastey. Born in 1781 to Marie Françoise Élisabeth Dumas and a Norman colonist, he became a leading Haitian political figure and historian during the early nineteenth century. Later traditions sought to link him to Dumas by claiming that they were related.⁵⁷ Streets and schools in Haiti continued to be named after Dumas and stamps often bore his image (Figure 10).⁵⁸ The government also built what

Figure 10: A mid-twentieth-century stamp printed in Haiti depicting a portrait of Alexandre Dumas and a scene from *The Count of Monte Cristo* (https://www.123rf.com/profile_boris15'>boris15/123RF Stock Photo).

2. A Hero of Assimilation

eventually came to be known as *La Place des trois Dumas* in Jérémie, bearing representations of Dumas's father, General Dumas; Dumas; and Dumas's son, Dumas *fils* (Figure 11).[59] In addition, *L'Habitation Latibolière*, a coffee farm traditionally believed to be the birthplace of Dumas's father, became a popular tourist attraction, reborn as the "*Habitation Davy de La Pailleterie*" (Figure 12).

Conclusion

Individuals deemed "primitive" or "backward," underwent profound cultural, social, political, psychological, and, in some cases as a result of the slave trade and labor needs, geographical dislocations as a result of Western determination to "civilize" the globe. French colonialism, spread through a "civilizing mission," generally sought to "Frenchify" those regarded as "primitive" and make them part of the French nation. Such a process required the colonized to internalize his or her inferior status of "backwardness" and accept the belief that "modern" French culture was superior and desirable to attain. Within the French Caribbean, Dumas thus became a beacon of light to follow in the quest for finding a sense of belonging, a "home." French Caribbean intellectuals, highly educated in

Figure 11: An early twentieth-century postcard depicting *La Place des Dumas* (Dumas Square) in Jérémie, Haiti.

Finding Monte Cristo

Figure 12: A mid-twentieth-century Haitian stamp depicting the *Habitation Davy de La Pailleterie,* a French Caribbean tourist attraction in Jérémie, billed as the home of Alexandre Dumas's father as a boy.

French culture and who often spent time in the metropole, did not generally perceive themselves as "black," "Caribbean," or as an "Other." Rather, they were dark-skinned Frenchmen. They viewed "blacks" as "Africans" and shared Western views regarding Africans' primitiveness. Dumas was understandably a hero to such individuals who felt that it was easiest for colonized "Frenchmen" to disavow their "backwardness," reflected in their dark skin, and to believe in their ability to become modern, and thereby achieve Frenchness.

This process of colonization displaced indigenous and locally developed cultures across the globe and ultimately led to the development of a "colonial complex" that created feelings of self-loathing, alienation, and an eventual search for a lost identity. While identities in the metropole were defined in opposition to colonial Others beyond Europe, how did colonized Others define their identities, particularly since colonialism socially conditioned them to accept a European identity that was defined in opposition to themselves? However, as conceptions about the relationship between the French Caribbean and the metropole shifted, so too did perceptions of Dumas, a topic we shall explore in Chapter 4. A crucial aspect of understanding these changing French Atlantic perceptions of Dumas was his growing importance within the African American memory.

3

Creating a Local Black Identity in a Global Context
Alexandre Dumas as an African American Lieu de Mémoire, *1840–1930*

With the rise of the global book trade, Alexandre Dumas became one of the most popular authors, not just in France, but also throughout Europe and the United States. His works, such as *The Three Musketeers* (1844) and *The Count of Monte Cristo* (1845–1846), were quickly translated for sale abroad. However, the transformation of literature as a form of "art" to one of popular commercial entertainment was not greeted with universal praise by American critics. The nineteenth-century reviewer Albert Southwick noted of Dumas that "in the book trade no name of [a] modern author has had a higher marketable value than his," yet "enlightened critics ... lament that he has abused his talent ... by degrading literature into a mere trade ... in utter forgetfulness of any high motive or aim."[1] Nevertheless, the rising global book trade enabled the works of popular writers from diverse European countries and the U.S. to transcend more easily their own national literatures and become part of a Western body of global literature. Dumas was such a famous figure in the U.S. that Charles Ranhofer, a noted nineteenth-century chef at New York's *Delmonico's* restaurant (then regarded as one of America's finest dining locations), created the Salade à la Dumas to honor the French writer, and the biographer Jacques Lucas-Dubreton claimed in 1928 that Dumas ranked after Napoleon Bonaparte in an American newspaper's survey of the most famous men of the nineteenth century.[2]

Despite his popularity, knowledge about Dumas's black ancestry had been largely unknown in the U.S. among the majority population during the 1830s and 1840s, the years in which he was at the peak of his fame in France. Many Americans generally assumed that such cultural acclivity was characteristic of "whites." In describing Dumas's family history, an 1843 edition of the *North American Review* declared simply that Dumas was "of honorable, though not wealthy, parentage." His father's status as the son of a French nobleman and an African slave from Saint Domingue (now Haiti) was omitted, for he was described only as a "general in Napoleon's army" who "served with distinction in Egypt."[3] This omission was not unique. For example, an 1849 review of Dumas's novel, *The Memoirs of a Physician*, also recounted the writer's background without mentioning his black ancestry and praised him as "a most extraordinary man."[4] Moreover, the omission of Dumas's black ancestry was often accompanied by images in English-language publications that emphasized his Caucasian features, a practice that would become more commonplace in France decades later during the New Imperialism (Figure 13). Such a practice, which contrasted sharply with his image in later contemporary photographs (Figure 14), maintained the illusion that he was not of black African descent.

Figure 13: A typical portrait of Alexandre Dumas as he appeared in English-language newspapers, this one taken from a February 27, 1847, edition of *The Illustrated London News*.

Dumas's black ancestry became widely known in the U.S. during the 1850s. From 1852 to 1855, Dumas published his multivolume memoirs, which gave details about his father's life and black ancestry. The memoirs, readily available in French for the educated elite as well as francophone Americans, were translated into English in abridged form in 1890 and in a complete edition in 1907–1909.[5] In the U.S., an advocate of the "one-

3. Creating a Local Black Identity in a Global Context

drop rule," individuals with any black ancestry were theoretically "black." Therefore, as the French literary scholar Michel Fabre has noted, "in American terms he [Dumas] was a Negro."[6] Not all American reviews of Dumas's memoirs noted his black ancestry, but many, such as *Littell's Living Age*'s 1852 review, certainly did. The review revealed that he had a grandmother "of color" and a father who was "a mulatto giant."[7]

While the knowledge of Dumas's black ancestry made him controversial among majority Americans, whose reactions ranged from disparaging Dumas and his works as "African" to marginalizing his black ancestry by rationalizing that his "white" ancestry was dominant (another practice that would gain in prevalence in France during the New Imperialism), it made him popular with other components of the population who identified with him because of his racial status in American terms. Dumas did not treat the black condition explicitly in his most popular works. Yet, many African Americans read *The Count of Monte Cristo* in particular as an allegory of their own condition and identified with the novel's themes of justice, emancipation, and hope. They, like Dumas in Chapter 1, seemingly related to the title character, Edmond Dantès, an innocent sailor imprisoned in the Château d'If, who escapes, finds a secret treasure, and seeks justice against those who had him imprisoned. As Michel Fabre has suggested, *Monte Cristo*'s popularity stemmed from the fact that Dantès's victory "over injustice could function as a parable for black endurance and eventual freedom."[8] The African American writer Charles W. Chestnutt, for example, noted in his journal in

Figure 14: French postcard, circa 1907–1915, reprinting a photo portrait of Alexandre Dumas, circa 1860s, published by J.L.C.–Legui.

Finding Monte Cristo

1878: "In some things, I seem to be working in the dark. I have to feel my way along, but by perseverance I manage to make better headway than many who have the light; and besides, like Edmund [sic] Dantes in Dumas' 'Monte Cristo,' I have become accustomed to the darkness. As I have been thrown constantly on my own resources in my solitary studies, I have acquired some degree of self-reliance."[9] Fabre has noted that, as a result of such identifications with Dumas and his works, it "would be hard to overestimate the magnetic appeal" the writer "exerted on black Americans ... even before emancipation."[10] As a testimonial to Dumas's status among African Americans during the Civil War era, his portrait graced the first issue's cover of the prominent African American publication *Anglo-African Magazine* in 1858.[11]

In the following decades, Dumas held an increasingly significant role in the consolidation of an African American identity. In this chapter, we will examine how African American intellectuals constructed Dumas into an African American *lieu de mémoire*.[12] Dumas has not been the subject of historical scholarship in this area, and his perception and reception in the U.S. in general has received minimal comments.[13] His popularity among African Americans has not gone unnoticed, but it has not been explored in any detail.[14] This chapter thus builds on the most significant item in this body of work, Fabre's brief article "International Beacons of African-American Memory," which first suggested the idea that Dumas could be analyzed as an African American *lieu de mémoire*, although he provided few reasons for this appropriation.[15]

Europeans placed their "civilized" state as an idealized norm to which others should aspire (or "progress" toward), and by which they should all be measured. Other cultures had to meet the European standard to be perceived as theoretical equals (or "modern").[16] Since most cultures beyond Europe were perceived as falling short of this standard, it was generally imposed on "backward" Others through "civilizing" colonialism, although some Others attempted to reach the standard on their own. The pursuit of modernity, therefore, "legitimized the subjugation" of Other cultures "to establish Western values."[17] Western expansion and domination in the form of internal and external colonial systems dating from the Age of Exploration ultimately served as a form of globalization, spreading white hegemony across the globe, particularly to the Western Hemisphere. Therefore, as Richard Mansbach has argued, "much of the global interconnectedness that we take for granted was produced by European [and American] imperialism."[18]

3. Creating a Local Black Identity in a Global Context

However, the hegemonic narrative of Western cultural development and global expansion, reinforced through colonial systems, did not include individuals of black African descent, who were perceived as "outside" Western culture and history. White Americans broadly perceived themselves as transplanted Europeans and therefore, along with Europe, comprised Western civilization. During the course of the nineteenth century, Western and white became synonymous. As a result, whites retained the monopoly on "modernity," while African Americans were perceived as "backward" individuals with a "primitive" culture. As the African American intellectual W.E.B. Du Bois claimed, "according to white writers, white teachers, white historians, and white molders of public opinion, nothing ever happened in this world of any importance that could not or should not be labeled 'white.'"[19] Beginning to think of blacks from the point of contact with Europeans at the birth of the modern age, thereby ignoring the great African civilizations and cultures of earlier eras, maintained the myth "that the Black man has always been reduced to slavery by the superior White race with which he has lived, wherever it may have been."[20] Such perceptions solidified the West as the exclusive writer of historical progress. No African American individuals were perceived as succeeding in Western terms in the arts, humanities, and sciences. Consequently, African Americans remained alienated from mainstream American society—a "nation within a nation"—despite formally gaining freedom and citizenship in the 1860s.

In the face of such discrimination, African American intellectuals forged a broad "counter-global" bloc, or collective movement, that challenged globalization conceived as hegemonic Western domination. They sought to insert African Americans as a whole into the history of America, (re)creating a local black *American* history that had been undocumented—and hence "forgotten"—because of slavery and Western power. A goal of African American intellectuals was, therefore, to create a "usable past," or counter-memory, that intentionally sought to reconstitute history through the inclusion of African Americans.[21] African American intellectuals sought to counter Western myths about black inferiority, which in turn supported white superiority, by arguing that being of black African descent was not the reason for the lack of African Americans' cultural achievements; that lack was, rather, the devastating legacy of slavery, which limited their abilities and created a break in their development. The want of nationally recognized African American historical figures of cultural achievement in Western terms during the nineteenth century forced intellectuals to rely on blacks of achievement such as Dumas from the Caribbean and Europe. From the mid nineteenth century to the early twentieth century, African American intellectuals subsequently constructed Dumas as a *lieu de mémoire* as part of wider efforts to appropriate historical individuals of black African descent across the globe within a transnational community produced by the Atlantic slave trade. Since all blacks were perceived as having a uniting "essence," the existence of past individuals of achievement such as Dumas meant that all such individuals of black descent had these abilities. Such identification efforts intended to demonstrate African Americans' social and cultural suitability in Western terms and the resulting right to be included in American society.[22]

In the process of identifying individuals in the Caribbean and Europe as "black" and "American" like them, however, African Americans expressed a new local black identity by expanding an "African American" identity to a wider range of individuals than was commonly applied, creating the foundations of a "black Atlantic." African American intellectuals therefore created a "decisive rupture" with the hegemonic geographic and cultural boundaries of "America," exceeding "bounded forms of the local" to create, ultimately, a transnational Atlantic community comprised of individuals of black descent from Africa, America, the Caribbean, and Europe united through a common history organized around the themes of slavery and emancipation, of Western domination and marginalization.[23] Such an application in turn served as a globalizing agent, prefiguring the complex transnational and hybrid identities characteristic of the global age.[24] In other words, while constructing a "usable past" as part of the counter-global movement, African Americans redefined "America" beyond the current hegemonic usage (which generally restricted the term geographically to the U.S.) to encompass an "Atlantic" world—a world in which Dumas was re-imagined as an integral component, transformed significantly into a figure of memory with strong connections to slavery and colonialism.

By using this strategy, African Americans were not concerned with the goal of uniting all people of black African descent around the globe into a transnational bloc. The ultimate objective of creating a "usable past" was to reconfigure Western history to open up "possibilities for shaping different futures" in which African Americans were integral components of American society.[25] By documenting black contributions to America's

3. Creating a Local Black Identity in a Global Context

development in the past, African Americans hoped to legitimize their right to be considered full members of the America of the present, for this new black American history would subsequently be integrated into mainstream American history. Forging a more counter-global transnational black memory would ultimately assist African Americans in their local struggle for equal rights and citizenship in the U.S. As time passed, African Americans gained increasing economic power, positions in elected office, cultural success, and support of local white reformers. Therefore, African Americans began to depend less on blacks from other parts of the globe (although not discarding them as "race heroes") and more on their own recent figures of achievement.

The Context of the African American Struggle to "Unveil" the Past

After the Civil War and emancipation, African Americans, despite gaining freedom and citizenship, generally remained outsiders to the national body, which was dominated by "white," or Western, American culture, and quickly became aware of their "blackness," or a sense of alienation from majority society because of their dark skin, which demonstrated the possession of an irremediable inferior essence that connected them, like their French Caribbean counterparts, to an imaginary and global mono-cultural "African" ethnicity. In contrast, white Americans perceived themselves as transplanted Europeans bonded as part of Western civilization. As Du Bois wrote in a 1922 article, it was white Americans' alienation of African Americans that contributed to a "black" identity. Consequently, the cultural theorist Paul Gilroy has argued that the black need "to acquire a supposedly authentic ... and stable 'rooted' identity ... is perhaps best understood as a simple and direct response to the varieties of racism which have denied the historical character of black experiences and the integrity of black cultures."[26] What was "white," however, was not fixed and quite subjective. Nevertheless, since whiteness was associated with advanced civilization, "proximity to whiteness symbolized the civilizational quotient of a group" and served as a way for majority American society to maintain the subservience of those deemed inassimilable, even while granting them citizenship.[27] African Americans were, therefore, forced into a paradoxical situation: born and raised in America, they found that they could not identify completely with non–Western African society and culture; yet, as a result of their "blackness," nor could they identify completely with existing Western American society and culture.[28]

Many scholars have viewed majority American society's attempt to exercise hegemonic control over non-whites in the post-emancipation era as internal colonialism. In internal colonialism, a minority is "subjugated" by a dominant majority, which defines, locates, and asserts its identity directly over the minority (rather than claiming identity and power from a distance, as was generally the case with European colonial empires).[29] Such hegemony was supported in part through control of the nation's historical memory, which served as a tool to justify certain groups' superior role and to determine who had the right to partake in being "American" and hence Western. Although the U.S. saw itself as an anti-colonial nation because of the American colonies' rebellion against the British, it nevertheless "incorporated many of the defining features of European colonial networks (including the color line) into its economic and cultural life."[30] As a result, mainstream America's social system of internal colonialism acted as an agent of globalization conceived as Western hegemony. The Reconstruction Era's Constitutional Amendments' promises of democracy were short-lived. During the 1870s, faced with little federal opposition, the Reconstruction freedoms began to be eroded, enabling segregation and further limitations on African Americans' rights as citizens.

In response to such broad developments, African American intellectuals began to develop a particular counter-global ideology to unite African Americans as a bloc, or collective movement, possessing solidarity; for it was crucial for African Americans to develop their own popular culture that could then undergo a transformation as part of the wider U.S. mass culture.[31] African American intellectuals (such as Frederick Douglass, W.E.B. Du Bois, and Booker T. Washington) sought to speak as leaders of the African American bloc. While not intellectually homogenous, these scholars generally favored African Americans' incorporation into the national body as equals to reconcile their feelings of being trapped in two worlds. However, the question remained of how to achieve such goals.

A common theme of late nineteenth- and early twentieth-century African American intellectual discourse was a firm belief in racial progress made since emancipation. African Americans, socially conditioned to accept notions that blacks were lesser than whites, identified their Western inferiority as based on their possession of a transnational "backward"

3. Creating a Local Black Identity in a Global Context

culture. As the black historian Arthur Schomburg noted in 1925, the "Negro has been a man without a history because he has been considered a man without a worthy culture."[32] African American intellectuals consequently took strides to demonstrate their cultural acclivity and worthiness of being "American," articulating the dawning of an era in which the global "gap" between blacks and whites was decreasing rapidly in the U.S. As Schomburg continued, expressing "backwardness" and "modernity" in familiar socio-temporal terms, "a new notion of the cultural attainment and potentialities of the African stocks has recently come about … [and] the mind of the Negro has leapt forward faster than the slow clearings of scholarship will yet safely permit."[33] The African American newspaper *Opportunity* repeated such sentiments, calling African Americans "a progressive people" making the "most remarkable advances … by any people in the world."[34] Du Bois also commended "the negro race in America," which had "more than indicated its ability to assimilate into modern [Western] culture."[35] In addition, African American chronicles of black history in America frequently bore titles implying that African Americans were "catching up" with whites because of education and cultural production.[36] Such sentiments were not confined to African Americans alone and gained credence among liberal-minded majority Americans. A 1912 *New York Times* article, for example, reported that African Americans were "making marvelous strides in all the elements of race building" even in the South, where they faced segregation and racial prejudice. Leading newspapers commonly reported on the ways in which "the emancipated race met the trust bestowed upon it" by proving their "capacity to develop and improve."[37]

The African American collective movement that emerged during the late nineteenth century increasingly sought to exert a counter-global hegemony to challenge majority America's authority based on blacks' inferiority and lack of assimilability. A central component was the use of popular culture to formulate a contested discourse of historical development that embodied the memory of a transnational black past and emancipation's significance. Historical memory, therefore, emerged as the battleground on which African Americans fought to be "Americans." We can broadly conceive the study of historical memory as one "of cultural struggle, of contested truths, of moments, events, or even texts in history that thresh out rival versions of the past which are in turn put to the service of the present."[38] As Du Bois, a "creator of black counter-memory," later argued

Finding Monte Cristo

in 1935, "with sufficient ... agreement among the dominant classes, the truth of history may be utterly distorted ... to any convenient fairy tale that the masters of men wish."[39] Consequently, the movement in general used methods that forced a public negotiation of both Western and American history, demonstrating African Americans' contributions to provide them with a present sense of legitimacy as "Americans."[40]

Slavery had not only robbed African Americans of their history but also of their cultural acclivity. Early African American intellectuals argued that their local preoccupation with achieving emancipation and equality prevented the pursuit of the arts for strictly creative purposes and thus the ability to achieve mainstream praise (like Dumas) for works of poetry, drama, and fiction. J.A. Rogers, a twentieth-century journalist and pioneering historian of black history who moved to the U.S. from Jamaica, noted that "luckily for the world, Dumas was ... not [born] in America, where he would have been circumscribed and might have used his genius in the struggle for elementary liberty like his notable Negro contemporary, Frederick Douglass."[41] Douglass, like other former African American slaves and prominent African Americans of the era, wrote "in the limited genres of slave narratives, protest oratory, and racial journalism."[42] He had noted that it was "a marvel" to him that, under such circumstances of racial inequality, he "learned to write at all." He was amazed that "such men as ... Dumas ... could have produced" such creative works, but "many have been the impediments with which I have had to struggle."[43] Individuals of black African descent like Dumas had still been affected by the Atlantic slave trade. However, as the African American scholar Carter G. Woodson argued in 1933, blacks of cultural achievement had risen to such "heights" because they were "farther removed from the influence of slavery and segregation. For this reason, we do not find ... [among African Americans] a Dumas."[44] Du Bois had posed a similar argument, citing only the African American poet Phillis Wheatley as having comparable mainstream praise in the U.S. as Dumas.[45] In *Darkwater* (1920), Du Bois also cited the black British musician Samuel Coleridge-Taylor, who was "fortunate ... to be born in Europe.... In America he could hardly have had his career.... He was one with that great company of mixed-blooded men: Pushkin and Dumas ... and many others."[46] The argument was, therefore, that African Americans' lack of creative production was not because of their dark skin but because of the late elimination of slavery, which prevented their development and left an enduring legacy of discrimination—the socio-cultural

3. Creating a Local Black Identity in a Global Context

condition of "blackness."[47] Dumas's literary works were depicted as a precedent for the achievement of future African American writers in the U.S.[48]

Linked to African American intellectuals' pursuit to create a black past and document black achievements and contributions to America's development was the need to demonstrate the suitability of African Americans as a whole for assimilation into the national body. To this end, African American intellectuals attempted to show that African Americans were on the "same level" culturally and socially as white Americans. Since there were few to be found who succeeded according to Western standards within the traditional definition of "America," African American counter-global discourse shifted its definitional criteria to refer to an Atlantic world in which "African Americans" were united through the common history of slavery. As a result, African American intellectuals developed a more transnational outlook, which sought to identify "African American" heroes of cultural merit beyond the limited local geographic confines of the U.S. African Americans used mainstream American conceptions of race to identify individuals "veiled" from the historical record by their classification as "symbolically white" in the U.S. and elsewhere because of their Western accomplishments both as a means to counter notions of African Americans' incompatibility with the national body and to create a black usable past. During the 1920s, Schomburg concluded that earlier individuals of achievement who were of black African descent were "by virtue of their being regarded as something 'exceptional' ... unfairly disassociated from the group, and group credit lost accordingly." In other words, individuals of black descent such as Dumas were categorized as "symbolically white," reinforcing blacks' incompatibility for cultural achievement and inclusion in the Western narrative of global development. Du Bois even specifically cited Dumas in public lectures to American audiences as among the great black men across the globe "veiled from your knowledge."[49]

Many of Dumas's majority American supporters had increasingly perceived him during the late nineteenth century as being predominantly "white" and thus a component of Western culture through his accolades and literary works. As J.A. Rogers alleged in 1946, Dumas's "'English-speaking' [supporters] ... were anxious to prove that he wasn't a Negro."[50] An 1896 edition of *Scribner's*, for example, argued that, despite the fact that Dumas's grandfather "with all the insolent pride of blood and superb disregard for the laws of God and man" settled in the Caribbean and married "a full-blooded negress," it is the "old aristocrat's pride [that] lives in ... his descendants."[51] In another example, the journalist Albert Southwick declared that Dumas, regardless of his "skin of a slight yellow tinge, and short, crispy, curling hair," was a "true Frenchman" and thus a member of modern Western culture.[52] In such a view—echoing that of some French intellectuals discussed in Chapter 1—Dumas's white ancestry was dominant and could "harness" his wild African characteristics, the result of which was his works of literature. As a result, Dumas's status as an individual of black African descent could be rationalized as being insignificant, demonstrating how the "one-drop rule" was not rigidly applied. In a lecture to the Society for Ethical Culture, Du Bois boldly declared that "you have [in] many great white men this negro element coming in to color and make wonderful the genius which they had." He criticized majority America's tendency to marginalize to the point of forgetfulness the black ancestry of prominent individuals, thereby making them "symbolically white." The *New York Times* article on the event, which expressed alarm at the "startling statement" that great "white" men could be secretly "black," bore the contradictory title "Mixed Blood Aided White Geniuses." If one strictly applied the "one-drop rule," individuals with "mixed blood" could not be classified as "white" in the first place.[53] As in France, various and competing interpretations of Dumas's biracial status existed, such as more "romantic racialist" views that Dumas drew from his African origins to add to his creativity and the opinion that Dumas's "Africanness" was reflected in the fact that his works were carelessly constructed and poorly written. Reflecting the influence of Mirecourt's scurrilous 1840s pamphlet discussed in Chapter 1, others argued that Dumas did not write any of the works attributed to him, but in fact oversaw a "literary factory" and placed his name on the work of subordinates. *Harper's* 1871 obituary of Dumas, for example, described his works as being written "with a carelessness, recklessness, and audacious pursuit of excitement that, happily, has but few parallels in America." He was criticized for using "scarcely any revision" and of producing a vast quantity of works via a "joint-stock company" that had no "scruple about plagiarizing ... whenever literary theft ... would serve their purpose."[54]

The conclusion that Dumas was essentially a "white" writer, however, became increasingly hegemonic in the U.S. during the decades following his death in 1870, as he became a topic for academics' debates rather than contemporary gossip. Dumas's works continued to be read by the

3. Creating a Local Black Identity in a Global Context

American public, but they largely concerned French history and had white heroes; consequently, readers assumed that he was French, which to them implied "white." A testament to the strength and longevity of this image in the U.S. throughout the twentieth century is provided by a 1991 *New York Times* article in which the African American activist Hugh B. Price (b. 1941), then vice president of the Rockefeller Foundation, admitted that he "was an adult" before learning that Dumas was "partly black," for "no literary anthologies in my high school or college courses mentioned this fact."[55] Images accentuating Dumas's Caucasian features were still frequently depicted in nineteenth- and early twentieth-century American editions of his works and on postcards. While the era's textual discourse (such as brief biographies that accompanied his works) admitted Dumas's black ancestry, the visual images generally portrayed a physically "white" Dumas, reinforcing the perception that he was not really a "black" writer at all. Figures 15 and 16 provide examples of such images, which sought

Left: Figure 15: A version of a popular image of Alexandre Dumas appearing in late nineteenth- and early twentieth-century publications (Lebrecht Music and Arts Photo Library / Alamy Stock Photo). *Right:* Figure 16: Image of Alexandre Dumas from a 1905 American edition of *The Count of Monte Cristo.*

to limit the physical characteristics that contemporaries had described as "African," including the kinkiness of Dumas's hair, his skin tone, and the shape of his lips. The journalist B. Phillips, for example, who encountered Dumas at the writer's Château de Monte Cristo, described Dumas as "about the average height, and portly.... The trace of his African blood, though not appreciable in ... [his ruddy] complexion ... was evident in the hair, the lips, and the eyes." In another example from 1871 presenting observations typical of the era, a *Harper's* reviewer declared Dumas as a "man with wooly hair, and deficient calves, and black pigment in the creases of his joints and fingers."[56] The visualization of Dumas and his racial conceptualization are inexorably intertwined. In such depictions, we see how the perceived moral, intellectual, or cultural accomplishments (or defects) of individuals of black African descent could influence how they were imagined physically as either white or black. If, as the adage goes, "a picture is worth a thousand words," such images negated the admission of his black ancestry, inscribing in the viewers' minds a lasting conception of Dumas as a "white" writer, not just symbolically but physically.

As a result, Schomburg argued that the "first true writing of Negro history," which had been in progress since the late nineteenth century, was the "rewriting of ... our common American history" to represent "historical truth," and that "the American Negro must remake his past in order to make his future."[57] In remaking this usable past, African American intellectuals increasingly expanded the African American bloc beyond hegemonically defined "America." Slavery and emancipation remained the key themes of this new American history. Beginning in the late nineteenth century, the production of books featuring heroes of black African descent from across the globe was a common means by which to create a counter-global black transnational collective memory. Such efforts built on the work of the famous French abolitionist and intellectual Abbé Grégoire, whose 1808 *De la littérature des nègres* (translated into English in 1810) illuminated black achievements through biographies of prominent individuals of black descent, including many "American" blacks who had gone to Europe.[58] Dumas consistently appeared in such collections, solidifying his reputation as a black writer among African Americans.[59] A 1921 piece on Dumas in *The Crisis* reflected the African American attitude that had developed toward Dumas, describing him as a "French and Negro" author "notable among the world's greatest writers."[60]

3. Creating a Local Black Identity in a Global Context

Dumas: A "Black" Symbol of Modernity

Dumas was an obvious early candidate for incorporation into the construction of a transnational black usable past because his works had been popular with majority American society, whose standards African American intellectuals aspired to meet. Therefore, although Dumas was "black," he succeeded on Western, or white, terms. Further, he had a long-standing popularity among African Americans. The exodus of whites, blacks, and *gens de couleur* from the French Caribbean to the U.S., particularly as a result of the Haitian Revolution, linked parts of the U.S., especially in the south, with the French Atlantic. Not surprisingly, many African Americans of French Caribbean extraction retained the French language and kept abreast of French affairs and culture. Francophone African Americans often sent their children to France for educations then unattainable in the U.S. Consequently, African Americans learned about Dumas's black ancestry through French newspapers and other media either at home or while abroad.

To such nineteenth-century African Americans, Dumas emerged as a heroic figure. For example, Martin Robinson Delany, an early black nationalist of French extraction, named his seven children after figures of black African descent whom he admired, including Dumas.[61] Further, many francophone African Americans who sojourned in France sought him out. Examples include Pierre Dalcour, who associated with both Victor Hugo and Dumas, and Eugene Victor Macarthy, who attended the Paris Conservatoire during the 1840s before returning to the U.S., where he starred in adaptations of Dumas's dramas *Antony* and *La Tour de Nesle*.[62] The most famous francophone African American in France at the time was Victor Séjour, who emerged as a noted dramatist and poet in French literature. Séjour copied the lifestyle and literary style of Dumas, with whom he also socialized, and dedicated his 1856 play *Le Fils de la Nuit* to Dumas.[63] Dumas's popularity among African Americans of French and francophone descent increased his appeal more generally to African Americans throughout the U.S. For example, African American acting troupes named themselves after notable figures involved in the dramatic arts. At least three during the late nineteenth and early twentieth centuries were named after Dumas.[64] In addition, there were "colored schools," particularly in the Midwest, named in his honor, and many African Americans named their children after him. An example is Alexandre Dumas Watkins,

Finding Monte Cristo

Princeton University's first African American instructor during the 1890s.[65]

William Wells Brown, a former African American slave and writer who traveled to England and France during the nineteenth century, described his first public encounter with Dumas. His account, published during the 1860s as part of a compilation describing the lives of prominent individuals of black African descent, was cited frequently and did much to solidify Dumas as a celebrity among African Americans. Brown wrote:

> In a double box opposite me [at the opera], containing a party of six or eight, I noticed a light-complexioned mulatto, apparently about fifty years of age, curly hair, full face, dressed in a black coat, white vest, white kids, who seemed to be the center of attraction, not only in his own circle, but in others. Those in the pit looked up, those in the gallery looked down, while curtains were drawn aside at other boxes and stalls to get a sight of the colored man. So recently from America, where caste was so injurious to my race, I began to think that it was his wooly head that attracted attention, when I was informed that the mulatto before me was no less a person than Alexandre Dumas. Every move, look, and gesture of the celebrated romancer were watched in the closest manner by the audience. Even Mario [the opera performer] appeared to feel that his part on the stage was of less importance than that of the colored man in the royal box.[66]

Brown remarked admiringly that no writer filled a more important place in the literature of his country than Dumas. Yet he clearly considered the writer's success as a tribute paid to the whole race, which naturally included African Americans. As a result, the celebration of Dumas was simultaneously a celebration of all African Americans. As the historian Elizabeth Bethel has argued, by the Civil War era, "largely as a result of Brown's compilation," the figures included in its pages became "firmly embedded in the popular historical consciousness of African Americans as race leaders and race heroes."[67] Such sentiments set the foundation on which lay Dumas's symbolic value to African American intellectuals in their efforts to construct a transnational black usable past that they perceived as having been lost owing to their time as slaves.

African American intellectuals appropriated Dumas as a symbol of the cultural potential of all African Americans in the U.S. to demonstrate that they were fully capable of achievement at the level of Western culture and of being assimilated into the American nation. Aspects of this symbolic transformation include the assertion of Dumas's black ancestry to counter his "symbolic whiteness" in the hegemonic narrative of Western development. African Americans praised Dumas for the same

3. Creating a Local Black Identity in a Global Context

accomplishments that majority Americans used as a rationale for his classification as "white." However, they also emphasized a rigid application of the "one-drop rule" to argue that Dumas's black ancestry made him a "black," rather than a "white," writer. The purpose was to counter the common perceptions that linked biology to culture, or, in other words, to assert that there was nothing biologically, or naturally, inferior about being of black African descent. Such individuals could attain the same cultural level as whites without having to explain their successes as "anomalies," or, in instances of biracial individuals, as a result of their "white" ancestry being dominant (an argument similarly applied to Dumas during his lifetime in metropolitan France). Du Bois, for example, argued frequently that the "mulatto descendants of Louise [sic] Dumas and the Marquis de la Pailleterie were a great gift to mankind" to counter global notions of black genetic inferiority, and that black blood had produced "mighty offspring" such as "Dumas and Pushkin and Coleridge-Taylor."[68]

One major obstacle to be overcome in solidifying this perception of Dumas as an accomplished "black" literary figure, however, was the longstanding accusation that he was not the "true" author of the popular works ascribed to him. As discussed in Chapter 1, the unsuccessful French writer Eugène de Mirecourt's 1845 pamphlet, *Fabrique de romans: Maison Alexandre Dumas et compagnie*, had declared that Dumas wrote none of the works attributed to him. Instead, he presided over a writing factory comprised of subordinates who produced works to which he ascribed his name.[69] Even though Dumas successfully sued Mirecourt for slander, the charges continued to be made. As a result, Dumas came to be regarded as a popular writer, but someone whose work lacked style, sophistication, and originality.

African American intellectuals, therefore, went to great pains to vindicate Dumas's literary reputation, almost as if they were defending their own. William Wells Brown, to name but one example, defended the French writer by posing the argument that, while Dumas's works were not entirely his own, he took the collaborator's initial idea, substantially revised it, vastly improved its dialogue, and added a "spirited scene" here and there to make the work "his own."[70] During the early twentieth century, the noted African American playwright Willis Richardson wrote an entire drama, *The Elder Dumas*, to vindicate the French writer. The play, set in Paris in 1843, focused on charges that Dumas stole other writers' ideas. Richardson used the drama to argue that Dumas's contributions were substantial. What he received was "rubbish" from unknowns that he "polished and painted and sent out under the name of Alexandre Dumas."[71]

However, some mid-nineteenth-century African Americans had mixed feelings about asserting Dumas's identity as a "black" writer and therefore a member of the expanding African American counter-global bloc, thereby implying fissures within the direction of the burgeoning collective movement. What were the criteria for belonging? Was being "black" strictly a biological condition? Although many attempted to read *The Count of Monte Cristo* as an allegory of emancipation, Dumas, at the peak of his fame during the 1830s and 1840s, did not write much about the "black experience" (that is, slavery, the African diaspora, and racial alienation) or take a highly active role in abolishing slavery, which occurred in France for the second and final time in 1848 and in the U.S. in 1863.[72] Nor did he consistently identify himself as black. As Phillips claimed upon meeting Dumas, he always identified himself simply as a "Frenchman."[73]

Frederick Douglass was the most prominent nineteenth-century African American intellectual to express dismay at Dumas's lack of a "black consciousness."[74] Douglass was an enthusiast for Dumas's work, particularly *The Count of Monte Cristo*.[75] As one biographer has argued, "Douglass had long held up the black author [Dumas] as an example for the race's capacity for genius."[76] Yet his feelings about Dumas were tarnished following a tour of France during the 1880s, when he met Victor Schoelcher, the French politician instrumental in legally abolishing slavery in 1848. Schoelcher, who, as discussed in Chapter 2, had been a political adversary of Dumas and his anti-slavery associates (such as Cyrille Bissette, a biracial abolitionist from Martinique), criticized Dumas, whom he portrayed as an individual who lived immorally and took no interest in working toward slavery's abolition or in improving blacks' social conditions.

Schoelcher's portrait of Dumas, however, was an exaggeration. As discussed in Chapter 1, Dumas did make some efforts to assist the struggle against slavery and inconsistently showed sentiments of solidarity with individuals of black African descent (particularly those who were of biracial descent and educated). During the American Civil War, Dumas received a letter from President Abraham Lincoln asking for an autographed picture to be sold at a June fair in Pittsburgh to benefit sick and wounded Union soldiers. As Lincoln wrote, "We know that we do not make our appeal in vain to you, whose heart and pen have always been in

3. Creating a Local Black Identity in a Global Context

the service of humanity, kindness, and charity." In addition, he asked for "a small donation."[77] Rather than send one autograph, Dumas sent one hundred. He even made "unfruitful" attempts with the French press to open a subscription for the benefit of the fair and sent an offering of U.S. $10 (FFr 50).[78] In France, Dumas may have written to the Bishop of Autun to thank him for his anti-slavery efforts.[79] In addition, his 1838 letter to Bissette, noted in Chapters 1 and 2, revealed his anger over the pro-slavery *Revue coloniale*'s incorrect claim that his poetry was to appear in its pages and expressed his position that "all my sympathies are instinctively and nationally for the opponents of the principles that these gentlemen defend." It was his hope to make this position known "not only in France, but everywhere I can count *my brothers in race and friends of color.*"[80]

Douglass, unaware of the complexities of French politics and the divisions that had existed within the French abolitionist movement, accepted Schoelcher's account. He recorded his conversation with Schoelcher in a private letter, writing that "we have nothing to thank Dumas for.... [This] brilliant colored man who could have let down sheets of fire upon the heads of tyrants and carried freedom to his enslaved people, had no word in behalf [of] liberty for the enslaved." When he visited the recently erected statue of Dumas in Paris, Douglass wrote that he perceived it as "an acknowledgment of the genius of a colored man"; yet he refused to "honor the character of the man himself."[81] Schoelcher's comments did not, however, prevent Douglass from voyaging with his wife to Marseilles to visit the Château d'If, the prison from which the fictitious Edmond Dantès, hero of *Monte Cristo*, escaped to seek his revenge on the men who had him falsely imprisoned. As Douglass recounted in an autobiography, he and his wife had an "irresistible" desire to visit the "Château d'If, the old prison anchored in the sea around which the genius of Alexandre Dumas has woven such a network of enchantment."[82]

Douglass's conflicted feelings about Dumas were thus shaped by the current African American struggles for emancipation and equality to which he devoted his life. His critique of Dumas at this early stage in the push for an African American counter-global movement revealed the opinion that it was the duty of all "black" individuals across the globe to contribute to a collective push for the advancement of equality, overcoming their transnational historical alienation. Some argued that admittance into the African American bloc was not automatically based on being of black African descent, or strictly a biological matter, but rather a sociocultural one. As a result, being "black" became a flexible social construction, mixing biological and cultural determinants.

However, many late nineteenth- and early twentieth-century African American intellectuals found this perception unrewarding. Being a "black" writer in the sociocultural sense was undesirable and "backward," for it meant alienation from, rather than integration into, Western culture and American society. African Americans often praised their race and their distinctiveness through the creation of a clear-cut counter-global collective movement. At the same time, however, they aspired to succeed on Western terms to be considered equal and hence integrated with majority Americans in a "new" America. Dumas's perceived lack of a "black consciousness," which had so offended the likes of Douglass, increased his cultural capital in the eyes of later African American intellectuals. While paradoxically asserting Dumas's biological black African heritage, such intellectuals simultaneously denied his sociocultural "blackness," or sense of alienation from Western culture and society. Dumas was not a "black" writer but rather a "French" one who happened to be of black African descent. As a result, Dumas "had little reason for thinking of the race from which he sprang."[83] Such perceptions led to Dumas being taken as an emblem for those African Americans who hoped to transcend the global color line, to be treated as "Americans" rather than "African" Americans. To them, Dumas was an incorporated "French" writer, rather than an alienated "Afro-French" writer who remained outside the French nation and Western culture. In the 1892 African American novel *Iola Leroy*, for example, the protagonist (who is of black African descent) wants to settle in France, where he believes he can gain greater educational opportunities and equality. As proof, he cites Dumas, "who was not forced to conceal his origin to succeed as a novelist."[84]

At the same time, however, African American intellectuals wished to assert that Dumas had pride in having a black heritage. Since Dumas was linked conceptually to African Americans as a whole, such pride would help foster in African Americans a sense of pride in themselves. J.A. Rogers, for example, in a brief biography of Dumas, cited examples of dubious authenticity to demonstrate Dumas's racial pride. First, he made the claim that Dumas embraced "as a brother" the African American Shakespearean actor Ira Aldridge after viewing the actor's performance as Othello and declared himself a "negro." In addition, Rogers attributed a quote to Dumas in which he reflected on the racism that he experienced

3. Creating a Local Black Identity in a Global Context

in Paris during the aftermath of the Haitian Revolution (1791–1804). According to Rogers, Dumas said, "When I discovered that I was black I determined to so act that men should see beneath my skin."[85]

Owing to his success, Dumas emerged among African Americans as a strong symbol of the potential of all blacks across the globe to achieve the "modernity" associated exclusively with the West and subsequent incorporation of African Americans into the American nation. As a result, he was used as a tool to criticize white racism. Du Bois argued that the "Negro ... resents ... any intimation that the Negro race is deficient in ability ... compared with other races ... [for] modern ... Negro genius has shown itself in ... Alexandre Dumas."[86] This opinion was not restricted solely to African Americans. In 1865, the liberal Carson City *Appeal* asked: "Is color distinctive of talent? I wot not. Is not Frederick Douglass an orator and Alexandre Dumas the chief of novelists? When will these invidious and unfair demarcations be obliterated in this free and enlightened Republic?" In another example from 1870, Albert Southwick argued that Dumas, "so distinguished as a writer and a man, belongs to a race that is generally considered by us incapable of those distinctions in literature and society which he has gained." Consequently, he was "living refutation of those prejudices which would necessarily condemn people of color to intellectual inferiority."[87]

Constructing an Atlantic Dumas

By virtue of identifying Dumas as a "black" writer (in either the biological or sociocultural sense), African American intellectuals affiliated him with the development of an African American counter-global collective movement, or bloc. A result of this affiliation was to extend "American" themes of slavery and emancipation to their remembering of Dumas. African Americans, therefore, embellished his connections with the history of both slavery and the Caribbean, since they generalized "America" to be synonymous with the Atlantic world. The African American identification with individuals of black African descent across the globe altered the perception of such individuals in the sense that they came to hold much in common with African Americans. By overcoming slavery in the Americas and achieving great literary success, the black Dumas of counter-global memory became more "American" and consequently more easily identifiable to African Americans in general. While this identification primarily provided a hero and pride to African Americans, it also generated greater sympathy from majority American reformers since Dumas was popular with both groups. Consequently, creating a counter-global argument that repositioned such a "white" writer as "black" created a "subversive rupturing of dominant geographical imaginations" of America and the West.[88]

By the mid to late nineteenth century, African American intellectuals had conceived a more "American" Dumas, portraying him, along with Haitian Revolutionary leader Toussaint L'Ouverture and the former slave Frederick Douglass, as one of the three great figures of an African Atlantic diaspora. Such connections demonstrated early attempts at conceptualizing a larger global community of "African American" individuals of black African descent to express transnational solidarity through the experience of the slave trade. As early as 1855, James M'Cune Smith connected Douglass to Dumas in his introduction to *My Bondage, My Freedom*, noting Douglass's "versatility of talent with which he wields in common with Alexandre Dumas." In a later example, George Ruffin wrote in his 1881 introduction to *The Life and Times of Frederick Douglass* that "I am glad ... to present a work which tells the story of our most celebrated colored man. To the names of Toussaint L'Overture [sic] and Alexandre Dumas is to be added that of Frederick Douglass. We point with pride to this trio of illustrious names."[89] As late as 1940, the African American scholar of French literature Mercer Cook noted that the black race in the Americas had "produced Alexandre Dumas to write about the world, and Toussaint-Louverture for the world to write about." As we have seen, J.A. Rogers even alleged that Dumas wrote a letter to the Bishop of Autun thanking him for his efforts on behalf of people of black African descent, for at that moment possibly his own relatives were "forming part of the cargoes of slave vessels."[90] Such passages asserted Dumas's black identity and connected him to America (via his association with the Atlantic world) and slavery (since Douglass and L'Ouverture had been slaves), even though it was Dumas's father who had been born a slave in the Caribbean. The connections between Dumas and the Atlantic slave trade have persisted in the African American and Afro-Caribbean memory. In 2007, for example, the Massachusetts Historical Society hosted the Boston premiere of Jamaican-born Ester Anderson and Gian Godoy's film *The Three Dumas*, which was "presented in honor of the bicentennial of the abolition of the

3. Creating a Local Black Identity in a Global Context

Atlantic slave trade." The film chronicled Dumas's life as the "grandson of a slave" who "overcame all the obstacles of prejudice to become a role model."[91]

However, in many instances during the nineteenth century, African American intellectuals wholly fabricated Dumas's ancestry to extend his links with the Caribbean (and by extension, America), thereby increasing his connections to the Atlantic world and slavery. During the 1860s, in his influential *The Black Man, His Antecedents, His Genius, His Achievements*, William Wells Brown perceived Caribbean individuals of black African descent as "American," particularly the primary figures of the Haitian Revolution. Using a more Atlantic connotation for "American," Brown attempted to portray the leaders of the first successful slave rebellion and first black republic as "African American heroes," thereby appropriating heroes of black African descent as part of a counter-global conception of "America."[92] He aimed to do the same for Dumas, claiming that Dumas's grandfather was the Marquis de la Pailleterie, "a wealthy planter of St. Domingo," while his grandmother was "a negress from Congo."[93] Citing the British writer Marcus Rainsford's *An Historical Account of the Black Empire in Hayti* (1805), which was among the first positive accounts of the Haitian Revolution, Brown made the false assertion that Dumas's father, Thomas-Alexandre, served in the "army of his own native land." In fact, Dumas's aristocratic grandfather brought his biracial son to France as a boy. When the French Revolution broke out, Thomas-Alexandre joined the French Revolutionary army. Brown correctly noted Dumas's father's short command of the Black Legion, which was comprised of free individuals of black African descent in France during the Revolution, and his service under Napoleon. However, Brown then falsely claimed that Dumas's father, "at the conclusion of the wars ... returned to his island home." In fact, he was captured leaving Napoleon's campaign in Egypt and held prisoner in Italy before returning to France, where he died in 1806. Brown's account, however, maintained that after his father's death *in Haiti*, Dumas "went to France destitute, where he obtained a situation as a writer." Such a claim contradicted the facts that Dumas was born in France and never set foot in the Americas, and provided the false image that Dumas was born and raised in the Caribbean before moving to France to become a great writer.[94] In Brown's version, therefore, Dumas was a francophone *African American* writer.

Such accounts further solidified Dumas's connections with the

Finding Monte Cristo

Atlantic world. By the early twentieth century, pioneering works on French-speaking writers in the Caribbean by such literary scholars as Mercer Cook featured Dumas. For example, Cook's classic work, *Five French Negro Authors* (1943), lists Dumas among its subjects, in addition to René Maran, Julien Raimond, Cyrille Bissette, and Auguste Lacaussade. In his review of the book, Carter G. Woodson argued that it depicted "the higher strivings of five of the *natives* [of the French Caribbean] who under the impact of colonial enterprise contrived to reach a higher level of expression than the economic imperialists contemplated." With specific regard to Dumas, Woodson argued that viewing Dumas in his "native" Atlantic context would help intellectuals think of him "as a branch from a root in dry ground."[95] Consequently, by the early twentieth century, Dumas had become firmly established in the African American counter-global movement as a black writer who overcame the adversities of slavery, had connections to the Atlantic world (and hence American), and symbolized the potential of all individuals of black African descent to achieve "modernity" on a global scale and of black contributions to Western development. As a result of the solidification of Dumas as a *lieu de mémoire* within the African American collective movement, scholarly reference works up to the contemporary era often include Dumas as an "African American" figure of merit.[96]

Dumas's status as one of the most prominent global black figures led many early twentieth-century African American sojourners to France to visit his grave and sites related to his works to honor his memory. In 1927, for example, the African American educator and civil rights leader Mary McLeod Bethune visited the Château d'If, noting in her journal (somewhat incorrectly) that it was "the place where Alexandre Dumas wrote his last book."[97] John Matheus, an African American playwright and scholar who edited *A Reader on Alexandre Dumas* (1936), also visited the prison during the 1920s.[98] Harlem Renaissance writers, including Arna Bontemps, Langston Hughes, and Gwendolyn Bennett, were all attracted to the persona of Dumas.[99] Langston Hughes recounted in his autobiography the day that he told his father of his literary ambitions. In response to his father's hesitations about such a career choice, Hughes could only think of Dumas as an example of a financially successful writer of black African descent.[100] When Gwendolyn Bennett went to France, she visited sites familiar to her through Dumas's works. When she entered Saint-Sulpice in 1925, for example, she noted that with its marvelous "organ [it] is a

3. Creating a Local Black Identity in a Global Context

veritable stage for romance, set as it is in the very heart of the quarters of Dumas' *Three Musketeers*."[101] Later, she visited the writer's grave, writing a notable poem on the topic.[102] Dumas continued to remain a point of reference for later twentieth-century African writers like Richard Wright.[103]

Conclusion

African Americans argued that one could be both African and American—that Africanness, or being of black African descent, did not automatically exclude one from Western culture and society. African Americans sought to overcome the stigma of their blackness in the U.S. by transcending the racial divide through the reimagining of the hegemonically conceived "American" geographical space to appropriate blacks of achievement in a transatlantic world. The paradox that faced African Americans was that, to be accepted as fully integrated "Americans," they had first to prove themselves independently according to Western standards. In declaring his statement of purpose, for example, Charles W. Chestnutt defiantly wrote: "I will live down this prejudice. I will crush it out. I will show to the world that a man may spring from a race of slaves, and yet far excel many of the boasted ruling race. If I can exalt my race, if I can gain the applause of the good, and the approbation of God, the thoughts of the ignorant and prejudiced will not concern me."[104] As this journal entry implies, many African Americans affirmed their black identity (which they came to see themselves as sharing with other black individuals across the globe), sought to exalt their race, and proclaimed their independence. Yet they paradoxically attempted to praise their race while simultaneously demonstrating their actual and potential cultural acclivity in white terms in their efforts to achieve Western "modernity." Such struggles remind us of the paradox of an individual trapped in two worlds. In *The Souls of Black Folk*, Du Bois used Dumas to help express such sentiments: "I sit with Shakespeare and he winces not. Across the color line I move arm in arm with Balzac and Dumas, where smiling men and welcoming women glide in gilded halls. From out the caves of evening that swing between the strong-limbed earth and the tracery of the stars, I summon Aristotle and Aurelius and what soul I will, and they all come graciously with no scorn or condescension.... Is this the life you grudge us, O knightly America?" Du Bois, both black and white, refutes neither identity. Each identity embraces him as he walks harmoniously with both a great white writer (Balzac) and great black writer (Dumas) to transcend the racial discrimination prevalent in America. In so doing, Du Bois enters a realm in which prejudice is displaced.[105] He articulated the African American's goal as being "to merge his double self into a better and truer self" without losing either former self; "to make it possible for a man to be both a Negro and an American, without being cursed and spit upon by his fellows, without ... the doors of Opportunity closed roughly in his face."[106] The problem lay not in African Americans' blackness but in the American nation's whiteness. Consequently, African Americans such as Du Bois posed a more pluralist conception of American national identity.[107]

In the pursuit of demonstrating African Americans' capacity for cultural accomplishments equal to "whites," African American intellectuals transformed the French Dumas (because of his celebrity status, cultural accomplishments, and popularity with both white and black Americans) into a francophone African American "cultural beacon" that they hoped would help undermine the existing social structures of inequality, forming a component of a broad counter-global alternative to white hegemony to force a negotiation of "Americanness" in the public sphere. Following his death in 1870, Dumas increasingly became an African American *lieu de mémoire* representative of blacks' global potential for "modernity" in Western terms, functioning as a black role model who evoked "a feeling of racial pride and 'togetherness' on a worldwide scale."[108] As a result, the Dumas of the African American usable past came to possess certain traits that were exaggerated from historical fact, including heightened connections to "America" through his Caribbean heritage and to the Atlantic slave trade.

The rising efforts that emerged during the late nineteenth century to remove the hallmarks of U.S. internal colonialism and white global hegemony in pursuit of an integrated national body reached their peak during the Civil Rights Movement of the 1950s and 1960s. Even at this time, Dumas was an established symbol within a collective African American memory of a global black past. For example, an issue of the publisher Bertram Fitzgerald's 1960s *Golden Legacy* African American comic book series, which detailed the lives of prominent individuals of black African descent, featured Dumas and his family. Early African American efforts against internal colonialism foreshadowed the era of post-war decolonization and identity struggles that faced contemporary western Europe,

3. Creating a Local Black Identity in a Global Context

including France. As the French sociologist Albert Memmi noted, "racism epitomizes and symbolizes the fundamental relationship between the colonist and the colonized."[109] External European colonialism may have increasingly trudged its way to its formal demise during the twentieth century, but the rising number of individuals moving to Europe from its former colonies created a form of internal colonialism within many contemporary western European societies. While Dumas came to occupy a critical role within the African American memory and their struggles for equality, Dumas was to be forgotten within the French Caribbean and African *Négritude* Movement, a topic we will explore in the next chapter. Individuals of black African descent around the globe were, therefore, engaged in the first stages of a transformation that would result in their achievement of political, economic, and cultural advances during the second half of the twentieth century. Africa, colonized by Europe, would gain its independence and individuals of black African descent in the U.S. and Caribbean—major centers of the African diaspora—would increasingly seek to free themselves from the consequences of slavery and quasi-slavery, such as racial repression and discrimination. As the twentieth-century African American writer Richard Wright argued, "the history of the Negro in America ... is the history of Western Man writ small. It is the history of men who tried to adjust themselves to a world whose laws, customs, and instruments of force were levied against them."[110]

4

Forgetting Alexandre Dumas

Négritude and the French Caribbean and Africa in the Mid-Twentieth Century, 1930–1970

By the early twentieth century, scholars of French culture had begun to analyze France as no longer a European, but rather a global polity as a result of its overseas territories. For example, in 1939, Mercer Cook, a Howard University professor, perceived "France" as being located in three areas: the European continent, the Caribbean, and Africa.[1] Similarly, African American intellectual W.E.B. Du Bois referred to France as "a world nation with one law-making body."[2] French colonial imperialism fostered the establishment of increased transportation, information, and communication networks that helped integrate the colonies with the metropole, enabling greater, mutual flows of ideas and people; the "contemporaneous" (modern) and "non-contemporaneous" (primitive or backward) worlds noted in Chapter 1 were becoming increasingly blurred. But the French sense of a "civilizing mission," which helped justify colonial imperialism, created difficulties as the goal of bringing "modernity" to the world continued. Everyone could not possess a culture equal to the imperialists, otherwise they would have had no purpose, no justification for domination of the world.[3] The superiority of modern European identities thus required the perpetual existence of inferior peoples and cultures, the exploitation of which provided Europe with its wealth (hence "Europe is literally the creation of the Third World," as French Caribbean intellectual Frantz Fanon suggested).[4] Colonials and overseas citizens who had assimilated French culture, however, found themselves excluded from the

4. Forgetting Alexandre Dumas

French cultural nation just as Dumas had been during his lifetime. Consequently, colonials and overseas citizens remained locked in a state of "non-contemporaneity" (or backwardness) that forced them to the margins of a global French civil society. The only way to abolish the sociotemporal "gap" between the two worlds, to escape from being "mired in the Dark Ages," as Fanon articulated it, would be "to dislocate the colonial world" by eliminating constructed borders of differences—a seemingly impossible task.[5]

However, there was a marked difference between the official political roles that French Caribbean and francophone African individuals held within the global French state. After slavery's abolition in 1848, the people of Martinique, Guadeloupe, and Guiana became French citizens with parliamentary representation, municipal self-government, and protective social legislation, as we saw in Chapter 2 when Dumas tried to run as a representative of Guadeloupe in the French government. However, in response to the declining sugar economy, the Second Republic (1848–1852) indemnified planters, restricted Caribbean social rights, and instituted restrictive labor regulations. The Second Empire (1852–1870) abolished national representation and municipal governments and instituted more severe forms of labor coercion.[6] The Third Republic (1870–1940) nominally reinstated Caribbean political rights, but it imposed an authoritarian colonial administration that governed a racially organized society.[7] Legal and political integration as overseas French departments in 1946, most of them in the Caribbean, instead of creating equality with the metropole and a sense of belonging, created new relations "of socioeconomic dependence and political marginalization."[8] As formal departments of "France," there should have been no difference between French citizens in the Caribbean and French citizens in the metropole. In addition to political unity, there was minimal "cultural distance" between the two: they were Catholic, spoke French, and received French educations.[9]

Meanwhile, although citizenship remained a central component of the Republic's core, its colonizing mission in Africa created subjects, not citizens. Being a citizen required certain dynamic qualities rationalized as being absent in individuals beyond Europe. Such qualities could likely be learned over time and such individuals could "catch up" to those of white Europeans. Early twentieth-century French traveler Jules Huret thus expressed a view held by many metropolitan Frenchmen when he observed that "for climatic or other reasons the African started out late on the road to civilization ... but I do not doubt that he will continue to progress rapidly in the future."[10] As elite Africans became "civilized," however, the problem of what rights they would obtain became a reality rather than a theory. The French colonial processes of missionary education, assimilation, and praise of the *évolué*; "training" in self-government; and other means taught the local elites ideas of universal liberty, equality, and fraternity. Once educated in French culture, African subjects increasingly used French ideology against the Republic's hypocrisies, challenging colonialism's inequalities based on unequal notions seemingly incongruent with the democratic and universal ideals inherent in Enlightenment rhetoric.

For much of the first half of the twentieth century, however, there were relatively few individuals in the metropole from the Caribbean and Africa.[11] As a result, blacks from these areas did not pose much of a social or cultural threat or economic competition for white metropolitan Frenchmen. Nevertheless, such individuals' experiences were in many ways similar to those of Dumas discussed in Chapter 1 in which he was often the subject of unwanted attention in the metropole because of his "exoticness." Fanon, for one, wrote often about the demoralizing (and de-humanizing) "white gaze" he and others encountered in the metropole. It was through the "dissecting" presence of this gaze that he "discovered" his "blackness ... deafened by ... backwardness."[12] Under such a gaze, Fanon argued, a black individual felt "the weight of his melanin" for it automatically made him or her a "prisoner" to the constructed "image of the black savage" rampant in French society.[13] Thus, the sight of black skin resulted in an automatic (unconscious) classification of the individual in the metropole as "backward," or primitive, thereby imprisoning him or her "at an uncivilized and primitive level."[14] This socio-cultural perception proved difficult to shake from the metropolitan French social imaginary, which often merged all individuals with dark skin as a mythical, monocultural "African"; a view particularly alarming to many Caribbean citizens because of their French cultural acclivity and belief in their "whiteness."[15] Consequently, metropolitan Frenchmen had difficulty in perceiving blacks, regardless of where they were from, as "French" instead of "foreigners."[16] This Othering could seemingly not be undone, even if the ostensible basis for difference (i.e., possession of a "primitive" culture as a result of its perceived figurative "distance" from Europe) had been actually overcome. As a result of such displacement, many French Caribbean and other colonial intellectuals came to increasingly reject the "inferiority" of having dark skin and the broader implication of dividing humanity into modern and unmodern peoples and cultures.[17] Similar feelings of exclusion, or "homelessness," were felt across the Atlantic.[18] The acceptance of the project of modernity, therefore, became a form of "self-enslavement."[19]

Within the French Atlantic world, and particularly in the Caribbean, local elites thus gradually came to the conclusion that despite their assimilation of French culture, they could never truly escape their perceived backwardness and find a "home" with France. In their search for "Monte Cristo," colonial and overseas intellectuals attempted to deal with these aspects of globalization by furthering the establishment of an ethnic (or minority) identity in response to their status as outsiders. Launching an ethnic identity search as a result of experiencing prejudice within the larger culture because of perceived differences that group members possessed, such intellectuals came to regard the possession and recognition of these differences as helping to constitute their "group." By learning about and documenting an ethnic heritage, as well as through much debate, such individuals sought to develop an ethnic identity that created an appreciation of the "ethnicity," or minority identity, to allow the members of the perceived ethnic group to develop a full sense of pride in themselves and a new understanding of their place within the larger culture.[20] In such efforts, the African American example served as inspiration.

The New Negro Movement and Négritude

Many African American intellectuals, particularly those of the New Negro Movement, often expressed African Americans' cultural advancement in temporal terms, a feeling of optimism that events were in motion that would help African Americans escape their "backwardness."[21] But elsewhere in the Atlantic, more pessimistic attitudes emerged. Some of early twentieth-century African intellectual Léopold Senghor's poetry, for example, reflected the inescapability of "non-contemporaneity," or as he wrote, of existing "out of time."[22] Later French Caribbean writers would repeat such sentiments. For example, the fictional character of Elmire in Patrick Chamoiseau's novel *Chronicle of the Seven Sorrows* (1986) recites: "And Haiti, mama wounded by/ that nightmare Doc/ who paints her life naively/ *outside of time and space.*"[23] Through their experiences as outsiders in the metropole, French Caribbean intellectuals reacted to national rejection through a contemplated search for identity elsewhere. Perceiving their "backwardness" as being based on their black skin, which signaled their colonial status, French Caribbean intellectuals began to perceive themselves as sharing a common identity with black Africans and other colonized individuals. They reacted through *Négritude*, which glorified their black African "primitiveness" and instead suggested the "backwardness" of the "modern" world. Through increased migratory flows now possible in an increasingly globalizing world, colonized and formerly colonized individuals from across the globe were thus able to converge in cosmopolitan locations like Paris, sharing their experiences and forming a sense of transnational solidarity.

Fanon, who had studied under the seminal French Caribbean writer Aimé Césaire, summarized *Négritude* as a black "superiority complex" that was a reaction to the long-standing treatment of blacks as inferior outsiders.[24] The broad concept of *Négritude* stemmed initially from the intellectual works of the Martinican Césaire, the Guianian Léon Damas, and the Senegalese Léopold Senghor, who met as students in interwar Paris. The term *"Négritude"* first appeared formally in Césaire's *Notebook of a Return to the Native Land* (1939), which won wider acclaim in 1947, when it was accompanied by a preface from surrealist artist André Breton.[25] Since Caribbean and African colonials had been "educated" to believe in the backwardness of Africa and "primitive" cultures, everything African was "savage, primitive, and pagan."[26] The West thus conditioned itself and those it colonized to perceive black as "the symbol of evil and ugliness."[27] This created a conflicted sense of self that even Dumas exhibited in his attitudes toward blacks and people of mixed racial descent. *Négritude*, borrowing from German intellectual Leo Frobenius's idea that "the barbaric Negro is a European invention," countered the negative socio-cultural connotations associated with blackness.[28] The invention of the "Negro," and by extension the fabrication of whiteness and the racial boundary policing that came with it, gave Europe "a monopoly on beauty, intelligence, [and] on strength."[29] In Césaire's adaptation of Shakespeare's *Tempest*, for example, the slave-master Prospero calls Caliban, a black slave, an "ugly ape," wondering how anyone could "be so ugly." Yet, Caliban challenges this accusation, replying defiantly, "You think I'm ugly ... well ... you're [not] so handsome yourself. With that big hooked nose, you look just like some old vulture ... with a scrawny neck!"[30] Since Caribbean individuals, in particular, often denied their black African heritage, Césaire

4. Forgetting Alexandre Dumas

observed that they "searched for all sorts of euphemisms for Negro: they would say a man of color, a dark-complexioned man, and other idiocies like that."[31] As one black journalist similarly noted in 1927, the "Martinicans and Guadeloupeans, who believe themselves to be of a superior essence, consider *nègres* from Africa ... to be inferior beings and forget their own origins; yet they know well that their own ancestors were African blacks sold as slaves and transported to the Antilles."[32] The terms *nègre* and *noir* generally signified blackness, but *nègre* was regarded as more derogatory since it had been associated with slavery and exploitation; it thus became symbolic of being outside modernity.[33] As a result, the term *nègre* had served as a form of what we can call "discursive ghettoization," or a label that establishes social boundaries that isolate one group in a given community from the larger community. As African American writer Richard Wright explained, "the word 'negro' ... is not really a name at all nor a description, but a psychological island ... within whose confines we live ... and ... its rocky boundaries have remained unyielding to the waves of our hope and dash against it."[34] *Négritude* writers consequently fought against the "embarrassment" of their "primitive" African heritage by picking "this word [*nègre*] up out of the mud ... in order to make it a symbol."[35]

In addition, Césaire and other proponents of *Négritude*, in a manner similar to that of African American intellectuals in Chapter 3, criticized Western history, which obliterated an African past prior to slavery at the beginning of the modern age. For example, Afrocentric historian Cheikh Anta Diop argued, "the memory of humanity concerning the past of Black people" had been "rendered amnesic" by slavery.[36] In *Notebook of a Return to the Native Land*, Césaire stated sarcastically, "No, we've never been Amazons of the king of Dahomey, nor princes of Ghana ... nor wise men in Timbuktu ... nor architects of Djenne, nor Madhis, nor warriors ... [only] mediocre dishwashers, shoeblacks without ambition."[37] In other words, Africa was omitted from accounts of world civilization, "as if Africa had made no contributions to the world." Césaire, for one, was determined to show that "Africa was not some sort of blank page in the history of humanity," but rather the source of a heritage worthy of respect "and that this heritage was not relegated to the past, that its values were values that could still make an important contribution to the world."[38] Further, *Négritude* proposed the argument that the Haitian Revolution birthed a universalistic concept of human rights. Although the French Revolution abolished slavery in 1794 after its agent, Léger-Félicité Sonthonax (1763–1813), had freed the slaves in Saint Domingue in 1793, this radical "promise" of change was not long lasting; Napoleon Bonaparte reintroduced colonial slavery in 1802.[39] As a result, many subsequent historians have assessed the Haitian Revolution as establishing the first modern state to implement universal and unconditional human rights. Advocates of *Négritude* consequently portrayed Haiti as the center of the movement against Western modernity and the birthplace of a more universal human civilization. In some of his poetry, for example, Damas depicted Africa and the New World as parts of a single body, suffering and crucified, "and its heart is beloved Haiti, Haiti which dared to proclaim Humankind in the face of the Tyrant."[40] As a result, the reclamation of the black memory emerged as a first step in the perceived liberation of the race and the restoration of black pride.

Négritude also attempted to emphasize black culture's uniqueness within a larger discourse of universalism in order to achieve acceptance within the larger cultural collective.[41] Césaire, for example, argued that "one should not oppose universal to particular. It is not by negating the particular that one reaches the universal, but by exploration and clear recognition of the particular." So, "the blacker we are going to be, the more *universal* we'll become.... Hence my way of relating (this is paradoxical) to this land, the tiniest township in the universe, this speck of an island that is, for me, *the world*."[42] Unless Western Europe, in its dealings with Africa, the Caribbean, and Asia undertook on its own initiative a new politics founded on respect for all peoples and cultures, there was no salvation for France and Europe.[43] As Ariel, a mulatto slave, declared to the black slave Caliban in Césaire's *Tempest*, he was trying to save all humanity, including Prospero, the symbol of Europe: "I'm not fighting just for *my* freedom, for *our* freedom, but for Prospero too, so that Prospero can acquire a conscience."[44] Rather than isolate "unmoderns" in a perpetual state of backwardness, it is suggested that the focus should be placed on relating to each other (what makes us similar) instead of comparing ourselves to each other (what makes us unique). As a result, identities would no longer be formed in oppositional relationships.[45]

Négritude writers thus initially reacted to their alienation from the West because of their black skin through the formation of an African identity. The decision to consciously associate oneself with "that place of barbarism about which no civilized map goes into detail" was a shock to

4. Forgetting Alexandre Dumas

traditional French Caribbean assimilationist currents described in Chapter 2.[46] Yet, as Caribbean writer Paulette Nardal argued in 1932, "the uprooting and the ensuing estrangement they felt ... had given them a real Negro soul, in spite of their Latin education."[47] Senghor similarly expressed *Négritude* as essentially the black man's quest for "the black essence in the depths of his heart."[48] Césaire examined the subject as a disembodied self seeking to escape solitude through solidarity with a "native land." Such a view reflected the shift in the quest for origins, or paternity, from France to Africa. At the heart of such a quest was the need to discover a missing element that would supplement (and hence "complete") the sense of self that would remove a sense of isolation. In his poem *"Dit d'errance,"* for example, Césaire suggested that "every island beckons/every island is a widow." As he wandered through his "dismembered" archipelago, the poet dreamt of a "lost body" for which his island is calling out in the hope of someday being reattached to it.[49] *Négritude* writers, therefore, defined themselves in relation to their cultural, racial, and historical connections to Africa as a way to reject French colonial hegemony and cultural, intellectual, racial, and moral domination. Such writers viewed the shared black heritage of members of the African Diaspora as a source of pride and power for those oppressed by the physical and psychological violence of the colonial project.[50] As Césaire contemplated in retrospect, if he and Senghor "spoke of *Négritude*, it was because we were in a century of exacerbated Eurocentrism, a fanatic ethnocentrism, that enjoyed a guiltless conscience. No one questioned all that—the superiority of European civilization, its universal vocation—no one was ashamed of being a colony. Europe really had nothing on its conscience and the colonized readily accepted this vision of the world; they had interiorized the colonizer's vision of themselves.... So *Négritude* was for us a way of asserting our own selves. First, the affirmation of ourselves, of the return to our own identity, of the discovery of our own selves."[51] In this sense, the rise of African, or black, identity, was "the child of European colonialism."[52]

Négritude celebrated the perceived existence of a black African essence that served as a common origin to transcend cultural differences between people of black descent scattered across the globe. Yet, *Négritude* built on earlier intellectual currents formulating in the Atlantic world, including pan-Africanism, which had been formulated by black intellectuals in parts of the Caribbean and United States to create solidarity between native Africans and those of the African diaspora as part of a macro-national global community.[53] French Guyanese writer René Maran's Paris salon in particular had emerged during the interwar period as an early center where black intellectuals from the Atlantic world met and exchanged ideas, thereby serving as a significant site for intellectual exchange between African American and French-speaking blacks from the Caribbean, South America, and Africa.[54] Maran in particular helped expand Harlem Renaissance writers' New Negro movement's popularity in the French-speaking world. For example, in the September 1, 1924, issue of *Les Continents*, a black newspaper founded in Paris, Alain Locke wrote an article that defined the New Negro movement's goals for a French-speaking public.[55] Maran also wrote articles on the movement for such publications as *Vient de Paraître* and articles on the French literary scene for African American periodicals like *Opportunity*. In a February 1928 letter, Maran wrote to Locke, "I continue to be involved with young American poets and you as much as possible.... My efforts are not in vain.... People speak of you from the Eiffel Tower radio-station."[56] As a result, Senghor claimed retrospectively that Maran was a true link between the continents, forging bonds across the Atlantic world.[57]

The New Negro movement's emphasis on pride in being black, documenting a black past in order to reshape their future, and emphasis on difference in order to achieve acceptance within the larger cultural collective created "a steady traffic of ideas across the Atlantic ... and the eventual take-over by the *Négritude* movement."[58] For example, Césaire wrote his thesis on the Harlem Renaissance writers and their representations of the American South, and both he and Senghor often acknowledged *Négritude*'s indebtedness to the New Negro movement. For example, in interviews, Césaire attributed the New Negro movement of expressing "the rudiments" of *Négritude*. To Césaire, it was the "beginning of a cultural revolution" that was not a refusal of the outside world, but rather an attempt to bring "things into focus" through "a desperate quest for the Negro 'self.'"[59] Similarly, at a conference in 1950, Senghor declared Harlem Renaissance writer Claude McKay "the true inventor of *Négritude*."[60] Sixteen years later, during a speech at Howard University, Senghor repeated *Négritude*'s indebtedness to African American culture, stating that "though the word was coined in France ... the thing itself, the ideology, was indeed a product of the Negroes of the USA."[61] Consequently, we can view *Négritude* as "a transatlantic reflection" of the New Negro movement. As a result of this cross-cultural exchange, African American ideas influenced

French culture and "helped reshape the very nature of racial identity in modern France."⁶²

Differing Views on Dumas

African American conceptions about a black identity thus influenced the French *Négritude* movement, including the concept of a black essence that united all individuals of black descent; the sense of an Atlantic Diaspora that connected Europe, the Americas, and Africa; the need to recover a black history lost as a result of slavery; pride in being black; and an emphasis on blackness in order to eliminate socio-cultural divisions. Yet, it is the two movements differing perceptions of Dumas that help illuminate just how the two movements radically differed. As we saw in Chapter 3, Dumas was a symbol to African Americans who hoped to transcend the global color line, to be treated as "Americans" rather than "African" Americans. To them, Dumas was an incorporated "French" writer rather than an alienated "Afro-French" writer, who remained outside the French nation and Western culture. Like Bissette and some other earlier Caribbean intellectuals discussed in Chapter 2, African Americans thus emphasized Dumas's black heritage to prove its irrelevancy. The Dumas of African American memory, similar to his early French Caribbean counterpart, was re-imagined as an integral component of a black Atlantic world with strong connections to slavery and colonialism. However, by overcoming Atlantic slavery and achieving great literary success, this conception of Dumas became more "American" and consequently more easily identifiable to African Americans as a whole. Consequently, by the mid to late nineteenth century, African American intellectuals conceived Dumas, portraying him, along with Haitian Revolutionary leader Toussaint L'Ouverture and former African American slave Frederick Douglass, as one of the three great figures of an African Atlantic Diaspora. Such connections demonstrated early attempts at conceptualizing a larger global community of "African American" individuals of black descent to express transnational solidarity through the experience of the slave trade. However, as we have seen, in many instances during the nineteenth century, African American intellectuals fabricated Dumas's ancestry to extend his connections with the Caribbean (and by extension, America), thereby increasing his connections to the Atlantic world and slavery. Nevertheless,

Finding Monte Cristo

by the early twentieth century, Dumas had become established in African American intellectual circles as a black writer who overcame the adversities of slavery, had connections to the Atlantic world (and hence "American"), and symbolized the potential of all individuals of black African descent to achieve "modernity" on a global scale and black contributions to Western development.

Within their historical contexts, both the New Negro and *Négritude* movements were essentially protest movements against a hegemonic culture that excluded people of black African descent from full equality and sought to use art and literature as a means through which to express this defiance at alienation, or "homelessness." Returning to Césaire's *Tempest*, the black slave Caliban, for example, defiantly warns his master Prospero of the coming "storm," the global demand from the oppressed for equality, in the play's finale:

> I bowed my head, for years I took it, all of it—your insults, your ingratitude.... But now, it's over! ... I don't give a damn for your power.... I'll impale you ... on a stake that you've sharpened yourself! ... Prospero, you're a great magician: you're an old hand at deception.... [Y]ou lied to me so much, about the world, about myself, that you ended up by imposing on me an image of myself: underdeveloped, in your words, undercompetent, that's how you made me see myself! ... I hate that image ... and it's false! ... [N]ow I know you, you old cancer. And I know myself! ... I know that one day, my bare fist ... will be enough to crush your [crumbling] world![63]

As a result, the French philosopher Jean-Paul Sartre argued that "black poetry in the French language is, in our time, the only great revolutionary poetry."[64] However, *Négritude*'s sense of protest did not go so far as to push for a break from France. Through the construction of an African essence, they hoped to relocate the position of blacks within French society, similar to the New Negro movement and American society. Despite their expressions of affection for Africa, *Négritude* writers still felt a connection to French culture and society.[65] Consequently, *Négritude* writers had no qualms about using the French language. Therefore, *Négritude* "vascillated between Black nationalism ... and the need to assimilate the Black world to the universal (i.e., French) culture."[66] Césaire, for example, described it as "a tool ... to use in developing a new means of expression. I wanted to create an Antillean French, a black French that, while still being French, had a black character."[67] Just as earlier French writers like Racine shaped French values and styles from their mastery of Greek fables and techniques of representation, Senghor believed that

4. Forgetting Alexandre Dumas

Africans, too, must "discover their blackness and a style to express it through the study of French letters."[68] At the same time, its proponents ambiguously argued that the use of French and admiration for French ideas did not automatically require one to be French. As Senghor argued, "to espouse the French language as the universal tool does not contradict the concept of association that implies a relationship between two autonomous states."[69] However, despite their affection for French, *Négritude*'s founders urged a decisive departure from much of existing Caribbean literature, which was largely a pastiche of metropolitan styles.[70]

The "revolutionary" aspect of *Négritude* literature in terms of style and presentation was significant in regard to the movement's reevaluation of Dumas. In the 1920s, amidst a rising fascination with African culture in Paris, metropolitan intellectual circles gave increased attention to colonial literature. While agreement existed on the importance of such literature, publications exploring the topic made little to no reference to writers from the Caribbean. Mercer Cook asserted in the 1940s that this neglect was the "general rule," in part because Caribbean authors had "become so thoroughly assimilated into the literary life of Paris as to lose their insular identity."[71] In other words, Caribbean writers wrote in metropolitan, or "mainstream," styles to such a degree that they were overlooked "colonial" writers. Haiti, in particular, maintained a hold on writers in French, particularly in the Caribbean, during the nineteenth and twentieth centuries, due to the slave revolution in the 1790s, and shaped *Négritude* conceptions of blackness.[72] Early Haitian leaders conceived the nation at first as a modern, socially progressive state. Elite attitudes toward Africa were similar to those held by white Europeans. For example, Baron de Vastey, who claimed to have fought in the revolution, asserted that Africa "can only be civilized by being conquered, a conquest which brings civilization…. [P]owerful means are required to change manners and customs [for] one cannot persuade people who are unable to be persuaded; that requires a degree of enlightenment."[73] Césaire once told an anecdote about a local Caribbean man who entered and won a poetry contest in the metropole. The man beamed with pride over the fact that when the judges read the poem, they had not even realized that his poems were written by a man of black descent.[74] Such a literary style indicated the larger issue of the lack of a strong distinct Caribbean identity and the effects of colonialism on the colonized psyche. Consequently, Haitian writer René Depestre called such literature "pseudo-literature," and reiterated the argument that the creation of an independent literary style, a symbolic break with the culture of the metropole, finished the work of the Haitian Revolution, which was only "a violent attack against the French presence in our country," since "our first authors did not attack French cultural values with equal force." As a result, the establishment of a unique literary tradition proceeded "toward a decolonization of their consciousness," thereby separating the existing socio-cultural alignment with the former colonial power.[75] Damas shared a similar view, suggesting that in the 1920s and 1930s, a "second revolution," or a radical shake-up of complacent elite moral and cultural values, was needed. He regarded Jean Price-Mars as a leader of this new generation, and thus a finisher of the Haitian Revolution.[76] However, Damas perceived this final revolution as aligning Haitian culture with that of Africa. Although Césaire's work on Haiti focused on the era of the Haitian Revolution, he too remarked on how Haiti was "the country where Negro people stood up for the first time, affirming their determination to shape a new world, a free world." Thus, Haiti represented the "heroic Antilles, the African Antilles."[77] He used Haiti's revolutionary heritage as a source of identity and symbol of anticolonial resistance, connecting the Revolution's resistance to colonial oppression to the postcolonial situation.[78] For example, in *The Tragedy of King Christophe*, he wrote, "Poor Africa! Poor Haiti! It is the same thing anyway."[79]

As a result, *Négritude* writers from the Caribbean had a very different problem than that of the African American New Negro movement. In the United States, African American writers had been perceived as "backward" because they did not have any literary figures who had achieved mainstream success. The genres of African American literature, such as the slave narrative, gave black American literature a unique identity. In response, African American writers attempted to produce literature on mainstream American terms to demonstrate their cultural acclivity. They sought a union between African American and American styles to overcome the cultural "gap" between the races that had existed because of slavery. As a result, Dumas, a writer of black African descent who succeeded on white terms, was a race hero because he was perceived as transcending the racial divide. French Caribbean writers, however, had the opposite dilemma. Many had successfully mimicked metropolitan styles, so thoroughly assimilated into mainstream literature as to lose any sense of differentiation. Consequently, *Négritude* writers in the Caribbean in

4. Forgetting Alexandre Dumas

particular sought to break this cultural union, intentionally creating a "gap" between Caribbean and metropolitan literature. As a result, Dumas was not a role model, but rather the epitome of what *not* to be. Some early-twentieth-century literary scholars noted that this "revolutionary" aspect of breaking against, rather than following French forms of literature, separated them from earlier black writers in French. Consequently, the break with earlier literary practitioners who had admired Dumas, meant a break with Dumas and his works. For example, Mercer Cook once declared in 1950 that "with old Dumas they [Césaire and Damas] had little in common."[80]

Dumas's actual nineteenth-century experiences of alienation and "outsiderness" as a result of his dark skin and perceived colonial origins in metropolitan France in many ways foreshadowed those of French Caribbean intellectuals in the first half of the twentieth century. Indeed, as we saw in Chapter 1, Dumas suffered under the exhibitic "white gaze" Fanon described. Further, Dumas, whose father was from Saint Domingue, had Haitian connections. Damas's and Césaire's sense of blackness reflected a sense of de-racination and loss influenced by Atlantic slavery and the plantation system. Consequently, both featured Haiti prominently in their works.[81] But the Haiti that Dumas symbolized to *Négritude* writers was not the Haiti of *Négritude*, the Haiti "where negritude rose for the first time and stated that it believed in its humanity."[82] Dumas was too assimilated, his life seemingly too devoid of the colonial complex, and his work too much a symbol of the metropole. In *Négritude*'s shift in identity from union with France to union with Africa, Dumas was in many ways the symbol of France. As a result, *Négritude* rejected (or at least ignored) Dumas as "one of them." In their glorification of "blackness," Dumas was distinctly not black. He was viewed as having never "decolonized his conscience," helping his black compatriots around the globe, and as denying his black ancestry. Consequently, while the Dumas of African American memory was re-imagined as an integral component of a black Atlantic world with strong connections to colonialism and the Caribbean, and hence more "American," the Dumas of *Négritude* became increasingly less connected to colonialism and the Caribbean.[83]

Négritude was fundamentally an early challenge to reconfigure French identity to meet the needs of the realities of ongoing globalization, which brought an increasingly connected and culturally diverse world. Its failure ultimately resided in its attempts to displace modernity within its own framework of reference. *Négritude* turned the ideology of non-contemporaneity "on its head and regard[ed] it as something to be cherished."[84] It situated the cruelties of modernity (i.e., genocide, mechanized warfare, racial and social inequality, slavery, colonial exploitation, symbolic violence, etc.) as signs of its hypocrisy. In *Discourse on Colonialism*, for example, Césaire summarized the dehumanizing character of colonialism on both the colonizer and colonized. The colonization process de-civilized the colonizer by turning him into an oppressor, serving "to brutalize him in the true sense of the word." More explicitly, Césaire explained that the colonial enterprise was "based on contempt for the native and justified by that contempt." It therefore inevitably transformed the person who undertook it. The colonizer, "in order to ease his conscience," adopted "the habit of seeing the other man as *an animal*" and therefore treated the other as an animal, which in turn transformed the colonizer into an animal. There was no true "human contact" between colonizer and colonized, "but relations of domination and submission" leading to "thingification," or the construction of Others into objects. Consequently, the modernity syndrome, or "pseudo-humanism," was "a poison ... [that had] been distilled into the veins of Europe" since it led to the destruction of humanity and compromised the theoretical Rights of Man.[85] *Négritude* writers were therefore proud to be "unmodern." Nevertheless, a positive spin on "backwardness" still situated the globe in different levels of sociotemporal development, thereby acknowledging Western worldview conceptions.[86]

Conclusion

The colonial process compelled the colonized to interpret Western culture as superior and the ideal culture to obtain. Local elites in the Caribbean and Africa, assimilated in French culture, for example, found that they could not escape their "non-contemporaneity," or state of "backwardness." By the mid-twentieth century, many intellectuals had concluded that the "continuity between the so-called primitive or backward world and the modern Western world" had made such divisions anachronistic. Fanon, for one, called for the end of a "backward" geo-psychology of socio-temporal difference conceiving blacks' ostracization from the French nation as a local variation of a lingering global problem: blacks'

4. Forgetting Alexandre Dumas

"amputation" from humanity.[87] Nevertheless, despite their belief in their Frenchness, their dark skin and colonial origins prohibited their grassroots acceptance into the French nation. The awareness of difference, especially for French citizens in the Caribbean, was a traumatizing event. One response, inspired in part by developments among African American intellectuals, was *Négritude*, which reflected the shift in the quest for a sense of belonging, or "home," from France to Africa.

Négritude intellectuals sought to reclaim a black African heritage obscured by Western domination and lost as a result of the slave trade. Yet, in accentuating their blackness, such intellectuals did not initially wish for independence from France, but situated their arguments within a larger humanist discourse. In essence, they argued for a new sense of Frenchness that was more open, since they sensed the discrepancy between theoretical French universalism and its realities. As demonstrated in Chapter 1, Dumas experienced much of the same outsiderness, alienation, and prejudice in nineteenth-century France as growing numbers of later-twentieth-century French Caribbean and African intellectuals would experience. Indeed, Dumas's need for recognition, low self-esteem, and struggle to rectify his own black and white identities in many ways exemplifies the colonized psyche documented in Fanon's *Black Skin, White Masks*. Nevertheless, Dumas expressed pride in his mixed heritage and colonial origins. Thus, while Dumas could have generated sympathy on the part of *Négritude* intellectuals, they too readily accepted the Dumas of memory constructed in the metropole in the immediate decades after his death. Dumas was rejected as a race hero because he was perceived as not experiencing anything that they did because of his "assimilation" into France (and hence not an outsider), and who wrote in a "traditional" French style. By the late twentieth and early twenty-first centuries, however, all that would change.

In 2002, Dumas's remains were transferred to the Panthéon, a mausoleum reserved for the greatest French citizens, amidst much national hype during the bicentennial of his birth. Contemporary France, struggling with the legacies of colonialism and growing diversity, transformed Dumas into a symbol of the colonies and the larger francophone (literally "French-speaking") world in an attempt to integrate its immigrants and migrants from its former Caribbean, African, and Asian colonies to improve race relations and to promote French globality. Presenting Dumas in a "francophone" context, intellectuals sought to present Dumas as a symbol of

Finding Monte Cristo

a "French" culture shaped by, and inclusive of, its (former) colonies and current overseas departments. But the general success of this re-conception stemmed from its acceptance by many French intellectuals with overseas ties, contrary to the earlier *Négritude* movement. As we shall see, such a re-conception of Dumas has made him a major figure in debates on French identity and colonial history. The road to this re-conception, which began to be paved in the post–World War II era, gained momentum during the 100th anniversary of his death in 1970. As we explore these developments, let us return to the Château de Monte Cristo, the construction of which we explored at the beginning of Chapter 1.

5

Alexandre Dumas *Métissé*

Celebrating Dumas as a Symbol of a Diverse France, 1946–2002

As the centenary of Dumas's death approached in 1970, it appeared as if the event would be marked by a rather "curious commemoration": a consortium with government consent planned to demolish the Château de Monte Cristo. Historian Alain Decaux gave local opposition a national voice in an article in *Le Figaro* mocking the obliteration of a monument to Dumas's "glory" at such a time.[1] French intellectual elites rallied to Decaux's call; further appeals were made in the press and thousands of protest letters were sent. Invigorated with such a response, Decaux established the *Société des Amis d'Alexandre Dumas* (Dumas Society), initially with one goal: "to protect the domain of Monte Cristo ... [for] the public and those dedicated to the memory of Alexandre Dumas." The association's goals rapidly evolved to include the promotion of the intellectual advancement of the writer's works in France and abroad.[2] By 1971, an Intercommunal Syndicate for the Protection and Management of Monte-Cristo, in conjunction with the local communities of Port-Marly, Le Pecq, and Marly-le-Roi, formed under government sanction to purchase the Château. Three years later, it obtained historical landmark status (Figures 17 and 18). However, much of the funding to renovate Dumas's former mansion came from a former French colony. King Hassan II of Morocco, a Dumas admirer, financed much of the restoration.[3]

The campaign to save Monte Cristo, with its broad rallying of French metropolitan intellectuals, symbolized Dumas's gradual, but steady rise within academic circles and a more flattering evaluation of his work than had existed previously.[4] Yet, the King of Morocco's involvement reflected the growing interest of intellectuals and politicians from former French

Finding Monte Cristo

Above: Figure 17: The Château de Monte Cristo, now a museum dedicated to Alexandre Dumas. *Right:* Figure 18: The châtelet at Monte Cristo wherein Alexandre Dumas worked on his writing projects, nicknamed the "Château d'If" in reference to the prison in *The Count of Monte Cristo*.

colonies, especially French overseas departments and territories, in Dumas's metropolitan legacy. French colonial expansion and domination served as a form of globalization, spreading white hegemony across the world. It also transformed France into a global nation-state. In the postwar world, whites in the metropole, as the exclusive writers of historical progress, retained the monopoly on "French" culture as the exclusive source from which it emanated to other world regions. French individ-

5. Alexandre Dumas Métissé

uals beyond the metropole, or perceived to originate beyond the metropole, were regarded consciously or subconsciously as separate from French culture largely because of their "colonial" status, despite colonialism having officially ended. Instead, they were often perceived as forming an inferior "francophone" culture—an impure French culture because it mixed (metropolitan) French culture with local ("inferior" or "backward") cultures.

In response, French overseas intellectuals, like their African American counterparts in Chapter 3, forged a counter-bloc to challenge notions of French culture as hegemonic metropolitan domination and francophone culture's inferiority. They sought to insert overseas Frenchmen as a whole into the development of France and its culture, (re)creating a local French overseas history "lost" because of slavery, colonialism, and French metropolitan power, for inclusion in the larger historical narrative. French overseas intellectuals thus also created a "usable past," or counter-memory, like African American intellectuals decades earlier, but with the goal of reconstituting French history and the development of French culture through the inclusion of overseas Frenchmen to counter myths of the (formerly) colonized's inferiority. French colonialism's devastating legacy was therefore posited as a cause of their exclusion. The general obfuscation of French overseas figures in French historical narratives left few individuals known in the metropole as having made significant contributions to French culture.

Consequently, intellectuals also constructed Dumas as their own *lieu de memoire* as part of wider efforts to appropriate historical and cultural individuals of colonial origins from across the globe within a global France produced by the slave trade and colonialism. In so doing, French overseas intellectuals sought to validate a new conception of French identity that extended a "francophone" identity to a wider range of individuals than usually applied, thereby "unveiling" heroes whose previous colonial/overseas connections had been ignored or marginalized. French overseas intellectuals thus promoted a conception of "francophone" that extended its dominant usage (which generally restricted the term geographically to areas beyond the metropole) to encompass the metropole as part of a global francophone world. Dumas was subsequently re-imagined as an integral component of this broader world, closely linked to slavery, colonialism, and overseas France, but also the metropole. Thus, Dumas's "French" works were presented as actually "francophone," since they mixed metropolitan and indigenous (colonial) styles; they symbolized France's long-standing cultural hybridity and challenged the notion that French culture emanated exclusively from the metropole. Therefore, the Dumas of memory became inextricably linked to France's postcolonial populations, enabling his commemoration and incorporation into the nation as such a figure to symbolize their inclusion into the national narrative. This image of Dumas influenced the one the state commemorated during Dumas's 2002 bicentennial as part of its efforts to identify past heroes of colonial origin to encourage cohesion among its increasingly diverse components. Consequently, as one biographer noted, "many hope to use Alexandre [Dumas] publicly, politically."[5]

The Context of the Need for a Dumas Métissé

French intellectuals' engagement with Dumas reflects the larger French social, intellectual, and cultural engagement with global diversity and increasing globalization facilitated through colonial enterprise. French colonialism from the early modern era was characterized by the desire to facilitate a "civilizing mission" across the globe. During the early modern period, the French state created a colonial empire centered in the Caribbean, which for most of the eighteenth century was a source of great wealth. After the Haitian Revolution (1791–1804) and the 1830 conquest of Algeria, French colonial efforts turned increasingly toward Africa and Asia. A unique component of French colonial efforts, however, was the relatively persistent perception that the conquest of the territories did not make them merely French possessions to administer, but rather integral components of the French nation-state. While perceiving peoples and cultures beyond metropolitan France as inferior, it nevertheless depicted the theoretical notion that "Frenchness" could be applied to the colonized. Such efforts expanded the French state into a global polity, especially after 1946 when several former colonies were incorporated as full-fledged French departments. However, the European colonial enterprise, built on the concept of modernity, necessitated the constructions of difference in order to exist. The French, therefore, had difficulty in conceiving individuals linked with the colonies as "French," despite a dominant belief in a theoretically "open" French political identity, and reconciling a restricted sense of Frenchness with its new global condition. Prior to the mid-twentieth century, individuals from the colonial world were relatively few

5. Alexandre Dumas Métissé

in number within the metropole. Consequently, debates about French identity's "openness" could remain largely philosophical exercises.

Despite his successes, as we explored in Chapter 1, Dumas faced forms of racial prejudice in France. Even though he was born in France, he faced difficulty in being accepted as "French" because of his Caribbean family origins. Dumas died in 1870 amidst the outbreak of the Franco-Prussian War. After a temporary burial, his remains were relocated in 1872 to a cemetery in Villers-Cotterêts. Following his death, Dumas, as one of his era's most popular writers, transcended the corporal realm into that of the imagination, becoming a myth, or "a symbolically treated historical reality."[6] French biographical studies on Dumas, particularly during the late-nineteenth century and first two-thirds of the twentieth century, generally downplayed his black ancestry's impact to support the myth of a color blind French society and perceptions of French culture as being the product of people of European stock, or "whites." Dumas and his works, especially his "Drama of France," which sought to portray in literature French history from the early modern period to Dumas's present as culminating in a destined republic, had been viewed as part of the French (metropolitan) patrimony and helping to consolidate a distinct national identity.[7] In 1902, Hippolyte Parigot, for example, wrote of the musketeers as "a living sense of France" in his biography of Dumas: "D'Artagnan, the adroit Gascon, caressing his moustache; Porthos, the muscular and foolish; Athos, the somewhat romantic *grand seigneur*; [and] Aramis ... the discreet Aramis, who hides his religion and his amours, able student of the good fathers ... —these four friends ... typify the four cardinal qualities of our country."[8] Further, Dumas was perceived as a *bon vivant*, or as one biographer dubbed him, a "laughing mulatto," whose only concerns were spending money, dining, late-night carousing, and women.[9]

Because of its French Revolutionary heritage, the Third Republic (1871–1940), which consolidated itself in the years following the Franco-Prussian War and lasted until World War II, conceived itself as the source of "liberty, equality, and fraternity" (despite its colonialism) and as the birthplace of the rights of man. France thus harbored a myth that it was not "racist" like its Western counterparts. As a symbol of France, Dumas posed a conceptual dilemma because of his black ancestry and past experiences with racism during the rise of the New Imperialism and scientific racism. In response, Dumas's portraits and caricatures generally reflected a departure in this era from those during his lifetime. Rather than accentuate his "black" features, as demonstrated in Chapter 1 in caricatures by artists like Cham (see Figure 4), it became common to accentuate his Caucasian features (see Figures 19 and 20). Therefore, Dumas's status as "symbolically white" by virtue of being part of the French heritage cast him in a contradictory role.[10] Consequently, French intellectuals generally cited him as a popular, though not great, writer. While his popularity was undeniable, his work's "quality" was often suspect. In 1950, for example, A. Craig Bell noted that "Dumas is a river which academicians, critics and literary snobs have been fouling for half a century." He felt that Dumas was largely ignored by French literary historians, who dismissed him "in a paragraph."[11] Similarly, French intellectual André Maurois noted in 1957 that previous generations of French literary critics "had denied ... [Dumas's] importance."[12] Since black African stereotypes depicted them as "childlike," Dumas's work was thus rationalized as being written at a low intellectual level. Consequently, his work, unlike that of other French Romantics (like Victor Hugo) was denigrated as solely adolescent literature. This served dual (but conflicting) purposes: it encouraged young people to read Dumas, which they largely enjoyed, to instill in their impressionable minds the basics of, and love for,

Figure 19: Several companies, such as Chocolat Lombart, used images of Alexandre Dumas to help sell their products during the late nineteenth and early twentieth centuries. In this advertisement, Dumas's date of birth is listed incorrectly as 1803 instead of 1802.

5. *Alexandre Dumas* Métissé

French history to help consolidate national sentiments. However, it simultaneously prevented him from being perceived as equal to truly great "French" literary figures, thereby allowing a means through which to criticize Dumas's "Africanness" without mentioning it directly to protect his symbolic whiteness bestowed as a symbol of France.[13] This image of Dumas was accepted not only in the metropole, but also in much of the colonial world, as we saw in Chapters 2 and 4. It buttressed the myth that Dumas's colonial heritage was largely insignificant in regard to his treatment in the metropole. Consequently, he was assimilated into French culture and thus the French nation, thereby experiencing minimal (if any) racial prejudice despite his biracial status and father's Caribbean origins.

Meanwhile, post–World War II metropolitan immigration and migration of people from former French colonies revealed increasingly within the metropole the global France created through its colonial endeavors. France already had an extensive history of *métissage*, as eastern and southern European, Armenian, and other groups had been immigrating to France for centuries. Cultural differences were generally short-term, however, as the politics of assimilation absorbed these minorities' differences. The

Figure 20: An early twentieth-century edition of one of Alexandre Dumas's works featuring a version of a popular late nineteenth-century French illustration by M. Léloir and J. Huyot depicting Dumas at work.

Finding Monte Cristo

rapid increase of citizens and permanent residents from beyond the European continent put many French at unease. How to deal with this postcolonial condition remained among France's most significant challenges at the dawning of a new millennium. Complicating matters was the decrease of the French state's global influence, particularly after World War II and the subsequent loss of its colonies.

The state sought to retain its authority during and after decolonization and the demise of its formal external colonial empire via alternative means viewed as more compatible with the changing times. The French Union, modeled on the British Commonwealth, emerged after World War II. In 1958, it was replaced by the French Community. By 1960, independence movements in Indochina and Algeria prompted French constitutional revisions allowing Community members to change their constitutions and obtain independence. The International Organization of *la Francophonie* (now *La Francophonie*), formed in 1970, evolved into an organization of polities in which there is/was a historical prevalence of French language and culture to consolidate French influence. The nineteenth-century term *francophonie* had referred to countries under French rule in which French was used widely. In its contemporary usage, it can mean many things (geographical areas where French is used, political organization, cultural heritage) and differs based on the social roles of French language and culture. Overall, these efforts imply a hierarchy situating the metropole as the active source/center of a true "French" culture adapted passively elsewhere, suggesting that "francophone" is an impure, or "French-like," culture because it blends French culture with other cultures in other global areas. The term is also often used to designate France's citizens from its overseas departments and territories, thereby denying that France's cultural and geopolitical borders extend beyond the European continent. Therefore, metropolitan France, often battling its mixed nature, often deploys *francophonie* to serve as a form of "discursive ghettoization," or the use of names or labels to figuratively segregate certain individuals from the national body in the collective imaginary. This view maintains the colonial perception recognizing the French in the francophone, but not the francophone in the French. French culture mixed with the cultures of those it colonized; this process reconstituted *both* cultures, which themselves were mixtures of diverse, fluctuating elements. Consequently, reimagining Dumas, long-perceived as a "French" writer, as having strong connections to the "francophone" world was part of broader attempts to

5. Alexandre Dumas Métissé

recognize the colonial influence on the metropole and to decentralize it as the source of "true" Frenchness. Dumas's francophone transformation, therefore, was not intended to divorce him from (metropolitan) French culture, but to help recognize that "French" culture *is* "francophone," constructed in part by its former colonial subjects in both the past and present.

Postwar immigration, the changing face of France, and efforts to adapt to a limited global role all came to a head by the twenty-first century. By the time of Dumas's 2002 interment in the Panthéon, France was at a crossroads. There had already been many concerted (and contradictory) efforts to realize greater socio-cultural cohesion among diverse and marginalized groups. As Pierre-André Taguieff has suggested, twentieth- and twenty-first century French racism emerged not from a white-black historical divide as in the United States, but as a tension between "authentic/native" citizens and increasingly-numerous "ethnic outsiders," arriving mostly from former colonies.[14] Consequently, the interaction between France and its former colonial peoples had undergone a fundamental shift. Rather than define identity in opposition to the colonial Other beyond France, French identity had to learn how to assimilate the former colonial Other, or de-Otherize former colonial peoples, within France for social cohesion. The Republic's universalistic framework expects immigrants to assimilate fully French culture and abandon their previous identities (a difficult "request" in our global age in which multiple, complex forms of simultaneous self-identifications that can extend beyond the nation-state exist), and refuses to recognize difference in the general view that treating all citizens equally means treating them the same. How to deal with this postcolonial condition remained among France's most significant challenges at the dawning of a new millennium.

Further, French Republican political culture has often been defined by forgetfulness, particularly in regard to French involvement and questionable actions in past "traumas" like the Holocaust and Algerian War. Another such trauma was slavery, which the republican state had largely obscured in its view of national history, thereby creating difficulty integrating overseas departments in which slavery had been a component of their local histories. In 1998, the 150th anniversary of the French abolition of slavery provided an opportunity to amend for the French past and reconfigure the national narrative. Such commemorations, however, focused neither on the heroism of the revolution in Saint Domingue (Haiti) nor Africans' resistance to the French slave trade and plantation system, but rather on Enlightenment values, anti-monarchism, and French liberals' generosity.[15] In the Caribbean, 1848 recalled the long struggle for identity and equality.[16] Caribbean intellectuals thus emphasized a local struggle that made abolition inevitable, shifting the source of freedom from the metropole to the colonies, thereby granting Caribbean individuals active roles in shaping their history.[17] The French state eventually declared slavery a crime against humanity in 2001, in part to channel French Caribbean frustrations.[18] President Jacques Chirac made May 10 a national holiday commemorating the injustice of slavery and its abolition.[19] However, minority advocacy groups continued to press for a greater awareness of black history in French society.[20] Some French civil rights movements even began to articulate reparations demands, as the 1990s was marked by the rise of reconciliation for past injustices amidst greater senses of human interconnectedness formed after World War II. As Philippe Moreau Defarges observed, this "time of repentance is that of another perception of history" in which previously excluded groups have a cooperative role in shaping its narrative. Such a "new" history echoed Frantz Fanon's postwar views calling for "a new history of man" written by the victors in conjunction with the vanquished to not only record Europe's accomplishments, "but also its crimes."[21]

To appeal to left-wing voters during the 1995 presidential campaign, the conservative right candidate Jacques Chirac condemned this form of exclusion, which he called *"la fracture sociale."* However, Chirac and the socialist coalition during the *cohabitation* of 1997 to 2002 did little to change the situation. During the 2002 elections, wide-spread disillusionment brought Jean-Marie Le Pen, leader of the extremist right-wing political party Front National, to compete against Chirac in the second round of voting. Chirac was re-elected by wide margins, largely because many voted for him simply to prevent Le Pen's victory.[22]

Consequently, ongoing agitation for social equality had forced France to reconsider who and what constitutes the nation, as the omission of segments of the nation in the national narrative creates a sense of disconnect to the past. Dumas was increasingly reconfigured within this context, celebrated by the state and society as a "francophone" writer, or a writer with connections to the French-speaking (colonial/postcolonial) world beyond metropolitan France, to help identify past heroes of colonial origin to revise the narrative of national development to include its contemporary

5. *Alexandre Dumas* Métissé

diverse components.[23] Dumas's "Africanness" was no longer a reason for his exclusion, as we saw in Chapter 1, but rather his inclusion into the French cultural nation. Dumas's visual portrayals on postcards, stamps, and other commemorative items increasingly began to depict him in ways that drew attention to his non-white features, but not in the caricature-like stereotypes typical of nineteenth- and early twentieth-century colonial France (see Figure 21).

Figure 21: "Alexandre Dumas outside the Château de Monte-Cristo," a French painting by Yves Le Boursicaud from the 1970s, depicts the author in typical fashion of the era with black African characteristics (akg-images/Gilles Mermet; Collection of the Société des Amis d'Alexandre Dumas).

Georges: A Masterpiece Against Slavery and the Color Complex?

During the late twentieth century, growing debates about French identity prompted a reevaluation about what it meant to be French. Amidst these debates, Dumas underwent a re-evaluation as some French intellectuals sought to use him to counter notions of French exceptionalism in regard to slavery, colonialism, and racism, and universal equality within the Republic. Establishing Dumas as a symbolic element of the post-colonial French population was a prerequisite for subsequent efforts to use Dumas as a means to incorporate them into the nation and its historical narrative. During the 1970s, after the efforts to save Monte Cristo discussed at the beginning of this chapter, intellectuals increasingly placed Dumas within a history of colonial contributions to France stretching centuries back. They steadily maintained Dumas's black colonial identity, constructing his image as a French colonial writer symbolic of former colonial populations. Dumas was presented as experiencing racism in France and his works reflected this experience and his struggles for equality. This limited French scholarship on Dumas during the 1970s through 1990s, during attempts to deal with decolonization, new immigration, and reduced French global influence, created the intellectual foundation for the Dumas of memory celebrated in the 2000s. A brief examination of the critical reception to Dumas's novel *Georges* reveals the evolution of this conception of Dumas, since its development paralleled the novel's rise in prominence.

Dumas's previously-ignored novel *Georges* (1843), his only major work with a hero of black descent addressing colonial racism and slavery, has now joined the ranks of his major works. *Georges* (set mostly in 1824) focuses on the struggles of the biracial elite on Île de France (Mauritius) in the Indian Ocean to obtain social equality within a race-based colonial society. Due to his rejection by the island's white elites, the title character, a member of its biracial elite, leads an unsuccessful slave rebellion. The relative commercial failure of *Georges*, which Dumas wrote in collaboration with Félicien Mallefille, a Creole from Mauritius, possibly deterred Dumas from returning to themes of racism. As biographer Henri Troyat observed of *Georges*, "neither the [French] public, nor the critics were interested by this confrontation between Whites, mulattoes, and Blacks under the torrid skies of the Indian Ocean."[24] Achille Gallet published the only full review of the novel in 1843. While not critical of its construction, he argued that all men who study the colonies' social state, and "not in the homilies of our philanthropists and the fantasies of our romancers," know the "truth, that the mulatto race is inferior to the white race, as the Negro race is inferior to the mulattoes. There are doubtless few exceptions … [Dumas] is himself clear proof."[25]

Due to Dumas's popularity within the Atlantic world and the novel's content, it might seem reasonable to conclude that *Georges* was well-known among African American intellectuals and French overseas intellectuals during the nineteenth and early twentieth centuries. American attention toward the novel, however, remained minimal at this time. African Americans, who, as we have seen in Chapter 3, had long expressed interest in Dumas and his works, exhibited only minor interest in *Georges* as indicative of the wider black struggle against racism.[26] Nevertheless, they did provide the first notable American interest in the work. In 1914, African American writer Charles Chestnutt, for example, delivered an address on Dumas, asserting that he had a "brown complexion and …

5. Alexandre Dumas Métissé

curly hair.... He was not ashamed of it, often mentioned it with not the least self-consciousness ... and he wrote one novel, *Georges, the Planter of the Isle of France*, of which the race problem in one of its aspects formed the motive."[27] Further, African American scholars John Matheus and W.N. Rivers edited a version of *Georges* in 1936 for use in French classes.[28] Scholarly reviews of the work, which identified Dumas as "a noble negro," described it as "a race novel," or a novel focused on "the African theme," and thus suitable "for use in negro schools." A reviewer for the *Journal of Negro History* even suggested that the novel's element of racial prejudice would resonate as "experience rather than fiction."[29] Nevertheless, the generally unflattering depiction of blacks (i.e., slaves) in the novel, as opposed to the more positive portrait of the educated biracial planters, repeated African stereotypes. The reviewer questioned the novel's effectiveness as a tract against racism, asking, for example, "How inspiring to young and impressionable readers of color might be the spectacle of oppressed Negroes suspending their dash to freedom in order to drain the kegs of rum that a wily enemy has placed in their path?" Nevertheless, the novel's biracial eponymous character's heroism outweighed such depictions, for Dumas, with "the conviction of a humanitarian," gave his hero the gumption to stand against prejudice.[30] However, the novel was not perceived as a particularly good one. One reviewer lamented that it was "characterized by rapidity of action and thinness of plot."[31] Dumas thus received several back-handed compliments for *Georges*. For example, another reviewer thought that while "from Dumas to Shakespeare is a far cry," there was nevertheless "something about the melancholy of the sensitive Georges Munier [the novel's hero] that recalls the dark outpourings of Hamlet."[32]

Reviews for Matheus's revised edition of *Georges* in 1970, however, were more positive. They sought to emphasize Dumas's colonial heritage, establishing for him a role as a defender of "his race." Such reviews, therefore, sought to situate Dumas within broader African Diasporic writing against racism and colonialism in an era marked by the American Civil Rights Movement and European decolonization.[33] The *French Review*'s reviewer, for example, commented that although *Georges* was still perceived as a "little known novel," it was relevant "despite the passing of 150 years" because it was an "early race novel." As Dumas's only work "concerned with the bars of prejudice ... it fairly shouts the eternal prayer for freedom shared by all members of the human race." Consequently, the novel allowed scholars to "acknowledge the impact of Dumas's concern with the social issues of a colonial régime."³⁴ Such comments implied three simple, yet complex conclusions: First, they suggested that racism existed (or, at least, had existed) in metropolitan France. Second, Dumas was a victim of this racism. Finally, he was involved actively in the fight against racism and colonialism. These two assertions offered a drastic contrast to the French metropolitan constructions of Dumas then in force that depicted him as a "symbolically white" writer and *bon vivant* lacking in sophistication.

American re-evaluations of the novel paralleled those in France, but with greater emphasis on Dumas's black identity, rather than his colonial one, to deal with each culture's respective form of prejudice. Léon-François Hoffmann's groundbreaking essay, "Dumas and Blacks," which served as the preface to Gallimard's 1974 edition of *Georges*, was the first major French work during the second half of the twentieth century to assert Dumas's biracial ancestry and that he faced racism as a result, contrary to the then common perception of a colorblind France that had allowed the French to perceive themselves superior to a United States engaged in a Civil Rights struggle. Hoffmann, too, asserted that the novel had "passed more or less unnoticed ... by scholars as well as the general public." It was "rare" for critics to mention the novel, which, consequently, had been designated a "secondary work."³⁵ Nevertheless, he argued, *Georges* ranked "among Dumas's best novels" and in some ways was superior to his best-known works.³⁶ Thus, it was time to give the novel its due, especially because of its cultural relevance to postcolonial French society. To Hoffmann, the novel was a "chronicle of a colonial society whose prejudices have far from disappeared.... Today, when the racial problem has assumed the intensity [that it has, it is even] ... more important that it [*Georges*] never falls into oblivion."³⁷ Hoffmann asserted the principle that every writer puts "a little of themselves" in every character. Consequently, the title character, to an extent, reflected Dumas himself. This observation was not entirely novel. Jacques-Henry Bornecque had noted in his 1956 introduction to *The Count of Monte Cristo* that Georges was a precursor to that novel's hero, Edmond Dantès, and that Georges was Dumas "recreated," or "a 'double' who is his creation." A 1903 British translation also included in its introduction the assertion that Georges, "who suffers humiliation and discouragement because of his 'dash of the tar brush,' but faces every obstacle and insult with irrepressible energy and spirit, is a fancy portrait of Dumas himself."³⁸

5. *Alexandre Dumas* Métissé

However, Hoffmann went further. In examining whether Dumas endured "racial prejudice," Hoffmann argued that despite Dumas's success, he suffered from a racist metropolitan society.[39] He then traced Dumas's family background, emphasizing his Caribbean heritage and his grandmother's slave status. While Dumas's Caribbean and biracial ancestry was common knowledge (even if minimalized from the late nineteenth century onward), his slave origins had been more publicly obscured. To identify someone as having biracial ancestry is not the same thing as saying that someone is descended from a slave, and both forms of identification carry different connotations.[40] Hoffmann strengthened Dumas's connections to the Caribbean and feelings of solidarity with French-speakers beyond the metropole by reprinting Dumas's letter to Bissette expressing solidarity with individuals of black descent and his letter to the Haitian government soliciting support for a statue for his father, both discussed earlier in this book.[41] Finally, Hoffmann explored Dumas's "rare" inclusion of black characters. He suggested that Dumas perceived biracial individuals as separate from blacks. Further, despite Dumas's sympathy for blacks, he had absorbed much of metropolitan society's stereotypes about blacks and Africa.[42] In summation, Hoffmann declared *Georges* not a "black novel," but a "mulatto novel," because its theme was not so much the abolition of slavery, but rather the "equality of races." Thus, *Georges* could be viewed as "a biographical document that illustrates Dumas's attitude toward his '*négritude*' and as a historical document that well illustrates the attitudes of biracial individuals during the middle of the past century."[43] The overall impression of Dumas was that he was a French writer with strong connections to the former French colonial world who faced metropolitan racism. The use of "*négritude*," a reference to the intellectual movement developed by French-speaking Caribbean and African figures earlier in the twentieth century, linked Dumas to overseas intellectuals and implied that he was a precursor to their cultural awakening.[44] This connection, based on what we saw in Chapter 4, was something that *Négritude*'s founders would have found startling.

Furthermore, since the 1970s, Gilles Henry maintained in his books that *The Count of Monte Cristo* was inspired by Dumas's Caribbean family history, an interpretation that steadily began to find its way into the press and popular biographies as uncontested fact.[45] Literary scholar Charles Grivel also wrote on Dumas's biracial background as influencing his work in indirect ways, since his heroes (like him) are "outsiders" in some form, and the writer's use of the color black.[46] Finally, during the 1990s, Dominique Fernandez's *The Twelve Muses of Alexandre Dumas*, the first major work to unequivocally declare Dumas a "francophone" writer, included a chapter on the "Black Muse" as a source of Dumas's inspiration. As Fernandez wrote, "Among all the Romantics in love with liberty, among all the righters of wrongs.... Dumas stands out because of a unique characteristic: his mixed blood. First of our 'francophone' writers, he brought with him something entirely new in French culture."[47]

Writers and intellectuals thus maintained Dumas's black colonial identity, constructing an image of the writer as symbolic of former French colonial populations. As a francophone writer, he experienced racism, and his works reflected profoundly this experience and his struggles for equality. Grivel, for example, asserted that Dumas's greatest crime was "the crime of color," and French writer Didier Decoin similarly made the "odious hypothesis" that Dumas had been "an excommunicate of honors ... because some blood of a black slave flowed through his veins."[48]

As such metropolitan French intellectuals suggested that Dumas's colonial and racial origins were deleted, or at least obscured, from the French memory to divorce him from his association with exploited colonial subjects to service the needs of colonialism, French overseas intellectuals ultimately argued that this realization created a cultural dismemory among members of the Caribbean and Africa. In turn, they sought to marry Dumas to the colonies, not to denigrate him or strip him of his Frenchness, but rather as part of broader attempts to reconstruct a global, or "creolized," French identity. Dumas's status as a symbol of "France," therefore, was used to demonstrate that what was "French" had long been "francophone" and the two terms could be perceived as equivalent, or even interchangeable. Notions of hybridity, or a creolized identity, which led to increasingly complicated interpretations of Dumas, had obtained particular credibility among French Caribbean intellectuals.

Édouard Glissant, from Martinique, began to describe the synthesis of diverse cultures as "not a process of bastardization" that violated "pure" cultures by creating "impure" ones, "but a productive activity through which each element is enriched."[49] Looking at the Caribbean, he was among the first to praise creolized cultures, to perceive such a state as having value, and which would not form a ("halfway") category in opposition to other ("pure") categories.[50] Later postcolonial intellectuals had rejected *Négritude*'s black essentialism, viewing it as seeking to replace a

5. Alexandre Dumas Métissé

longing for France with one for Africa. By the mid-twentieth century, such intellectuals favored notions of hybridity, or anti-essentialism, in national cultures.[51] In 1937, for example, Senegalese writer Ousmane Socé wrote that "if you think about it, everything is *métis*. On this earth there is no pure race, no civilization that is not *métis*."[52] Rather than to "totalize" (or essentialize) cultures and groups, Glissant insisted on formlessness, latency, and mutation, which he called "a cross-cultural politics." He conceived a world in a state of continuous flux. The Caribbean—a "chaos-world" that resulted from the constant "clash of so many cultures which flare up, repel each other, disappear, subsist, die, or transform each other, slowly, or at lightning speed"—depicted in miniature what was happening globally.[53] Consequently, the project of modernity, which had attempted to impose an orderly structure on the world, was always doomed since it tried to suppress globalization's "permanent revolution."[54] Further, creolization was not a geographic concept limited to the Americas; creoleness became a characteristic of the globalizing world, "an integrating process of world diversity."[55] He displaced the notion of a center influencing its periphery, perceiving all peripheries as centers exchanging as equals. Glissant asserted that the French had to replace their efforts to control the world with recognition that they "are part of the world." French culture could then thrive, embracing its "creole," or hybrid, heritage from its union with the world, especially its former colonies.[56]

Glissant thus argued that a collective memory, erased by slavery, was needed to assert a Caribbean identity.[57] French slavery's temporary abolition during the French Revolution (1794), its final demise (1848), the granting of adult male suffrage (1877), and departmentalization (1946)—often used as benchmarks in French Caribbean history—are the results of events in the metropole.[58] Caribbean intellectuals thus argued that the world had been presented to them "through the filter of western values," giving them an inferior image of themselves that led to a condition of dependence. This condition, the "syndrome of the colonized," could be overcome by reclaiming a Caribbean history.[59] During the 1980s, Caribbean intellectuals Jean Barnabé, Patrick Chamoiseau, and Raphaël Confiant built on Glissant's ideas to establish the philosophy of *Créolité*. Using Creole and local languages emerged as a way for former colonial subjects to assert their cultural acclivity against the metropole as equals.[60] Glissant perceived language as a symbol of the power imposed on colonial subjects to obliterate their native "backward" cultures. Creole had thus suffered "linguistic impoverishment" because it has been perceived (like Dumas) as vulgar, childish, and lacking in sophistication.[61] Such developments came to be applied to Dumas's novel, *Georges*.

By the 1990s, *Georges* was still described in a critical essay as a "forgotten novel," despite being one of Dumas's "most important" since its "hero is black" and dealt "with feelings that Dumas seems to have felt."[62] Nevertheless, intellectuals in the Caribbean and Africa now frequently embraced the francophone Dumas constructed in the metropole, reshaping this image within the intellectual contexts of hybridity and complex identities, recognizing Dumas as influencing their works and as part of their collective memory. Earlier twentieth-century Caribbean intellectuals, like Anténor Firmin, had begun to assert Dumas's "hybrid" status.[63] Dumas's popularity and success also made him a "conqueror of Paris," which was an important site as the seat of colonial power, thereby restoring pride to the colonized and their descendants.[64] Chamoiseau, for example, paid homage to Dumas in his Goncourt Prize-winning 1990s novel *Texaco*, set in Martinique. He named a minor character "Dartagnan," a black guard and paramour known by his bombastic hat and brash behavior.[65] Further, in an interview, Guadeloupean writer Maryse Condé described her novel *Segu* as building on popular writing formulas Dumas established.[66] Due to this renewed interest in Dumas, schools in former French colonies became increasingly named after him.[67]

The most significant document to establish Dumas as a francophone writer by his bicentennial, however, was the 1998 preface to *Georges* by Calixthe Beyala, a French writer from Cameroon. Two years earlier, she had been twice accused of plagiarism amidst receipt of the French Academy's *Grand Prix du roman* for one of the novels in which she had allegedly plagiarized.[68] In the second epigraph to one of her novels, she included a parody of Pierre Assouline, an editor and a key figure in the affair, expressing her contempt for those hoping that the events would have ended her career. Beyala, who associated the plagiarism accusations levied against her to those against Dumas, implied that Assouline, like Mirecourt, could not accept such literary accomplishments as not being the works of whites. Seeking solace through Dumas, she wrote that such critics, "as Alexandre Dumas said, bring nothing to the literary world apart from the crowns of thorns they've woven to push deep onto the head of the conquering or conquered poet, laughing as they go."[69] Consequently, Beyala developed a sense of kinship with Dumas that was reflected

5. Alexandre Dumas Métissé

in her preface, written for an edition of *Georges* issued to coincide with the 150th anniversary of the French abolition of slavery. Written about a generation after Hoffmann's, Beyala's preface, written in the first person to Dumas, was notable for bearing a non-metropolitan voice. It appropriated the conception of Dumas conceived within Hoffmann's preface within broader French overseas intellectuals' construction of a usable past. In her preface, Beyala thus established Dumas as a writer who expressed solidarity with an African Diaspora, as a victim of racism who responded by forming pride in his blackness and cultural hybridity, and as a forerunner to later literary traditions in francophone Africa and the Caribbean. She claimed that Dumas was a pioneer, among the first writers of color to pen an anti-slavery novel. Despite facing metropolitan injustices, however, Dumas championed the French ideals of liberty, equality, and fraternity; thus, he was a better "Frenchman" than those who mocked him. Further, his "French" work was really "francophone," since it mixed metropolitan and indigenous (African) styles, and was thereby symbolic of the long-standing hybridity of global France. Beyala positioned Dumas as a hero for oppressed colonial subjects and their descendants, arguing that the past struggles he faced had not subsided; the legacies of slavery and colonialism were still faced by his contemporary brothers "in spirit."[70]

Beyala argued that *Georges*, still treated as a "minor work," was receiving more attention as "the central book" for understanding Dumas the person since the 1970s. Addressing Dumas's spirit, she asked forgiveness for addressing him as "Georges," for she argued that the character was Dumas's thin cover for himself. The novel, she claimed, was his own story, his "autoportrait."[71] Therefore, both Georges and Dumas, "despite their fortune and talent," earned many of their contemporaries' contempt because of their skin color.[72] Beyala, like Hoffmann, recalled Dumas's letter to Bissette to suggest that he had felt solidarity with his "brothers in blood ... and friends of color."[73] She observed that seemingly all of Dumas's (white) biographers had felt compelled to debate if he suffered "from color prejudice." She asserted, "Permit me, my dear Dumas, to respond, 'YES!'" All the riches, fame, and glory, she argued, could not overcome being treated as a "*nègre*." Dumas was, therefore, presented as experiencing all the "moral suffering and epic scorn that black people" have endured.[74]

Beyala thus argued that *Georges* was Dumas's response to this racism, a vehicle for his "pride and revolt" against color prejudice that reflected his "*négritude*."[75] She acknowledged Hoffmann's and others' criticism that it was a "*métis* novel" (or "mulatto novel") that fought essentially against white prejudice toward people of biracial descent rather than blacks in general. She also conceded that the novel was not "militant" in its attack on slavery or racism and could have been more assertive.[76] Dumas, like how he described Georges, was a "*Nègre blanc*"; his "*négritude*" was thus mixed with his "*métissitude*."[77] However, Beyala "confessed" to Dumas that she understood his attitude. He was depicted as a lone (black) voice in his era's literary arena, and it therefore took great courage to criticize color prejudice at all.[78] Beyala, in turn, condemned those who argued that Dumas was only concerned with people of multiracial descent, calling them "detractors." The fact that Georges, a biracial character, leads the black revolt to freedom is therefore of minor significance, because it represents "the black cause."[79]

Beyala also depicted the novel as against slavery and colonialism. She credited it as one of the first anti-slavery books in literary history written by a person of color. It thus occupied a crucial role in "the memories of black peoples." She asserted that *Georges* was "a condemnation of blacks' oppression," as well as "racist theories and advocates of slavery." Slavery, she argued, was a "crime" in Dumas's era revealing a "cruel" act of man toward man, treating certain people as "vulgar merchandise" based on their skin color and cultural "inferiority" by self-proclaimed "masters of the universe." Beyala thus argued that Dumas's "mulatto complex" was an attempt to eradicate this complex, itself "a fight against Western civilization" as imposed via colonialism. Therefore, "under a hierarchization of human beings" based on "their skin color and blood," Dumas provided an "indictment denouncing the prejudices which give pretext to insanity" to restore dignity to blacks and claim the liberty that they deserved. He was portrayed as criticizing the hypocrisy of his contemporaries, who praised the equality of man and allowed color prejudice.[80] In adopting racism, the French were not truly French; the bearers of "French" ideals were its former colonial subjects like Dumas; they sought to push France to realize itself, to create in reality the France existing in the social imaginary.

Furthermore, Beyala presented Dumas as "a visionary poet," since his work anticipated the themes of future African and Caribbean writers. Continuing the counter-factual links between Dumas and *Négritude*, she described *Georges* as "a black novel" that revealed the "cry of revolt of the mocked," an allusion to Martinican writer Aimé Césaire's "cry" of *Négritude* in his *Return to the Native Land*. Through the portrayal of the

5. Alexandre Dumas Métissé

culturally-mixed world ("a *métissé* universe") in which *Georges* occurs, Dumas additionally claimed "cultural *métissage*, 100 years before this notion" enlightened the pens of contemporary French-speaking African and Caribbean intellectuals. Therefore, Dumas was an early advocate of "cosmopolitanism." His work was also interpreted as demonstrating African influences. He was a great storyteller, a "griot ... in the grand African tradition," whose narration had "a musical quality."[81]

Finally, coinciding with the edition's marketing information underlining Dumas's "torment" as an accomplished writer "confronted with prejudices that ... endure to the present day," Beyala noted that while slavery had been abolished formally, it has changed in form to still exist, as people continue to maltreat and exploit other human beings.[82] She apologized to Dumas for the "late acknowledgement" of his part of the "combat" against injustice.[83] Paraphrasing Dumas that the pen is "the sword of the intellectual," she asserted that he used it to attack slavery, giving blacks an "immaterial liberty" through his words that led ultimately to "their physical liberty." He thus continued to inspire those struggling to achieve equality in the present, "a little light in the black night, a little less suffering in an ocean of tears, some more respect to the unloved."[84] Consequently, Dumas became a symbol of a composite France, but also a symbol of the "injustices" committed against former colonial subjects and the state's debt to their descendants.

Such a position was controversial and challenged lingering conservative conceptions of Dumas and his works initially forged during the late nineteenth and early twentieth centuries. Those seeking to depict Dumas as a fighter for racial rights and against slavery have often turned toward *Georges* to defend their arguments. However, the novel's message in regard to racial equality and slavery's abolition are ambiguous. As Jean Lacouture observed, those in France who argue that Dumas was "conditioned by his '*négritude*' [blackness]" often turn toward *Georges* as evidence, since the novel has become associated with "the prejudice of color." Consequently, "a good number of literary historians have presented the character of Georges as a self-portrait and the novel as an anti-racist tract."[85] While Lacouture conceded that one could be tempted to see in *Georges* an autobiography or a work in which Dumas contributed to the fight for the abolition of slavery and racism, "*Georges* can be neither a self-portrait of ... [Dumas] nor a manifesto for the liberation of Blacks," for the novel is more complex. Lacouture pointed to the portrayal of Georges's brother, a wealthy slave trafficker, who rescues the hero from death after the failed slave rebellion. Therefore, although he is involved in the slave trade, he is a hero (rather than a villain). Further, Lacouture argued that Laiza, the only slave to be depicted heroically, has mixed Arab and black African ancestry. Consequently, he claimed that no black African character was depicted positively.[86] Such arguments maintained that Dumas's black ancestry and experiences with color prejudice were not major influences on the novel (and by extension, his body of work), which in turn implied that Dumas could not be perceived as a black or colonial writer.[87]

However, scholars' seemingly unanimous emphasis on *Georges* as a literary source for determining Dumas's position on slavery is tenuous. A better approach to determining Dumas's stance on slavery would be to survey his wider body of work. Superficially, *Georges*'s plot and themes would make it the ideal novel for this purpose, even though some have argued that the novel is uncharacteristic of Dumas and have cast doubts on his authorship. The debate over Dumas's authorship began following Mirecourt's accusation in his infamous 1845 pamphlet discussed in Chapter 1. Scholars examining *Georges* have thus felt the need to defend Dumas's authorship.[88] Dumas's authorship seems certain, but it is important to emphasize a known fact that gets lost in this debate: Dumas wrote the novel in collaboration with Mallefille. A novel written in collaboration is the product and reflection of both authors. Based on the lack of existing evidence to determine who wrote what, it is difficult to ascertain how much of the novel is Dumas's and how much is Mallefille's (who is usually assumed to have supplied details about local conditions). However, it is inconceivable that Mallefille, as a white Creole from a French colonial outpost, left no trace of his own opinions and attitudes. Therefore, using the co-authored *Georges* alone to determine Dumas's sole opinion seems fallacious. While *Georges* should certainly not be dismissed *en masse* when gauging Dumas's literary stance on slavery, it needs to be interpreted within the broader context of Dumas's literary output. Viewing *Georges* in comparison with other works reveals elements of consistency that suggest the hand of their common author: Dumas. Although Dumas's stance on slavery in *Georges* is ambiguous, he would turn to the issue repeatedly and less ambiguously by concentrating on slavery's inhumanity in several works of historical fiction in which he chose to focus primarily on different (i.e., more distant) historical eras. Some of these works dealing with slavery include: *Charles VII at the Home of His Great Vassals* (1831), a play set in fifteenth-century France with a Muslim slave hero named Yaqoub; *Captain Pamphile* (1839), a satirical fantasy in which the title character is shipwrecked and taken as a slave by an Iroquois chief, only to later escape and become an African slave trader; *Acté* (1838), a novel in which the title character is a Greek slave in Ancient Rome; *Joseph Balsamo* (1846–1848), a novel set in eighteenth-century France in which one of the main aristocratic characters has a black slave to serve her at the French court; and *The Count of Monte Cristo* (1845–1846), which features Haydée, a Greek princess sold into slavery after the French military betrays her father and who becomes an instrumental component in Monte Cristo's quest for revenge.

Georges (and Dumas), therefore, continue to present mixed interpretations. Nevertheless, the image of Dumas articulated in Beyala's preface was largely the Dumas the state celebrated during his bicentennial and interment in the Panthéon, and the one gaining cultural hegemony in France. The rise of civil society, the media, and other factors have forced the state into increased negotiations that have limited its authority in certain domains, creating a public space to contest French identity.

Imagining Dumas During His Bicentennial

In 2001, the Dumas Society, then led by Didier Decoin, initiated a request to President Chirac to transfer Dumas's remains to the Panthéon for the upcoming bicentennial of his birth. Decoin's letter compared Dumas to Victor Hugo, whom posterity had praised at Dumas's expense. But Decoin also argued that Dumas merited inclusion in the Panthéon to honor an "exemplary" Frenchman. In explaining "exemplary," he focused on Dumas's symbolic nature, his "blackness" and struggles against racism, his connection to former colonial subjects, and his global popularity.[89] Decoin even suggested that Hugo alluded to Dumas's fight against "a latent, but very real, racism" in a letter to Dumas *fils*. Again making the now commonplace, but dubious connections between Dumas and *Négritude*, Dumas was described as being descended from a slave and possessing frizzy hair and thick lips that "sparked in him a sense of *Négritude*, to take the expression of Léopold Sédar Senghor." Finally, Dumas's interment would delight the French people in all its "composite dimensions," an allusion to a global Republic inclusive of its overseas citizens and postcolonial

Finding Monte Cristo

immigrants.[90] After contemplating on the proposal, Chirac declared in March 2002 at a National Library exposition dedicated to Hugo that Dumas deserved a place next to him in the Panthéon.[91] He subsequently authorized the transfer, praising Dumas's efforts to support "republican ideals" and his accomplishments, which were especially significant because "slavery had yet to be abolished" and Dumas "was the grandson of a slave."[92]

The year of 2002 became the year of Dumas as events dedicated to the writer swept across the nation. Publishers released new editions of his works, commemorative stamps and editions of magazines and journals flooded the market, banners celebrating his literary masterpieces floated triumphantly throughout Paris, and adaptations of his works saturated television screens.[93] Not to be outdone, museums, libraries, and academic institutions held film festivals, exhibits, conferences, and events.[94] The Dumas Society saw its membership leap over 20 percent and its then new website was inundated with over 135,000 hits, a trend which continued for the next few years.[95] A state committee charged with organizing the interment ceremony included the Society's leaders and state representatives. Granted nearly one million euros for expenditures, the planners intended the event, the "pinnacle of the bicentennial celebrations," to be "jubilatory," thereby different in nature "from the seriousness" of recent past interment ceremonies.[96]

The decision to inter Dumas was reported as overwhelmingly popular.[97] Villers-Cotterêts, however, refused to let the central government remove from its soil the remains of its most famous native without compensation, particularly since Dumas and related sites remained the town's significant tourist attractions.[98] Writer Geneviève Dormann summarized the town's opinion to the press, arguing that the "monstrous" project "deprived a small provincial village of its only great wealth ... to lock up in an honorific Parisian icebox."[99] Ultimately, a compromise was reached. The state commissioned a replica for Villers-Cotterêts of the bronze Dumas statue erected there in 1885, but removed in 1942 during World War II (Figure 22). Further, a plaque would cover his former grave explaining his remains' transfer.[100]

Building on the reasons for Dumas's interment outlined in the Dumas Society's letter, in turn influenced by changing perceptions of Dumas from metropolitan and overseas intellectuals since the 1970s, Dumas was depicted regularly within the public sphere as the "incarnation of social

5. *Alexandre Dumas* Métissé

Figure 22: An early twentieth-century postcard depicting the original statue of Alexandre Dumas erected in his hometown of Villers-Cotterêts. The statue was destroyed during World War II and recreated for the town after the state government made the decision to transfer Dumas's remains to Paris.

and racial *métissage*" and a symbol of a "mixed" France.[101] Individuals interred in the Panthéon must personify the qualities attributed to "French genius."[102] Thus, the simultaneous celebration of Dumas's "certain ethnic traits" and his nature as a French symbol helped facilitate a de-territorialized conception of "French" from the metropole that allowed its more equal union with its overseas departments and former colonial territories.[103] Such a Dumas helped create a retrospective perception that minority groups from the former colonies had existed in the metropole for centuries, contributing to the nation's development.[104] Such discourse indicated that it was not only Dumas's role that was to be vindicated in the construction of "France," but that of former colonial subjects as a whole. Dumas, although connected to those from the former colonies and their descendants, was not merely a "colonial" hero, but also (and simultaneously) a "French" hero because he was emblematic of France's republican values, like "liberty, equality, and fraternity."[105] Since Dumas was descended from a black slave from the colonies and his works had long been part of "France," the refusal to accept a mixed France was presented as to deny something that had already long existed. Therefore, *Le Monde*'s article on Dumas's interment boldly declared that he was a "symbol of the *métissage* ... at the heart of our national identity."[106] Honoring Dumas was projected as a way to foster amends (rather than separation) between metropolitan and overseas France as part of an ongoing project to realize the Republic's ideals within French borders. The media thus declared that since Dumas symbolized "plural and mixed identities," his commemorations served as "a call for national reconciliation."[107]

Descendants from France's colonial populations, in a similar fashion to that of African American intellectuals in Chapter 3, became involved in identifying past heroes to "unveil" their past contributions to the development of France and French culture to posit role models for subsequent achievement. Writer Daniel Picouly, for example, noted in a discussion of literature that Dumas "was black." It was important to note this because "there is a problem of identification. When one is a boy of color, one says to himself, 'How can I be a writer?' It is very important that that child knows that he exists: if one sees a writer, a lawyer, an athlete of color ... one knows that it is possible. For Dumas this is important because our accounts are conditioned to our origins, our context."[108] Dumas's origins, which lay in the "history of colonialism and racism," could serve as a reminder to all Frenchmen of "the black face in our national history" by helping insert citizens descended from colonial subjects "into the national novel."[109]

During Dumas's bicentennial, he was therefore noted as having a "complex ... identity."[110] First, Dumas was connected to the Caribbean, attaching him to the former colonial world. From the 1990s onward, he

5. *Alexandre Dumas* Métissé

had become increasingly described as an "Antillean,"[111] "Caribbean,"[112] "Haitian,"[113] or "Franco-Haitian"[114] writer. It became customary to comment publicly on his "black blood" from his "Caribbean grandmother" and his "Haitian family history."[115] Second, Dumas was routinely connected to Africa and the larger African Diaspora. Dumas's surname, which had belonged to his slave grandmother and which his father had assumed on entering the military, was suggested as being a "distortion of an African name," even though Dumas is a common French surname.[116] Consequently, some intellectuals, like Fernandez, suggested that Dumas's retention of his "African," or "black," surname was "an act of solidarity with his *nègre* origins."[117] Further, Dumas developed a newfound solid footing in France as a member of a global African Diaspora.[118] *Le Monde* linked Dumas to recent African immigrants, suggesting that his father arrived "*sans-papier*" from Saint Domingue to leave his slave past to become a French Revolutionary commander.[119] Dumas's "blackness" as a result of these connections was perceived as a primary (and revealing) component within his multifaceted identity.[120]

Similarly, public discourse on Dumas largely focused on his experience with racism, which in France, has been viewed "primarily as an incorrect or unjust invocation of culture."[121] The routine admittance of such racism and the allusion that it still existed marked a dramatic change in perceptions of French society and history since World War II, implying that Dumas's interment was an act of repentance.[122] Dumas was therefore depicted as a figure destined to "eternal exile" because he was a man "of mixture," a Frenchman who "never ceased being regarded as the Other" by his fellow Frenchmen.[123] Even the Château de Monte Cristo's souvenir booklets noted that he "had black blood in his veins, which gained him ... racial critiques throughout his life."[124] Dumas was depicted as a man who actively resisted his racist treatment. In so doing, however, he did not necessarily assert his blackness, but rather his Frenchness because he fought against treatment that unjustly severed him from the French cultural nation.[125] The "imbecile racism" of men like Balzac and Mirecourt was also routinely criticized.[126] Consequently, it was observed that Dumas's egalitarian sentiment of "all for one and one for all" was not held by his contemporaries, making him a man ahead of his era.[127] Some, like Decoin, also suggested the honors bestowed on Dumas, one of France's "children," went beyond struggles against racism, but more broadly "against all forms of the exclusion of man."[128] Dumas was thus depicted as a defender of human rights and some newspapers even praised him as an early feminist.[129]

Dumas was also described routinely as a descendant of a slave.[130] Intellectuals like Decoin asserted that Dumas, as "the grandson of black slave Marie-Césette," endured similar "humiliations and ... sorrows" as that of his fictional character Edmond Dantès.[131] Such connections echoed those made by African American readers over a century earlier. Meanwhile, other intellectuals noted that Dumas was born the same year that Napoleon "ruined the projection of the French Revolution's ideals by reestablishing slavery and purging the army of all *métis*" like Dumas's father.[132] Chirac, however, linked Dumas to Hugo and Victor Schoelcher, and argued against fact to claim that the trio led the Republic in the battle to open the "gates of emancipation."[133] He thus ignored the animosity that had existed between Dumas and Schoelcher, as discussed in Chapters 2 and 3. Ultimately, UNESCO's slave route project included Dumas in its literature and he became connected with May 10 celebrations.[134]

Although Dumas's popularity had never been in doubt, his reimagination in the 1990s and early 2000s included a widespread reevaluation of him as a "great" writer because of his popular longevity, style, depth, pioneering of new genres, and contributions to modern drama.[135] *Le Monde*, for example, declared him a writer of the people, who, shunned by the Academy, was an "immortal" only through his work; continued popularity was thus his "revenge."[136] He was described in "the past" as being treated "with condescendence" and having "never been an official Great Writer."[137] Lyonel Trouillot, a professor of Haitian literature, provided a typical view from the academic arena, noting in an article his admiration for Dumas in his youth. But as an adult, he revealed, there is a need to be taken seriously "in the world of literature." Therefore, "I admired Dumas, but guarded it as a secret," a type of guilty pleasure.[138] Dumas's association with literary figures like Voltaire, Rousseau, Hugo, and Émile Zola already interred in the Panthéon indirectly elevated Dumas to the same standards.[139] By the bicentennial, both the French and international press observed that growing intellectual interest in Dumas during the last decade had resulted in the writer's "rehabilitation."[140] Claude Schopp, a specialist on Dumas from when being one was unfashionable, commented in an interview, "studying Dumas today is no longer scandalous."[141] Consequently, Dumas ranked with, if not eclipsed, the best of his contemporaries. It became the norm to describe him as equal (or superior)

5. *Alexandre Dumas* Métissé

to already highly-regarded writers like Balzac, Stendhal, and Zola.[142] Others sought to link Dumas's series of novels (his *Drama of France*) as a prequel to Balzac's *Human Comedy*, which examined in literature the lives of individuals from varying French social classes during the 1830s and 1840s, and Zola's *Les Rougon-Macquart*, which similarly examined across several novels the lives of individuals from different French social classes, but during the 1850s and 1860s.[143] As a "visionary," there was an intellectual attempt to divorce Dumas from the image of being a children's author. He was reevaluated as being "more complex and innovating" than formerly conceived.[144] Dumas's work was described as full "of stylistic novelties" and he was praised for inventing new literary genres.[145] He was also praised as a leader of contemporary theater and an influential travel writer.[146] Finally, there was an attempt to definitively dismiss the long-standing accusations that Dumas was not the true author of his works. Dumas's use of collaborators was not denied, but their roles were marginalized because "his style" was detectable in all his works. Defenders pointed out that during the Renaissance, for example, the master's name was always placed on the final project, even though subordinates assisted him.[147]

Perhaps most importantly, however, Dumas was connected to francophone writers beyond the metropole, particularly those of the Atlantic world. Therefore, his "francophone dimension" received much attention.[148] The simultaneous elevation of Dumas's literary reputation and emphasized connections with writers beyond the metropole indirectly elevated "francophone" literature within French culture. Canadian scholar Réginald Hamel, for one, interpreted Dumas within the realm of "American *créolité*," positioning him as a francophone writer, even if he insisted that Dumas "wrote as an observer, without taking a position against slavery and racial prejudice." Hamel also asserted Dumas's influence on minorities in the U.S. and francophone writers in the Americas.[149] Dumas was inevitably associated with the *Négritude* movement, with some newspapers linking him to Césaire.[150] While no one argued explicitly that Dumas was a forerunner to *Négritude*, many writers and politicians suggested or implied (often quite strongly) that the movement expounded on some of his ideas and attitudes. This link materialized an intellectual and experiential continuity between past and present (post)colonial immigrants, even if the forerunners of the *Négritude* movement might have been puzzled over the connection (see Chapter 4). One Dumas biographer argued that although the writer was "[not] the precursor of *Négritude*," he nevertheless was not fully accepted as a Frenchmen and reacted through a sense of pride in his mixed heritage. Consequently, Dumas "invokes *Négritude*" in some of his works, while maintaining "an ambiguous position," since he "refused to condemn France" while retaining "a sense of sentimental attachment" to his colonial origins.[151]

Dumas's innovative, "revolutionary" literary styles similarly gained attention as reflecting his roots overseas and in Africa.[152] Dumas's "French" work was therefore presented as influenced by the native cultures of former colonial subjects.[153] As Decaux, for example, pondered in an article, the writer's "black blood takes us back to Africa where in the villages ... griots narrate the past of their tribe to amazed audiences. How much of Dumas's genius did he inherit from them?"[154] In connecting Dumas to "Africa," however, some intellectuals, politicians, and journalists invoked a sense of exoticness that reflected black stereotypes. For example, his works were noted as having a musical, "jazz-like" rhythm.[155]

Dumas Enters the Panthéon

The ceremonies surrounding Dumas's interment in the Panthéon, the culmination of a year's worth of events and anticipation, launched on November 26, 2002. Unsurprisingly, these ceremonies largely repeated in miniature the themes surrounding Dumas's reconceptualization that had dominated public discourse during the year. To launch the spectacle, Dumas's remains were exhumed from his grave in Villers-Cotterêts and placed in a casket exhibited at the town hall for the population's final respects. Two days later, the hype leading up to the final interment began.[156] On November 29, Dumas's casket arrived at the Château de Monte Cristo, Dumas's former home outside Paris and now a museum dedicated to the writer. Local politicians, Dumas Society members, and an escort dressed as musketeers, recognizable by their blue tunics with crosses, received the casket, which spent the evening at the château. There, during a soirée, notable French writers and actors, including Calixthe Beyala, read or performed extracts from Dumas's works, or texts by contemporaries about him.[157]

The next day, Dumas's casket left Monte Cristo. A republican guard formed a line of honor as "musketeers" escorted Dumas to his first stop in Paris, the Senate.[158] Senate President Christian Poncelet and French

5. Alexandre Dumas Métissé

Caribbean intellectual Claude Ribbe gave speeches evoking Dumas's colonial origins.[159] Ribbe declared that Dumas must be thought of as "a writer of color," a "black Romancier," and a "Caribbean author," for "one must speak of his creoleness, Africaness, blackness, and black blood." Poncelet argued that "in evoking Dumas ... we cannot miss to think of [French politician] Victor Schœlcher ... with his victorious battle for the abolition of slavery [in 1848]." The "universal Republic," he declared, "draws its radiance from its capacity for integration" and "makes amends for the horrific crimes" of racism and slavery of past generations. He also connected Dumas to the *Négritude* movement, by then a standard observation, arguing that Dumas "had an acute conscience of his *négritude* before the concept was invented."[160] After these solemn speeches, a festive parade to the Panthéon opened with a fanfare.[161] A float depicting scenes from the writer's dramatic works led the procession.[162] Actors portraying a nineteenth-century audience cheered to demonstrate their delight. Cast in a bluish light and decked in a blue velvet cloth bearing the musketeers' motto, "All for One, One for All," Dumas's casket slowly brought up the procession's rear. The casket, still escorted by musketeers, was carried by four men in plain period dress.[163] A biracial woman dressed in white with the red Phrygian cap associated with the French Revolution arrived on a white horse. Representing Marianne, the Republic's female embodiment, she greeted Dumas's casket as mother France welcoming a cherished son.[164] "Marianne" then accompanied the entourage to the Panthéon to conclude the homecoming, her white and red combining with Dumas's blue to form the French flag, the tricolor. "All for one, one for all" thus became appropriated fully by the Republican flag. While the musketeers stepped aside, the four bearers brought the writer before the Panthéon, lit with the tricolor's hues for the ceremony. An orchestra saluted the personality of Dumas in an oratorio.

Dumas's most famous protagonists, the musketeers—Athos, Porthos, Aramis, and d'Artagnan—have become a literary myth through countless theatrical adaptations, films, sequels, and rewritings that have perpetuated the characters' existence in the cultural environment. In *The Three Musketeers*, as Roxane Petit-Rasselle argues, Dumas's musketeers and their valets originate from different social classes and French regions. This diversity, appropriated symbolically for various national and republican purposes, represented metropolitan France's regional and social diversity. Thus, the musketeers' unity, embodied in the slogan "all for one, one for all," came to symbolize French plurality. During Dumas's bicentennial, the collective memorial symbol of the musketeers was transferred to Dumas's persona to represent France in its contemporary, postcolonial diversity.[165] Through this reconfiguration, Dumas's republican canonization thus glorified unity while celebrating diversity. The bearers' plain tunics indicated their "ordinariness," like that of the musketeers' valets, but they occupied as prominent a ceremonial position. For Dumas's interment, the casting of a biracial figure to embody Marianne sought to reinforce a global conception of France. Together, she and Dumas symbolized not just the unity of the geographic regions of the French metropole, but the unity of a broader French state that included overseas departments across the globe. Marianne thus echoed the notion that France, in its global diversity, could be united and indivisible like Dumas's musketeers. Each member of the group is different, yet all of them work together in unison for a collective cause. By transposing their unity and diversity onto the persona of Dumas, Dumas was recast as a symbol for a global France. In recalling France's multiracial diversity, Marianne and Dumas allied the past with the future, evoking nineteenth-century historian and politician Ernst Renan's conception of a nation, which rejected race as the foundation for national belonging in favor of a collection of individuals willing to live together.[166]

For the final act, Alain Decaux, the Dumas Society's founder and honorary president and French Academy member, paid tribute to Dumas's literary "genius." So, too, did President Chirac, who also presented Dumas as a victim of past French racism and slavery, suggesting his celebration served as "national healing." France was thus honoring Dumas's "genius" and "repairing an injustice": the racism that "marked Dumas at childhood just as shackles previously marked his slave ancestors."[167] Chirac commented on the author's entrance in the Panthéon next to writers Hugo and Zola, calling the trio "the musketeers" of the Republic who with their pens defended "with so much tenacity that genius of Liberty, Equality, and Fraternity."[168] He argued that Dumas's works, which address all citizens due to their popular nature, make everyone feel "French," of belonging to the same community. Moreover, Dumas's international appeal made him a global herald of French values. Dumas's casket then entered the necropolis, ending the ceremony.

Such praise (and the general intellectual enthusiasm greeting Dumas's interment), would have surprised French literary critics a century earlier

5. Alexandre Dumas Métissé

or during the height of Dumas's fame. Consequently, such celebrations represented a radical reassessment. As we saw in Chapter 1, Dumas, a prodigious writer, was accused falsely in an 1845 pamphlet of establishing a writing factory in which he placed his name on works by others. Many critics did not respect Dumas as a writer during his lifetime despite (and, perhaps, because of) his popularity, and he never gained admittance to the prestigious French Academy. The half century after Dumas's death in 1870 did not result in more positive reassessments.

During Dumas's bicentennial and interment in the Panthéon, the reevaluation of Dumas's "genius" and biraciality were linked, reflecting the evolution of the Dumas of memory since the 1970s. For example, Chirac's praises of Dumas's genius did not fail to cite a specific source of this greatness: "his roots overseas and in Africa."[169] One journalist even asked rhetorically if Dumas's upcoming panthéonization was "another celebration or a celebration of the Other" and historian Jean Tulard made the cynical accusation that Dumas had been "transferred to the Panthéon ... less for the quality of his writings ... than for having a black slave grandmother."[170] While Dumas's biracial background was not the sole reason for his interment, it was nevertheless an aspect of Dumas that separated him from his literary contemporaries and came to occupy a crucial role in the conceptual portraits of him constructed after his death and during the interment (whether through marginalization or glorification). Therefore, Dumas's biraciality was a significant and crucial factor in his commemoration and celebration and makes him a unique symbol of France particularly poignant to contemporary society. Debates about Dumas's biraciality linked to his perceived colonial origins thus shed light on shifting French attitudes toward its national identity and colonized and the (former) colonized's (in)ability to achieve acceptance in the French cultural nation.

Conclusion

During the ceremony for Dumas's interment in the Panthéon in the same chamber as Hugo and Zola, President Chirac had compared the three literary figures to Dumas's fictitious trio of Athos, Porthos, and Aramis. As a result, "the Republic also has its musketeers."[171] The state's transformation of the motto "All for one and one for all" into a slogan for national unity suggested that "France" was comprised of diverse global elements. Although not mentioned during the ceremony, the figures of Hugo, Zola, and Dumas represented in miniature the history of French immigration. In a long-forgotten 1883 *Atlantic Monthly* article, Havelock Ellis attempted to create a map of France in which he attached the "most illustrious Frenchmen" to the geographic location where "there is reason to believe that ... [each] had set down his deepest ancestral roots." However, existing globalizing effects on migration complicated his efforts. Literary figures he perceived as having connections to more than one place were listed multiple times. He also noted several omissions "in the case of individuals whose ancestry is so mixed that it is difficult to find anything like a taproot." Consequently, Ellis excluded "many eminent persons who are not only of mixed, but largely of foreign ancestry," like Dumas. However, he also excluded Zola, who, along with Hugo, were positioned as "marked examples of the influences of cross-breeding." By "foreign," however, Ellis did not exclusively mean from other European "races," a term customary of his era, but from beyond the European continent. He thus concluded that the "rich and varied genius of France" was due to its history of immigration from other parts of the European continent and, because of colonialism and increased transportation networks, from "the commingling of remote foreign elements." Ellis therefore created a broad, general history of immigration to France symbolized by French literary figures. He perceived a wave of immigration heralding from parts of Western Europe, especially "German" areas, symbolized by Hugo because of his descent "from the Germanic race of Lorraine and the Breton race." Zola, because of his Italian and Greek ancestry, emerged as a symbol of another wave that included immigrants from Southern Europe. The "negro blood which it is still easy to trace in the face of Alexandre Dumas" and "the Iroquois blood in Flaubert" made them symbols of the influx of new "races" from the French American colonies, which included both New France (on mainland North America) and the Caribbean.[172] Since Ellis's article was published during the late nineteenth century, he did not discuss subsequent waves, or broad categories, of immigrants to the metropole from the French colonies in Africa and Asia. Just as the three musketeers became four in Dumas's novel upon the arrival of the brash "outsider," d'Artagnan, from the "remote" region of Gascony (and therefore the margins of France), the trio of Hugo, Dumas, and Zola await a fourth member with ties to the second wave of French colonialism to assist in the ongoing

5. Alexandre Dumas Métissé

transformation of the Panthéon from a "metropolitan" to a more global French site of memory.[173]

Yet, Ellis's article, which sought to connect national identities as natural to specific geographic places, implied another revelation about "modern" national identities. In constructing identities derived from notions of sociotemporal difference based on distance, Europeans linked national identities to specific global spaces (or places), dividing the world into multiple (and presumably independent, or partially independent) areas. During the early modern era, the West thus developed a geo-psychology that organized the globe temporally, creating contemporaneous (in the present, or "modern") and non-contemporaneous (backward, primitive, or "unmodern") peoples even though all existed in the same present to justify European dominance over an "expanding" globe. This process, examined in Chapter 1, formed individual European identities in opposition to "distant" Others since individual national identities are formed through complex, comparative interaction with individuals, societies, and cultures encountered beyond the geopolitical boundaries of the nation-state. Consequently, such constructions created senses of difference between Englishmen, Frenchmen, etc., and "Africans" and other native peoples across the globe. This modern conception of global difference linked geographical distance with social and cultural difference.[174] Therefore, as we saw in Chapter 1, Dumas had difficulty in being accepted during his lifetime as part of the French cultural nation. He and "others" like him faced feelings of alienation, or "homelessness," that prompted them to seek "Monte Cristo," or a figurative sense of belonging. Transportation, communication, and information networks spread via colonialism integrated the colonies with the metropole in a more tangible sense, allowing increasingly higher levels of migration from the colonies to the metropole, thereby enabling greater flows of ideas and people. Consequently, the contemporaneous and non-contemporaneous worlds became increasingly blurred. By the early twentieth century, France was no longer a European, but rather a global polity due to its overseas territories.

Individuals deemed "backward," however, underwent profound cultural, social, political, psychological, and, in some cases (because of the slave trade and labor needs) geographical dislocations due to Western determination to "civilize" the globe. French colonialism, spread through a "civilizing mission," generally sought in theory the francization of those regarded as "primitive" to make them part of the French nation. This

Finding Monte Cristo

process required the colonized to internalize his or her inferior status of "backwardness" and accept the belief that the contemporaneous, or modern, French culture was superior and desirable to attain. To many individuals, as we saw in Chapter 2, Dumas emerged as a symbol of the potential to master French culture and (perhaps ironically) gain acceptance in mainstream French society.

This process of francization, however, displaced indigenous (or local) cultures across the globe and created feelings of self-loathing, alienation, and an eventual search for their own "Monte Cristo." While identities in the metropole were defined in opposition to colonial Others beyond Europe, how did colonized Others define their identities since colonialism socially conditioned them to accept a European identity defined in opposition to themselves? Colonials who had assimilated French culture, and in some cases had French citizenship, found themselves excluded from the French nation. Consequently, overseas territories and their inhabitants remained on the margins of a global French society. Colonial intellectuals grappled with this situation, often establishing an ethnic, or minority, identity in response to their outsider status. *Négritude* can be viewed within this context and its proponents generally accepted notions that Dumas was accepted in French society and thus an assimilated Frenchman; consequently, they ignored Dumas, viewing him as a model of how not to be.

French expansion and domination through colonialism, then, not only served as a form of globalization, spreading white hegemony across the world, but also transformed France into a global nation-state. In the postwar world, whites in the metropole, as the exclusive writers of historical progress, retained the monopoly on "French" culture as the exclusive source from which it emanated to other global regions. French individuals from outside the metropole, or perceived to be from areas outside the metropole, were regarded as separate from French culture largely because of their "colonial" status, even though colonialism had officially ended. Instead, as we explored in this chapter, they were perceived as forming an inferior "francophone" culture; an impure French culture because it mixed (metropolitan) French culture with local ("inferior" or "backward") indigenous cultures. Consequently, there were limited individuals from the overseas departments, territories, or former colonies perceived as contributing to "French" cultural and historical development. In response, French overseas intellectuals forged a counter-bloc that

5. *Alexandre Dumas* Métissé

challenged notions of French culture as hegemonic metropolitan domination and francophone culture as inferior. They sought to insert overseas Frenchmen as a whole into the development of France and its culture, (re)creating a local French overseas, or Atlantic, history "lost" because of slavery, colonialism, and French metropolitan power to insert into the larger historical narrative. For example, Martinican intellectual Édouard Glissant opposed the narrative of perpetual (Western) progress that placed the Caribbean on the margins. He described History with a capital "H" as representing this narrative, which was the West's creation.[175] History sought to fix reality in terms of a rigid hierarchical discourse of superiority and inferiority to normalize Western culture. Glissant dated History from the start of the modern age, during which increased exploration and contact with diverse global cultures created a state of confusion in terms of "finding where one must establish one's place in the sun." History, he argued, resulted from this confusion. The West built a "fantasy" that "it alone 'made' the history of the World."[176] African intellectual V.Y. Mundimbe similarly argued that colonization included the integration of local histories "into the Western perspective."[177] African history prior to the Atlantic slave trade and its contributions to global developments had thus been marginalized to maintain Africa's inferiority. Contemporary French intellectuals from France's former colonies thus asserted that "our history (or ... histories) is shipwrecked in colonial history," for it "is just the history of ... [our] colonization." Within the "the currents of the history of France ... there was the obstinate progress of ourselves."[178] As we saw in Chapter 3, such sentiments echoed those of African American intellectuals during the late nineteenth and early twentieth centuries.

The collapse of the popular consensus that constituted the French nation-state in the postwar era thus enabled the negotiation of the nation's history in the global age. A crucial component of this process of rewriting the nation (and group belonging) is to acknowledge certain groups' positive contributions to the nation's development. Group memory selects certain landmarks and past individuals and invests them with symbolic and political significance as *lieux de mémoire*. Since national histories can be tools of exclusion, *lieux de mémoire* can be posed as a counter-history, or as Foucault calls it, "counter-memory," to challenge the "false" generalizations of an exclusionary history. Official historical interpretations, which proceed "from domination to domination," are carried out "in rituals, in meticulous procedures that impose rights and obligations."[179] Since

Finding Monte Cristo

"France" has been defined, debated, and redefined in its symbols and commemorations, the state's adoption of "counter-memories" can serve as the start of new collective memories. Past-oriented politics thus revise national histories in a global age to meet the challenges of a citizenry comprised of individuals from diverse origins. History, therefore, reflects the politics of the era in which it is composed.

In this sense, Dumas has been used as a symbol in the reconstruction of French identity, both by the hegemonic ruling class and those on the margins seeking to expand its definitional borders for their firm inclusion, through commemoration and personification. In the public sphere, the Dumas of memory was a French writer of Afro-Caribbean heritage and a descendant of a slave who became a celebrated "genius" in France during the Romantic Age, fighting valiantly for the nation, the Republic and its principles, even if it treated him "unjustly." French intellectuals' rehabilitation of Dumas as one who contributed to the development of France and republicanism was simultaneously accompanied by his casting as a symbol of citizens in the former colonial overseas departments. Dumas, as one who helped forge contemporary France, was part of French national history and thus the French nation. As representative of citizens from the overseas departments, his rehabilitation also provided them a positive role in the nation's development and thus "France." Consequently, Dumas's rehabilitation as a *lieu de mémoire* embodying the Caribbean overseas departments as part of the French collective memory was an attempt to rewrite the French nation, a validation for national inclusion and reconciliation for past exclusion.

Dumas's 2002 interment offered an opportunity to repair "the injury to the memory" of the citizens of the overseas departments and former colonies while simultaneously celebrating him as a great Republican literary hero. Commemorations of Dumas focused on the importance of the writer, but also his works' appeal to the public and different media, including film and television. Consequently, it allowed the nation to feel good about its history even as it acknowledged and "repaired" the "memory wounds" regarding slavery and colonialism. When it comes to the construction of a collective memory of the nation's history, statements of "truth," or what happened in the past, are not necessarily descriptions of what was, but rather exhortations to produce what was not. As actor Carleton Young, in the role of Maxwell Scott, declared in the 1962 film *The Man Who Shot Liberty Valance*, "When the legend becomes fact, print

5. *Alexandre Dumas* Métissé

the legend." Consequently, Dumas presented an opportunity for contemporary France to make public amends for the "forgetfulness" of slavery and its legacy of discrimination as a means to help realize in the present the universal Republic. Dumas's transformation thus revealed a renegotiation of French identity formed in relation to France's changing ethnic makeup and status as a global entity.

Chapter Notes

Introduction

1. *The Man in the Iron Mask* does not exist in French. It is the last part of *Le Vicomte de Bragelonne*, which English-language publishers divided into multiple books due to its length (and the Musketeer sequels' popularity) to generate more revenue.

2. Sometimes Dumas's grandmother is identified as Louise-Césette (or Céssette). Thomas-Alexandre's marriage record lists her as Marie-Céssette. Davy de la Pailleterie adopted Thomas-Alexandre and took him to France. When the French Revolution (1789–1799) began, Thomas-Alexandre joined the revolutionaries, having already discarded his father's aristocratic surname for that of his mother. He later served with Napoleon Bonaparte in Egypt, but was captured returning to France and held prisoner in Southern Italy. Thomas-Alexandre was eventually released, but his reunion with his family was brief due to his deteriorated condition from his incarceration. See record of marriage between Citoyen Thomas-Alexandre Dumas and Citoyenne Marie Louise Élisabeth Labouret, 28 November 1792 (First Year of the French Republic), Records of Marriage in Villers-Cotterêts, 1791–1792, Archives départementales de l'Aisne, accessed 23 January 2018. http://archives.aisne.fr/.

3. Jules Michelet, *La Femme* (1860), excerpt in *Alexandre Dumas en bras de chemise*, ed. Claude Schopp (Paris: Maisonneuve et Larose, 2002), 6–7.

4. The stage play, presented in the early 2000s, was entitled *Signé Dumas*. See Cyril Gely and Eric Rouquette, *Signé Dumas* (Paris: Les Impressions Nouvelles, 2003). A performance was also filmed and released on DVD. For sample reviews, see "*Signé Dumas*," *La Dépêche du Midi*, 20 October 2004, accessed 29 September 2017. http://www.ladepeche.fr/article/2004/10/20/263089-signe-dumas.html; André Lafargue, "*Signé Dumas*: magnifique Perrin!" *Le Parisien*, 11 October 2003, accessed 29 September 2017. http://www.leparisien.fr/loisirs-et-spectacles/signe-dumas-magnifique-perrin-11-10-2003-2004458696.php; Didier Sénécal, "Théâtre: *Signé Dumas*," *L'Express*, 1 November 2003, accessed 29 September 2017. http://www.lexpress.fr/culture/livre/theatre-italique-signe-dumas-italique_808477.html&title=Th%E9%E2tre+%3A+%3ACItalique%3ESign%E9+Dumas%3C%2FItalique%3E.

5. This collaboration was known to Dumas's associates and peers. Further, in 1919, Gustave Simon published a well-known book extensively documenting Dumas's and Maquet's collaboration, particularly on *The Three Musketeers*.

6. American producers and directors have shared this view. For example, Orson Welles was involved in an unrealized project to make a film starring himself as Dumas. Welles was set to write a script and likely star in the film, but actor Kirk Douglas had also been approached about that possibility. See A.H. Weiler, "Welles's *King of Paris*," *New York Times*, 25 November 1962. Later, Welsh actor John Rhys-Davies played Dumas in two episodes of the television series *The Secret Adventures of Jules Verne* (2000).

7. Examples: André Soares, "Gérard Depardieu Too White to Play Alexandre Dumas," *Alt Film Guide*, 2010, accessed 29 September 2017. http://www.altfg.com/blog/actors/gerard-depardieu-alexandre-dumas-mixed-race-81901/; "Depardieu Dismisses Controversy Over Dumas Role," *CBC News*, 19 February 2010, accessed 29 September 2017. http://www.cbc.ca/news/entertainment/depardieu-dismisses-controversy-over-dumas-role-1.876656.

Chapter Notes—Introduction

8. These five overseas regions are French Guiana, Guadeloupe, Martinique, Mayotte, and Réunion. Despite their location beyond the geographical entity of Europe, French overseas regions are integral components of the French Republic: they are represented in the National Assembly, Senate, and Economic and Social Council; elect a member of the European Parliament (MEP); and use the Euro as currency.

9. For an example of this "new "conception of France, see Lucien Febvre and François Crouzet, *Nous sommes des sang-mêlés: Manuel d'histoire de la civilisation française,* ed. Denis and Élisabeth Crouzet (Paris: A. Michel, 2012).

10. See Claude Ribbe, "*L'autre Dumas,* de Safy Nebbou, avec Depardieu: un film français nul et ouvertement négrophobe," *Le blog de Claude Ribbe,* 7 February 2010, accessed 29 September 2017. http://www.claude-ribbe.com/dotclear/index.php?2010/02/07/145-lautre-dumas-avec-depardieu-un-film-ouvertement-negrophobe; Calude Ribbe, "*L'Autre Dumas*: un film raciste?" *Jeune Afrique.com,* 12 February 2010, accessed 29 September 2017. http://www.jeuneafrique.com/Article/ARTJA20100212154551/; Soares, "Gérard Depardieu Too White to Play Alexandre Dumas"; Patrick Lozès, "*L'Autre Dumas*: Un polémique très … clairement justifiée," *Le blog de diversiteé,* 18 February 2010, accessed 29 September 2017. http://diversite.20minutes-blogs.fr/archive/2010/02/18/l-autre-dumas-un-polemique-tres-clairement-justifiee.html; "*L'Autre Dumas*: Gérard Depardieu critiqué par Sonia Rolland," *Voici,* 10 February 2010, accessed 29 September 2017. http://www.voici.fr/news-people/actu-people/l-autre-dumas-gerard-depardieu-critique-par-sonia-rolland-341567; Colin Grant, "Could Gérard Depardieu Play Marcus Garvey?" *History News Network,* 2010, accessed 29 September 2017. http://hnn.us/article/124001.

11. For example articles on this controversy, see Soares, "Gérard Depardieu Too White to Play Alexandre Dumas"; Emma Jane Kirby, "Dumas Film with White Actor Depardieu Sparks Race Row," *BBC News,* 19 February 2010, accessed 29 September 2017. http://news.bbc.co.uk/2/hi/europe/8523212.stm; "Depardieu Dismisses Controversy Over Dumas Role"; Peter Allen, "Gérard Depardieu Sparks Race Row after He 'Blacks Up' to Play Author Alexandre Dumas," *Daily Mail,* 21 February 2010, accessed 29 September 2017. http://www.dailymail.co.uk/news/article-1252278/Gerard-Depardieu-sparks-race-row-darkens-skin-wears-black-wig-play-mixed-race-author-Alexandre-Dumas.html?openGraphAuthor=%2Fhome%2Fsearch.html%3Fs%3D%26authornamef%3DPeter%2BAllen; Joel Dreyfuss, "Depardieu Plays Dumas Amid Some Controversy," *Star Tribune,* 19 March 2010, accessed 29 September 2017. http://www.startribune.com/entertainment/movies/88566612.html; Charles Bremner, "Gérard Depardieu as Dumas Poses Race Question," *The Australian,* 15 February 2010, accessed 29 September 2017. http://www.theaustralian.com.au/arts/film/gerard-depardieu-as-alexandre-dumas-poses-race-question/story-e6frg8pf-1225830446832.

12. Étienne Balibar, "The Nation-Form," in *Race, Nation, Class: Ambiguous Identities,* eds. Étienne Balibar and Immanuel Wallerstein (New York: Verso, 1991), 86.

13. Pierre-André Taguieff, *The Force of Prejudice: On Racism and Its Doubles,* trans. and ed. Hassan Melehy (Minneapolis: University of Minnesota Press, 2001).

14. Arthur Schomburg, "The Negro Digs Up His Past," in Alain Locke, ed., *The New Negro: Voices of the Harlem Renaissance* (1925; reprint, New York: Touchstone, 1997), 232.

15. Fred Constant, "Pour une lecture sociale des revendications mémorielles 'victimaires,'" *Esprit* (February 2007): 105–116.

16. John Torpey, "'Making Whole What Has Been Smashed': Reflections on Reparations," *The Journal of Modern History* 73, no. 2 (2001), 337.

17. Frantz Fanon, *The Wretched of the Earth,* trans. Richard Philcox (New York: Grove, 2004), 238.

18. Alexandre Dumas, *Adventures in Algeria,* trans. and ed. Alma Elizabeth Murch (Philadelphia: Chilton, 1959), 199.

19. Gilles Henry has been at the forefront of making this assertion. See Gilles Henry, *Monte-Cristo ou l'extraordinaire aventure des ancêtres d'Alexandre Dumas* (Paris: Perrin, 1976); Gilles Henry, *Les Dumas: Le secret de Monte Cristo* (Paris: France-Empire, 1999); Gilles Henry, *Dans les pas des …Dumas. Les mousquetaires de l'aventure: Normandie, Haïti, Paris* (France: OREP, 2010).

20. Henry, *Les Dumas,* 200; Henri Troyat, *Alexandre Dumas: Le cinquième mousquetaire* (Paris: Grasset et Fasquelle, 2005), 534. See also Catherine Toesca, *Les 7 Monte-Cristo d'Alexandre Dumas* (Paris: Maisonneuve and Larose, 2002).

21. On the sociological concept of "home-

lessness" as a form of alienation, see Peter Berger, Bridgette Berger, and Hansfried Kellner, *The Homeless Mind: Modernization and Consciousness* (New York: Random House, 1973); Kathleen Arnold, *Homelessness, Citizenship, and Identity: The Uncanniness of Late Modernity* (Albany: State University of New York Press, 2004).

22. Antonio Benitez-Rojo, *The Repeating Island: The Caribbean and the Postmodern Perspective*, trans. James Maraniss (Durham: Duke University Press, 1996), 201.

23. Chris Bongie, *Islands and Exiles: The Creole Identities of Post/Colonial Literature* (Stanford: Stanford University Press, 1998), 18.

24. Benitez-Rojo, *The Repeating Island*, 235.

25. Jean Barnabé, Patrick Chamoiseau, and Raphaël Confiant, *Éloge de la Créolité/In Praise of Creoleness*, trans. M.B. Taleb-Khyar (Paris: Gallimard, 1993), 89, 90.

26. Pierre Nora, "Introduction: Between Memory and History," *Realms of Memory: The Construction of the French Past*, eds. Pierre Nora and Lawrence Kritzman, trans. Arthur Goldhammer, vol. I (New York: Columbia University Press, 1996), xvii.

27. Alexandre Dumas, *My Memoirs*, trans. E.M. Waller, 6 vols. (New York: Macmillan, 1907–1909), V: 337.

28. *Le Mousquetaire* (2003), 13–14.

29. Claude Schopp and Fernande Bassan, eds., *Cent-Cinquante Ans après: Les Trois Mousquetaires et Le Comte de Monte Cristo* (Marly-le-Roi, France: Champflour/Société des Amis d'Alexandre Dumas, 1995); Michel Arrous, ed., *Dumas, une lecture de l'Histoire* (Paris: Maisonneuve & Larose, 2003); Angels Santa and Francisco Lafarga, eds., *Alexandre Dumas y Victor Hugo: Viaje de los textos y textos de viaje* (Lleida, Spain: Pagès, 2006); Chantal Massol, ed., *Stendhal, Balzac, Dumas: Un récit romantique?* (Toulouse: Presses Universitaires du Mirail, 2006); *Le Rocambole: Bulletin des Amis du Roman populaire* 36 (Fall 2006) was dedicated to Dumas and the theater; Charles Grivel, ed., *Les Vies parallèles d'Alexandre Dumas* (Villeneuve d'Ascq, France: Presses Universitaires du Septentrion/Revue des Sciences humaines, 2008); Pascal Durand and Sarah Mombert, eds., *Entre presse et littérature:* Le Mousquetaire, *journal de M. Alexandre Dumas* (Liège, Belgium: Bibliothèque de la Faculté de Philosophie et Lettres/Diffusion Droz, 2009); Eric Martone, ed., *The Black Musketeer: Reevaluating Alexandre Dumas in the Francophone World* (Newcastle upon Tyne: Cambridge Scholars, 2011); a special *Cahiers de l'Association internationale des études françaises* (2012); and Matthieu Letourneux and Isabelle Safa, eds. *Mousquetaires! (Cahiers Alexandre Dumas 43)* (Paris: Classiques Garnier, 2017).

30. Of the over 100 contributions collected in these works, only entries in *The Black Musketeer* and seven others have a focus on Dumas's Caribbean heritage or connections to the francophone world beyond Europe. See Sarga Moussa, "Orientalisme et récit de voyage: l'exemple du *Véloce*," in *Dumas, une lecture de l'Histoire*, 361–377; Daniel Desormeaux, "Portrait d'Alexandre Dumas en personnage romanesque dans *Les Mille et un fantômes*," in *Dumas, une lecture de l'Histoire*, 477–505; Ana Monleón, "Alexandre Dumas et les Antilles," in *Alexandre Dumas y Victor Hugo: Viaje de los textos del viaje*, 589–606; Christine Prévost, "D'un rôle convenu à la promotion d'un personnage original: le maure de *Fiesque* à *Charles VII*," *Le Rocambole: Bulletin des Amis du Roman populaire* 36 (Fall 2006): 33–42; Didier Blonde, "Mes Mémoires ou la naissance du nom," in *Les Vies parallèles d'Alexandre Dumas*, 9–18; Claude Schopp, "Fabrique d'impressions: Quatre jours à Alger," in *Les Vies parallèles d'Alexandre Dumas*, 155–170; Léon-François Hoffmann, "Les personnages noirs et mulâtres, la traite et l'esclavage dans l'œuvre d'Alexandre Dumas," in the *Cahier de l'Association internationale des études françaises*, 171–186.

Chapter 1

1. "The Palace of Marly," *The Living Age*, 26 May 1849. See also L. Henry Lecomte, *Alexandre Dumas* (Paris: Tallandier, 1902), 51. Some thought that the cost ruined Dumas financially. See Gabriel Ferry, *Les Dernières années d'Alexandre Dumas, 1864–1870* (Paris: Calmann Lévy, 1883), 110.

2. Honoré de Balzac, *Lettres à Madame Hanska*, ed. Roger Pierrot, 4 vols. (Paris: Du Delta, 1967–71), IV: 478; On Dumas's and Balzac's relationship, see Claude Schopp, "Balzac et Dumas, ou Ennemis et rivaux," in *Honoré de Balzac: Camins creuats*, ed. Angels Santa (Lleida, Spain: Pagès, 1997): 95–122; Dumas, *My Memoirs*, V: 455.

3. Léon Gozlan, "Le Château de Monte-Cristo," in *l'Almanach comique pittoresque, drolatique, critique et charivarique, pour 1848*, reproduced in Charles Glinel, *Alexandre Dumas et son œuvre* (Rheims, France: F. Michaud, 1884), 407–408.

Chapter Notes—1

4. Percy Fitzgerald, *Life and Adventure of Alexandre Dumas*, 2 vols. (London: Tinsley, 1873), II: 141.

5. "The Palace of Marly," *The Living Age*, 26 May 1849; Gozlan, "Le Château de Monte-Cristo," 408–409.

6. *The Living Age*, 26 May 1849; Christiane Neave and Hubert Charron, *Monte-Cristo: Château de Rêve* (Marly-le-Roi, France: Champflour/Syndicat Intercommunal de Monte-Cristo/Société des Amis d'Alexandre Dumas, 1994), 11.

7. *The Living Age*, 26 May 1849.

8. Gozlan, "Le Château de Monte-Cristo," 409–410.

9. *The Living Age*, 26 May 1849; Gozlan, "Le Château de Monte-Cristo," 411–412.

10. Other components of the estate received names from the novel. The chatêlet was named the Château d'If after the prison in which Dantès escaped to find a treasure on Monte Cristo and subsequently seek revenge for his false imprisonment as the "Count of Monte Cristo." In addition, the garden was named after Haydée, the former Greek slave who becomes Dantès's companion.

11. *The Living Age*, 26 May 1849.

12. As Dumas relates the anecdote: "I was expecting [the actor Étienne] Mélingue to dinner.... My château was only just built, and as yet had no name. I had explained as well as I could its situation to my guests, but not so accurately as to enable the family to find their way there on foot. At Le Pecq they took a conveyance. 'To M. Dumas,' Madame Mélingue told the driver. "M. Dumas'— where's that?' the man asked.—'Why, on the Marly road.'—'There are two Marly roads ... which is it? ... But surely M. Dumas' house has got a name?'—'A name? Why, of course: It's the Chateau de Monte-Cristo.'" See Alexandre Dumas, *Adventures with My Pets*, trans. and ed. A. Craig Bell (Philadelphia: Chilton, 1960), 5–6.

13. *The Living Age*, 26 May 1849.

14. Fitzgerald, *Life and Adventures of Alexandre Dumas*, II: 142; Dumas, *Adventures with My Pets*, 6–7; Contemporaries came to gawk at the zoo and aviary, see Ferry, *Les Dernières années*, 103–116.

15. Dumas, *Adventures with My Pets*, 45.

16. *Ibid.*, 6.

17. Comtesse Dash, *Mémoires des autres* (1896–1898), excerpt in *Alexandre Dumas en bras de chemise*, 66.

18. Wolf Schäfer, "Global History and the Present Time," in *Wiring Prometheus: Globalisation, History, and Technology*, eds. Peter Lyth and Helmuth Trischler (Aarhus, Denmark: Aarhus University Press, 2004), 103–125.

19. The term "Others" evokes French philosopher Michel Foucault's notion derived from the antagonistic subject/object relationship established by Freud and Lacan that nations establish the Other as a "bad race" or "inferior race (or the degenerate, or the abnormal)" whose elimination "will make life in general ... healthier and purer." See Michel Foucault, *"Society Must Be Defended": Lectures at the Collège de France, 1975–1976*, trans. David Macey (New York: Picador, 1997), 255.

20. Ernst Bloch, *Heritage of Our Times*, trans. and ed. Neville Plaice and Stephen Plaice (Berkeley: University of California Press, 1991), 97.

21. Johannes Fabian argues that nineteenth-century evolutionism treated travel to distant *places* as if it were travel to earlier *times*, depicting *contemporary* Others as "our primitive *ancestors*." Western representations of physical and cultural differences as differences in time have shaped anthropology. He refers to this phenomenon as "the denial of coevalness." See Johannes Fabian, *Time and the Other: How Anthropology Makes Its Object* (New York: Columbia University Press, 1983).

22. Joseph Marie de Gérando, *Considerations on the Methods to Follow in the Observation of Savage Peoples* (1800), quoted in Fabian, *Time and the Other*, 7.

23. As black nationalist J.A. Rogers noted in 1947, "the African slave trade is essentially the story of the ... rise of Europe" for "the opening of the territory called the new world ... and in motion ... the dehumanization of Africa ... in European textbooks, geographies, and travel books." See J.A. Rogers, *World's Great Men of Color, Volume II: Europe, South and Central America, the West Indies, and the United States* (1947; reprint, New York: Touchstone, 1996), xx, xvi.

24. Marc Augé, *An Anthropology for Contemporaneous Worlds*, trans. Amy Jacobs (Stanford: Stanford University Press, 1999), 66; Edward Said makes a similar case regarding Asian and Middle Eastern peoples and cultures in *Orientalism* (New York: Vintage, 2003).

25. William Cohen, *The French Encounter with Africans: White Response to Blacks, 1530–1880*, reprint ed. (Bloomington: Indiana University Press, 2003), xvii, xxi–xxii, 1–34, 155–180, 263–282; Guy Thilmans, ed., "La Relation de François de Paris" (1682–1683)," *BIFAN* 38 (1976), 41.

Chapter Notes—1

26. Quoted in Cohen, *The French Encounter with Africans*, 221–222.
27. Although the number of blacks in France during Dumas's father's lifetime was small, it was large enough to cause the French government to issue legislation to control their numbers and curb their legal freedoms. Pierre Boulle asserts that the total number of all non-whites registered in France in 1777 was 2,329 individuals. See Pierre Boulle, *Race et esclavage dans la France de l'Ancien Régime* (Paris: Perrin, 2007), 109; Sue Peabody, "*There Are No Slaves in France*": *The Political Culture of Race and Slavery in the Ancien Régime* (New York: Oxford University Press, 1996); Cohen, *The French Encounter with Africans*, 110–120, 128–129.
28. After the French Revolution, the British gained control of most French colonies. In an 1815 peace settlement, France regained most of them, but had to join the British in banning the slave trade.
29. Timothy Mitchell, *Colonising Egypt* (Berkeley: University of California Press, 1991), 1–33.
30. In 1827, for example, six Osage Amerindians arrived in France wearing indigenous dress as part of a traveling spectacle that caused a brief cultural phenomenon.
31. Claude Schopp, *Alexandre Dumas: Genius of Life*, trans. A.J. Koch (New York: Franklin Watts, 1988), 330.
32. Dumas's father was descended from slaves and likely born a slave. He came to enjoy a life of luxury and education in metropolitan France during the Old Regime as a recognized son of a noble. Thus, Dumas's father was simultaneously descended from the highest and lowest ranks in the social hierarchy. Dumas's mother was from a bourgeois family. Consequently, while Dumas's occasional pretensions to nobility were mocked, he was generally perceived as an individual of the middle class.
33. Rogers Brubaker, *Citizenship and Nationhood in France and Germany* (Cambridge: Harvard University Press, 1992), 1, 6–8, 35–49.
34. *Ibid.*, 1–8, 35–49.
35. Jules Michelet, *Historical View of the French Revolution*, trans. C. Cocks (1890). Excerpt in Hans Kohn, ed., *Nationalism: Its Meaning and History* (Malabar, FL: Krieger, 1982), 98.
36. Hippolyte Romand, *Revue des deux mondes*, January 1834, in *Alexandre Dumas en bras de chemise*, 42–43; From 1790 to 1794, those residing in France automatically became naturalized citizens. Consequently, Dumas's father was a French citizen at the time of Dumas's birth in France and could pass citizenship on to his son. See Patrick Weil, *How to be French: Nationality in the Making since 1789*, trans. Catherine Porter (Durham: Duke University Press, 2008), 4, 14–19.
37. Théophile Gautier, *Histoire du Romantisme* (Paris: Charpentier, 1874), 166–171.
38. Hippolyte de Villemessant, *Mémoires d'un journaliste: Les Hommes de mon temps* (Paris: E. Dentu, 1872), 233–235.
39. Schopp, *Alexandre Dumas: Genius of Life*, 113.
40. Fernand Calmettes, ed., *Mémoires de général Baron Thiébault*, 5 vols. (Paris: E. Plon, 1893–1895), II: 32; Jules Lecomte, *Lettres de Van Engelgom*, reprint ed. (Paris: Boissard, 1925), 111; Benjamin Pifteau, *Alexandre Dumas en manches de chemise* (1884; reprint, Montreal: Joyeux Roger, 2009), 20; de Villemessant, *Mémoires d'un journaliste*, 235.
41. Mathilde Shaw, "Alexandre Dumas père: Mes souvenirs sur lui," *La Nouvelle Revue*, 1 August 1899, in *Alexandre Dumas en bras de chemise*, 225.
42. Audebrand, *Alexandre Dumas à la Maison d'or*, 49.
43. Charles Maurice, *Histoire anecdotique du théâtre, de la littérature et de diverses impressions contemporaines*, 2 vols. (Paris: H. Plon, 1856), I: 428.
44. The poem is quoted in Bernard Falk, *The Naked Lady* (London: Hutchinson, 1952), 182.
45. Christiane Neave and Digby Neave, eds., *Iconographie d'Alexandre Dumas père* (Marly-le-Roi, France: Champflour/Société des Amis d'Alexandre Dumas, 1991), 49.
46. Dumas, *My Memoirs*, VI: 123.
47. In *Souvenirs de la princesse Pauline de Metternich, 1859–1871* (Paris: H. Plon, 1922).
48. Arthur Davidson, *Alexandre Dumas: His Life and Works* (Westminster, UK: Archibald Constable, 1902), 45; André Maurois, *The Titans: A Three-Generation Biography of the Dumas*, trans. Gerard Hopkins (New York: Harper and Brothers, 1957), 80.
49. Dumas, *My Memoirs*, IV: 41–43.
50. For reproductions of Cham's caricatures, see Neave and Neave, *Iconographie*, 36, 41, 42, 44, 47, 52–56, 64, 67–69, 71, 74, 76–77, 82, 87–89, 90–92, 94, 99, 100, 102, 106, 108; For Nadar's, see Neave and Neave, *Iconographie*, 24, 57, 62, 66, 74, 85–86, 88, 90; For similar caricatures from other

artists, see Neave and Neave, *Iconographie*, 25–26, 34–35, 38, 40, 42, 44, 46, 47, 50, 56–59, 64–65, 69–71, 74, 78, 80–81, 83, 85, 90, 94, 96, 98–99, 102.

51. See Neave and Neave, *Iconographie*, 105; Charles Oulmont, "Un portrait d'Alexandre Dumas par Daumier," *Les Arts* 186 (1920), 23.

52. Dumas, *My Memoirs*, IV: 77–343.

53. Léon-François Hoffmann, *Le Nègre romantique: Personnage littéraire et obsession collective* (Paris: Payot, 1973), 102–3.

54. The terms *nègre* and *noir* were generally reserved for individuals dark in appearance and perceived as "pure" Africans. The term *gens de couleur*, or "people of color," was a neutral term for Caribbean individuals with less than 50 percent black ancestry often offended by "mulatto." See Jeremy Popkin, *Facing Racial Revolution: Eyewitness Accounts of the Haitian Insurrection* (Chicago: University of Chicago Press, 2007), 23, 24.

55. Dumas, *My Memoirs*, IV : 230–231; For the story of last white French survivors on St. Domingue, see Mlle De Palaiseau, *Histoire des Mesdemoiselles de Saint-Janvier: Les deux seules blanches conservées à Saint-Domingue*, 2nd ed. (Paris: J.J. Blaise, 1812).

56. Quoted in Charles Grivel, "Alexandre Dumas: mal écrire, bien écrire," in *Cent-Cinquante Ans après: Les Trois Mousquetaires et Le Comte de Monte Cristo*, 191; In the French context, "Creoles" referred to people born in the Caribbean regardless of race.

57. Jean Tulard, *Alexandre Dumas, 1802–1870* (Paris: Figures et plumes, 2008), 10; Neave and Neave, *Iconographie*, 17, 24.

58. Alexandre Dumas, *Histoire de mes bêtes*, 2nd ed. (Paris: Michel Lévy, 1868), 76–81; Dumas, *Adventures with My Pets*, 51–55; The account is also in Ferry, *Les Dernières années*, 149–154.

59. *Every Saturday*, January 28, 1871.

60. "Editor's Literary Record," *Harper's New Monthly Magazine*, March 1871; see also J. Brander Mathews, "The Dramas of the Elder Dumas," *The Atlantic Monthly*, September 1881.

61. Junius Henri Browne, "A Few French Celebrities," *Harper's New Monthly Magazine*, November 1873.

62. "Editor's Literary Record," *Harper's New Monthly Magazine*, March 1871; John Bigelow, "A Breakfast with Alexandre Dumas," *Scribner's Monthly*, April 1871, 598.

63. Bigelow, "A Breakfast with Alexandre Dumas."

64. Maurois, *The Titans*, 80; Dumas wrote at great length about Byron in his memoirs (III: 8–41, 51–53). Although Balzac's "immorality" was criticized, for example, it was not perceived as indicative of physical degeneracy or as a reason to cast him outside the French nation.

65. Michel Foucault, *History of Sexuality, Volume One: An Introduction*, trans. R. Hurley (New York: Vintage, 1990), 122–127.

66. Cohen, *The French Encounter with Africans*, 33.

67. *Ibid.*, 245–248.

68. F.W.J. Hemmings, *Alexandre Dumas: The King of Romance* (New York: Charles Scribner's, 1979), 64; Dumas, *My Memoirs*, IV: 40; Comtesse Dash, *Mémoires des autres*, in *Alexandre Dumas en bras de chemise*, 65.

69. Antoine Jay, a member of the *Académie Française*, published an article calling *Antony* obscene and immoral. See *Le Constitutionnel*, 28 April 1843; Critic Gustave Planche wrote: "Dumas is not in the habit of thinking. With him, action follows on the heels of desire with childlike rapidity. Consequently, he has rushed into doing battle without having considered the value of the monument which he has wished to tear down.... Dumas has all serious artists against him." Quoted in Maurois, *The Titans*, 135–136. See also Patrick Berthier, "Dumas, l'immoral: quelques images du dramaturge dans la presse des années 1830," *Dix-neuf Vingt: Revue de littérature moderne* 5 (March 1998): 55–65.

70. Cited in Maurois, *The Titans*, 136; see also Fernande Bassan, "Alexandre Dumas père et le théâtre romantique," *The French Review* 47, no. 4 (1974): 767–772.

71. Eugène de Mirecourt, *Fabrique de Romans, Maison Alexandre Dumas et compagnie* (Paris: Hauquelin et Bautruche, 1845), 33–47.

72. For examples, it was reported incorrectly that Dumas had died in 1832 and again in 1870. See Alexandre Dumas, *Adventures in Switzerland*, trans. and ed. R.W. Plummer and A. Craig Bell (Philadelphia: Chilton, 1960), 3–4; *Le Moniteur universel*, 20 October 1870.

73. Schopp, *Alexandre Dumas: Genius of Life*, 325; Bell, *Alexandre Dumas*, 166.

74. Charles Robin, *Galerie des Gens de lettres au XIXe siècle* (Paris: V. Lecou, 1848), 257.

75. For Dumas's account, see Dumas, *My Memoirs*, VI: 91–92, 129–141, 142–185, 186–197; The drama remained Gaillardet's most successful work and he came to like the attention he received for having such a famous

Chapter Notes—1

"collaborator." In an 1861 letter to the Théâtre de la Porte Saint-Martin, which was contemplating a revival of play, Gaillardet wrote: "I give you permission ... to join to my name that of Alexandre Dumas, my collaborator." Quoted in Glinel, *Alexandre Dumas et son œuvre*, 320. See also Fernande Bassan, "Histoire de *La Tour de Nesle* de Dumas *père* et Gaillardet," *Nineteenth-Century French Studies* 3, no. 1–2 (1974–1975): 40–57; Barbara Holland, *Gentleman's Blood: A History of Dueling from Swords at Dawn to Pistols at Dusk* (New York: Bloomsbury, 2003), 232.

76. See Harry Spurr, *The Life and Writings of Alexandre Dumas, 1802–1870* (1902; reprint, Honolulu: University Press of the Pacific, 2003), 96; Schopp, *Alexandre Dumas: Genius of Life*, 325–333; Gustave Simon, *Histoire d'une collaboration: Alexandre Dumas et Auguste Maquet* (Paris: G. Crès, 1919).

77. The literary Goncourt brothers claimed that Dumas read the novel first to determine its suitability to be published under his name. Yet, Paul Foucher related that when Meurice later claimed authorship, Dumas openly supported him, stating that he had not even read it. See Edmond de Goncourt and Jules de Goncourt, *Journal des Goncourt: mémoires de la vie littéraire*, ed. Jean-Louis Cabanès, 2 vols. (Paris: H. Champion, 2005–2008), I: 69; Paul Foucher, *Les Coulisses du passé* (Paris: E. Dentu, 1873), 442.

78. See Tilar Mazzeo, *Plagiarism and Literary Property in the Romantic Period* (Philadelphia: University of Pennsylvania Press, 2007).

79. Examples: Dumas referred to Maquet as his "friend and collaborator" in Alexandre Dumas, *Adventures in Spain*, trans. and ed. Alma Elizabeth Murch (Philadelphia: Chilton, 1959), 6; "I hope that my collaborator Anicet [Bourgeois] will allow me to say the same in the case of *Theresa*," in Dumas, *My Memoirs*, V: 491; "I [put] ... forth his [Maquet's] name with mine as author of the drama of *Les Mousquetaires*. This was but fair, however, since we did not only the drama, but also the romance, in collaboration," in Dumas, *My Memoirs*, V: 350; *Le Constitutionnel* announced the premier of *Le Fils de l'émigré* as a "drama by MM. Anicet Bourgeois and Alexandre Dumas," in Dumas, *My Memoirs*, VI: 402–408, 409–411; For examples of other contemporary remarks on Dumas's collaborators, see de Villemessant, *Mémoires d'un journaliste*, 238–239; Pifteau, *Alexandre Dumas en manches de chemise*, 30.

80. See Charles Glinel, *Le théâtre inconnu d'Alexandre Dumas père* (Paris: Revue Biblio-Iconographique, 1899); A. Craig Bell, *Alexandre Dumas: A Biography and Study* (London: Cassell, 1950), 399–400; An early biographer and contemporary, Henri Blaze de Bury, noted that he had seen Dumas "deny himself any credit for twenty works which have been signed with other names, but of which he had written two-thirds." See *A. Dumas, sa vie, son temps, son œuvre* (1885; reprint, Montreal: Joyeux Roger, 2008), 58; In his memoirs, Dumas noted that "since 2 June 1832 ... I have composed upwards of forty dramas ... it will, therefore, be taken for granted that I have no interest whatever in laying claim to one paternity more or less." See Dumas, *My Memoirs*, VI: 91.

81. Charles Grivel, *Alexandre Dumas, l'homme 100 têtes* (Villeneuve d'Ascq, France: Presses Universitaires du Septentrion, 2008), 19–86.

82. Antoine Fontaney, *Journal intime*, ed. René Jasinski (Paris: Presses Françaises, 1925), 115–118.

83. Jean-François Féraud's *Dictionnaire critique de la langue française* (Paris: France-expansion, 1787) defined "*nègres*" as people from sub-Saharan and North Africa "transported to European colonies where they serve as slaves." A decade later, in the 5th edition of the *Dictionnaire de L'Académie française* (Paris: J.J. Smits, 1798), the term was noted as referring "to all black slaves employed in work in the colonies." In the 6th edition of the *Dictionnaire de L'Académie française* (Paris: Firmin-Didot frères, 1835), the term was noted as referring "to the black race, especially those inhabitants of certain African countries," but "particularly to the black slaves employed in work in the colonies."

84. Alphonse Toussenel, *L'Esprit des bêtes: Vénerie française et zoologie passionnelle* (Paris: Librairie Sociétaire, 1847), 2, 392.

85. Mirecourt, *Fabrique de Romans*, 7.
86. *Ibid.*, 7–8.
87. "The Literary Leviathan," *Littell's Living Age*, 12 July 1856. [Emphasis added.]
88. Victor Pavie, *Les revenants: Alexandre Dumas père* (1881), in *Alexandre Dumas en bras de chemise*, 48; The Goncourt brothers similarly perceived Dumas as devoid of creativity and merely a copier: Dumas "talks fluently but without sparkle, colour, or wit; all he does is fish facts with a hoarse voice from the depths of an immense memory, with

Chapter Notes—1

childish vanity." See Edmond de Goncourt and Jules de Goncourt, *Pages from the Goncourt Journals*, trans. and ed. Robert Baldick (1962; reprint, New York: New York Review of Books, 2007), 103.

89. Quoted in Maurois, *The Titans*, 185.

90. Théodore de Banville wrote a poem about the affair in his "Odes Funambulesques." See *Poésies complètes* (Paris: E. Fasquelle, 1909), 94–95.

91. In Henri d'Alméras, *Alexandre Dumas et les Trois Mousquetaires* (Paris: Edgar Malfère, 1929), 65–66.

92. Quoted in Troyat, *Alexandre Dumas*, 410.

93. Eugène de Mirecourt, *Alexandre Dumas* (Paris: Gustave Havard, 1856).

94. *Ibid.*, 66, 47–48. [Emphasis added]

95. de Villemessant, *Mémoires d'un journaliste*, 236.

96. Pavie, *Les revenants*, in *Alexandre Dumas en bras de chemise*, 56.

97. Nadar, *Quand j'étais photographe*, reprint ed. (Le Plan-de-la-Tour, France: Éditions d'Aujourd'hui, 1979), 242–243.

98. Born in 1802, Dumas's name in the official register was "Alexandre Dumas." In 1813, a judgment from the Tribunal Civil de Première Instance in Soissons certified his descent from nobility, enabling the addition of "Davy de la Pailleterie," which was later posted on the register of civil certificates of Villers-Cotterêts. Dumas claimed in his memoirs that as a boy he opposed the addition. See Schopp, *Alexandre Dumas: Genius of Life*, 18; Maurois, *The Titans*, 41–42; Glinel, *Alexandre Dumas et Son Œuvre*, 11–13, 17–18; Dumas, *My Memoirs*, I: 2, 345–347. "Acte de Naissance de Alexandre Dumas," 5 Thermidor, Year 10 of the Republic (24 July 1802), Records of Birth in Villers-Cotterêts, 1793–1803, Archives départementales de l'Aisne, accessed 23 January 2018. http://archives.aisne.fr/.

99. Dumas's grandfather left behind his other children with Césette. Dumas seems to have been unaware that he had relatives in Haiti. Biographer F.W.J. Hemmings argues that Dumas's unawareness "seems certain." See *Alexandre Dumas*, 5.

100. Dumas's formal name is found on the paternity documents recognizing his son, Alexandre Dumas *fils*; documents pertaining to his son's marriage; and his death certificate. See Alexandre Dumas, *Lettres à mon fils*, ed. Claude Schopp (Paris: Mercure de France, 2008), 33–34, 287–289, 325–326.

101. The most noted instance where Dumas signed his name as the "Marquis de la Pailleterie" was in 1846 on a request to build a theater. See Spurr, *The Life and Writings of Alexandre Dumas*, 6; Schopp, *Alexandre Dumas: Genius of Life*, 338; Gilles Henry, *Les Dumas: Le Secret de Monte Cristo* (Paris: France-Empire, 1999), 181.

102. In his memoirs, Dumas claimed that his grandparents were married (although they most likely were not) and cited a marriage certificate. In the colonies, a child's status was dependent on that of the mother only. Evidence exists to support that Césette was a slave (a contemporary recorded that Alexandre-Antoine Davy de la Pailleterie paid a M. de Maubielle "un prix extraordinaire" for Césette, who was unusually beautiful). Since a marriage between a master and his slave enfranchised his wife and their children, Dumas's grandparents' marriage would have meant that his father had never been a slave and, as de la Pailleterie's eldest and only acknowledged son, he would have had the moral right to the title of marquis. See Dumas, *My Memoirs*, I: 3–4; Henry, *Les Dumas*, 55.

103. Dumas, *My Memoirs*, I: 12–13, 202, 228, 238.

104. *Ibid.*, I: 13, 21.

105. *Ibid.*, I: 21.

106. For example, Julien Joseph Virey, a pioneer of scientific racism, argued in his *Histoire naturelle du genre humain* (Paris: Crochard, 1824) that "the negro does not habitually support himself as straight as the European.... The negro leans forward; the ape holds himself in a transversal position." In addition, blacks have "smaller calves" than Europeans. Similarly, Abel Hovelacque argued in *Les nègres de l'Afrique sous équatoriale* (Paris: Lecrosnier et Babé, 1889) that blacks had calves like apes and that their feet were rather large in order to better climb trees. See also Claude Ribbe, *Le Diable Noir: Biographie du général Alexandre Dumas, père de l'écrivain* (Monaco: Alphée, 2009), 51–53; Grivel, *Alexandre Dumas, l'homme 100 têtes*, 113, 157.

107. Dumas, *My Memoirs*, I: 218–220.

108. As Dumas writes: "I was quite a pretty child: I had long, fair, curly hair, which fell on my shoulders, and which did not turn crisp until my fifteenth year; large blue eyes…; a straight nose, small and well-shaped; thick red sensitive lips; white but uneven teeth. In addition to this, my complexion was dazzlingly white, due, so my mother believed, to the brandy my father had made her drink during her pregnancy; it turned darker when my hair became crisp." See Dumas, *My Memoirs*, I: 296.

Chapter Notes—1

109. Grivel, *Alexandre Dumas, l'homme 100 têtes*, 144–168.

110. Dorothy Trench-Bonett, "Alexandre Dumas: Black French Author," in Alexandre Dumas, *Charles VII at the Homes of his Great Vassals*, trans. Dorothy Trench-Bonett (Chicago: Noble, 1991), 14.

111. Heidi Murkoff and Sharon Mazel, *What to Expect When You're Expecting*, 4th ed. (New York: Workman, 2008), 285, 291–293, 480–481.

112. Daniel Zimmerman, *Alexandre Dumas le Grand* (Paris: Phébus, 2002), 40.

113. Upon meeting Thomas-Alexandre during the French Revolution when his unit was in Villers-Cotterêts, Dumas's mother wrote to a friend that he was "very gentile," tall, and well-mannered. In addition, he was "a handsome young man." Yet, there was also an element of mystery about him: "His comrades say that ... [Dumas] is not his real name. He is the son of a seigneur from Saint-Domingue." This letter is printed by Ernest Roch in "Le Général Alexandre Dumas," *Bulletin de la Société Historique Régionale de Villers-Cotterêts* (1907), 91–92.

114. Dumas, *My Memoirs*, I: 204–205.

115. African American writer James Baldwin expressed similar feelings and negative perceptions in his fiction, in which he argued that blacks "saw themselves as others had seen them. They had been formed by the images made of them by those who had had the deepest necessity to despise them." Such images formed the "cornerstone of their identities." See James Baldwin, *Tell Me How Long the Train's Been Gone* (London: Corgi, 1970), 166.

116. Dumas, *My Memoirs*, II: 257; IV: 41.

117. While he may make "all kinds of mistakes" in life, Dumas wrote, he was incapable of "a disgraceful action ... because bad and dishonourable actions are the result of reflection and calculation, and when I act, it is on the spur of the moment; and this impulse is ... done before I have had time to consider the consequences or to calculate the results." See Dumas, *My Memoirs*, II: 220.

118. Dumas, *Adventures with My Pets*, 44.

119. *Ibid.*, 6; One early twentieth-century biographer included an anecdote, meant to amuse, revealing Dumas's alienation: on hearing Dumas laughing and talking in his study one day, a visitor asked who was with the great writer. "No one is with him," the maid replied, "he's having a good time with his characters." See Henri Clouard, *Alexandre Dumas* (Paris: Albin Michel, 1955).

120. Cited in Bell, *Alexandre Dumas*, 6; The anecdote appeared in *Blackwood's Magazine*.

121. Dominique Fernandes makes this point in *Les douze muses d'Alexandre Dumas* (Paris: Grasset, 1999), 257.

122. Claude Schopp, for example, has suggested that Dumas was a man who gave the "impression of happiness," but was ultimately "very melancholy." Such views replace "the longstanding view of Dumas as the naive bon vivant" with the image of a man who succeeded in a society that expressed "its disdain for him." François Tallandier even observed that the Count of Monte Cristo, a "victim of social injustice and legal hypocrisy," who lives in solitude and behind masks that separate him from the human community, was in large part Dumas himself. See Yves-Marie Lucot, "Claude Schopp: Dumas au-delà de sa légende," *Le Magazine Littéraire*, September 2002, 24; Victoria Foote-Greenwell, "The Life and Resurrection of Alexandre Dumas," *Smithsonian*, July 1996, 110–121; François Tallandier, "Introduction," in Alexandre Dumas, *Le Comte de Monte-Cristo*, 2 vols (Paris: Le Livre de Poche, 1995), I:19.

123. Arsène Houssaye, *Les Confessions: souvenirs d'un demi-siècle 1830–1880*, 6 vols. (Paris: E. Dentu, 1885–1891), I: 251.

124. Raphaël Lahlou, *Alexandre Dumas ou le don de l'enthousiasme* (Paris: Bernard Giovanangeli, 2006), 6; *Pages from the Goncourt Journals*, 103.

125. Paul Laurence Dunbar, *The Collected Poetry of Paul Laurence Dunbar*, ed. Joanne M. Braxton (Charlottesville: University Press of Virginia, 1993), 71; Frantz Fanon, *Black Skin, White Masks*, trans. Richard Philcox (New York: Grove, 2008).

126. There was also the worldly Dumas, "distinguished in manners" and the "*bon enfant* Dumas, the witty Dumas.... The Dumas ... whose sparkling conversation, whose words ... amuse all of Europe." See Comtesse Dash, *Mémoires des autres*, in *Alexandre Dumas en bras de chemise*, 65–67.

127. Dumas, *My Memoirs*, VI: 98–99.

128. In 1859, the Vicomtesse de Saint-Mars claimed that Dumas "often lies, but he does not know that he is lying. He begins ... by telling some ... careless, untruth," which he repeatedly retold until a "week later, both story and untruth have become, for him, the truth. He is no longer lying, but believes implicitly in the accuracy of what he has been saying. He persuades himself, and so persuades other people." See Jacques Reynaud

(Vicomtesse de Saint-Mars), *Portraits contemporains* (Paris: Amyot, 1859), 17–21.

129. Quoted in Schopp, *Alexandre Dumas: Genius of Life*, 383.

130. Pier Angelo Fiorentino, *Comédies et comédiens*, 2 vols. (Paris: Michel Lévy, 1866), II: 358.

131. Charles Hugo, chapter VI, *Les Hommes de l'exil* (Paris: Alphonse Lemerre, 1875); As Dumas confessed, "Often, after my long nights spent working, when I have only had an hour or two's sleep, my eyes close and if I happen to be sitting near a wall, I rest my head on the wall; or if I am sitting at a table, my head falls on the table. Then, however awkward the position ... I sleep for five minutes, and ... I wake up sufficiently refreshed to start work again immediately." See Alexandre Dumas, *Le Caucase*, 3 vols. (Paris: Calmann-Lévy, 1889), III: 134–135.

132. Audebrand, *Alexandre Dumas à la maison d'or*, 23; *Pages from the Goncourt Journals*, 103.

133. Maurois, *The Titans*, 12.

134. Schopp, *Alexandre Dumas: Genius of Life*, 307.

135. Letter from Victor Hugo to Alphonse Karr, printed in Alphonse Karr, *Le livre de bord: souvenirs, portraits, notes au crayon*, 3rd series (Paris: Calmann-Lévy, 1880), 129.

136. "Letter 51: Dumas to Taylor, 15 January 1842," in *Frères d'armes de la révolution romantique: Lettres d'Alexandre Dumas au Baron Taylor et à Adrien Dauzats*, ed. Claude Schopp (Paris: Fondation Taylor, 1993), 97–98.

137. Letter in Étienne Charavay, *Lettres autographes composant la collection Alfred Bovet* (Paris: Librairie Charavay frères, 1885), 318.

138. Maurois suggests a similar argument. See *The Titans*, 160.

139. "Lettre IV: 5 mai 1845," in Vicomte de Launay (Delphine de Girardin), *Lettres parisiennes*, vol. 4 (Paris: Michel Lévy, 1857), 192.

140. Dumas, *My Memoirs*, V: 256–264.

141. Maurois, *The Titans*, 80.

142. Dumas, *My Memoirs*, IV: 230–231.

143. Jean Lacouture, *Alexandre Dumas à la conquête de Paris, 1822–1831* (Brussels: Complexe, 2005), 28, 29; Spurr, *The Life and Writings of Alexandre Dumas*, 125, 142.

144. Jean-Paul Sartre, *Being and Nothingness: An Essay on Phenomenological Ontology*, trans. Hazel E. Barnes (London: Routledge, 2003), 246; Comtesse Dash, *Mémoires des autres*, in *Alexandre Dumas en bras de chemise*, 66.

145. Dumas, *Adventures with My Pets*, 137.

146. "Lettre d'Alexandre Dumas à un groupe d'Haïtiens," 5 August 1838, in *Cahiers Alexandre Dumas* 29 (2002), 75–76.

147. " À Cyrille Charles Auguste Bissette, directeur de la *Revue des colonies*," 10 March 1838, in *Cahiers Alexandre Dumas* 29 (2002), 74–75

148. See Dantès Bellegarde, *Haïti et son peuple* (Paris: Nouvelles Éditions Latines, 1953).

149. Henry, *Les Dumas*, 260; "Lettre à Demesvar Delorme," 29 December 1869, in *Cahiers Alexandre Dumas* 29 (2002), 337–339.

150. Dumas published a werewolf tale that Hippolyte allegedly told him. In the preface, Dumas wrote that his childhood home included "a negro, a valet of my father's, named Hippolyte, a sort of black merry-andrew, whom my father, I believe, only kept that he might be well primed with anecdotes." See Alexandre Dumas, *The Wolf-Leader*, trans. Alfred Allinson (London: Methuen, 1904), 2.

151. Dumas, *Adventures with My Pets*, 66–68, 69.

152. Soulouque was a black general and self-declared imitator of French emperor Napoleon I who became president of Haiti in 1848 and emperor in 1849. Soulouque was described in the French press as an extravagant and authoritarian despot to criticize the current French emperor, Napoleon III, who also modeled himself on his uncle, Napoleon I.

153. Popkin, *Facing Racial Revolution*, 26; Christopher Miller, *The French Atlantic Triangle: Literature and Culture of the Slave Trade* (Durham: Duke University Press, 2008), 190–194.

154. Fernandez, *Les douze muses*, 255.

155. Dumas, *Adventures with My Pets*, 69–71.

156. *Ibid.*, 73–76.

157. *Ibid.*, 77–80.

158. *Ibid.*, 81–85.

159. Neave and Charron, *Monte-Cristo*, 23; Gilles Brochard, "La Caravane Dumas," in *Le Grand Livre de Dumas*, ed. Charles Dantzig (New York : Belles Lettres/toExcel), 120.

160. Alexandre Dumas, *Adventures in Spain*, trans. and ed. Alma Elizabeth Murch (Philadelphia: Chilton, 1959), 7–9; Some variations in the account given in *History of My Pets* include an extended account of Paul's drunken debauchery and outburst, and that it is the French colonel (rather than Dumas's

gardener) who has the same name of Pierre (Peter) and who forces Eau-de-Benjoin to change his name to Paul. See Dumas, *Adventures with My Pets*, 141–152.

161. Alexandre Dumas, *Adventures in Algeria*, trans. and ed. Alma Elizabeth Murch (Philadelphia: Chilton, 1959), 157.

162. Dumas, *Adventures in Spain*, 12, 161.

163. Audebrand, *Alexandre Dumas à la Maison d'or*, 50.

164. Dumas, *Adventures with My Pets*, 141–152.

165. For an example of an advocate for such views, see Abbé Grégoire, *Considérations sur le mariage et sur le divorce adressées aux citoyens d'Haïti* (Paris: Badouin Frères, 1823), 14–15; On Grégoire's Haitian involvements, see Alyssa Goldstein Sepinwall, "Exporting the Revolution: Grégoire, Haiti, and the Colonial Laboratory," in *The Abbé Grégoire and His World*, eds. Jeremy Popkin and Richard Popkin (Dordrecht, Netherlands: Kluwer, 2000), 41–69; Chapter six of Ruth Necheles, *The Abbé Grégoire, 1787–1831: The Odyssey of an Egalitarian* (Westport, CT: Greenwood, 1971).

166. See Claude Blanckaert, "Of Monstrous *Métis*? Hybridity, Fear of Miscegenation, and Patriotism from Bufon to Paul Broca," in *The Color of Liberty: Histories of Race in France*, eds. Sue Peabody and Tyler Stovall (Durham: Duke University Press, 2003), 42–70.

167. Dumas, *My Memoirs*, I: 231, 295–304, 347–354, 359–360, 435–436; Alexandre Dumas, *The Three Musketeers*, trans. anonymous (Norwalk, CT: Easton, 1978), 1–3.

168. Similarly, Dumas would appropriate Grégoire's notion that "all men are my brothers" in his literary works advocating republicanism. For an example, see *The Return of Lord Ruthven*, trans. F.J. Morlock (Encino, CA: Black Coat, 2004), 224.

169. Alexandre Dumas, *The Woman with the Velvet Necklace*, trans. anonymous (1898; reprint, Amsterdam: Fredonia, 2002), 73–74.

170. Alexandre Dumas, *The Last Vendée; or, The She-Wolves of Machecoul*, trans. Katherine Prescott Wormeley, 2 vols. (Boston: Colonial Press, n.d. [1894?]), I: 29, 37.

171. Alexandre Dumas, *The Progress of Democracy; Illustrated in the History of Gaul and France*, trans. anonymous (1841; reprint, Honolulu: University Press of the Pacific, 2002).

172. Hippolyte Romand declared Dumas "cosmopolitan by taste." See *Revue des deux mondes*, January 1834, in *Alexandre Dumas en bras de chemise*, 42–43.

Chapter 2

1. Dumas, *My Memoirs*, V: 217–218.

2. Ferry, *Les Dernières années*, 139–148; Maurois, *The Titans*, 238; Henry, *Les Dumas*, 213.

3. *Cahiers Alexandre Dumas* 25 (1998), 332–334; "Dumas *père*'s Earnings," *New York Times*, 29 October 1883, 2.

4. Quoted in Bury, *Alexandre Dumas*, 153–154.

5. French society, as one Dumas biographer put it, had been "contaminated by the racist theories of Vacher de Lapouge and Drumont as well as Rousseauist themes of the noble savage that were always present." Consequently, Dumas suffered "from the racial prejudice that infested—and continues to infest—European society." See Lacouture, *Alexandre Dumas à la conquête de Paris*, 27.

6. *Cahiers Alexandre Dumas* 25 (1998), 367, 368, 369.

7. Maurois, *The Titans*, 238; Henry, *Les Dumas*, 213.

8. *L'Avenir*, 9 January 1850, in *Cahiers Alexandre Dumas* 27 (2000), 319.

9. "À Cyrille Charles Auguste Bissette, directeur de la *Revue des colonies*," 10 March 1838, in *Cahiers Alexandre Dumas* 29 (2002), 74–75

10. Cyrille Bissette, *De la situation des gens de couleur libres aux Antilles françaises* (Paris: J. MacCarthy, 1823), 6–7.

11. Cyrille Bissette, *Examen rapide des deux projets de loi relatifs aux colonies* (Paris: De l'imprimerie d'Éverat, 1833), 8, 12.

12. Mercer Cook, "The Literary Contribution of the French West Indian," *Journal of Negro History* 25, no. 4 (1940), 524.

13. In many ways, the *Revue* was a precursor to Martinican Aimé Césaire's *Négritude* journal *Tropiques* in the early twentieth century. See Bongie, *Islands and Exiles*, 171.

14. Quoted in Bongie, *Islands and Exiles*, 273–27; see also Kelly Duke Bryant, "Black but Not African: Francophone Black Diaspora and the *Revue des Colonies*, 1834–1842," *International Journal of African Historical Studies* 40, no. 2 (2007): 251–282.

15. Bongie, *Islands and Exiles*, 279–87, 323–341; Bissette's conflict with Schoelcher has largely reduced his legacy. See Chris

Chapter Notes—2

Bongie, "A Street Named Bissette: Nostalgia, Memory, and the *Cent-Cinquantenaire* of the Abolition of Slavery in Martinique (1848–1998)," *The South Atlantic Quarterly* 100, no. 1 (2001): 215–257.

16. Cyrille Bissette, *Réfutation du livre de M. Victor Schoelcher, intitulé* Des colonies françaises (Paris: Imprimerie Breton, 1843), 6.

17. Cyrille Bissette, *Réfutation du livre de M. V. Schoelcher sur Haïti* (Paris: Ébrard, 1844), 28.

18. Cyrille Bissette, *Réponse au factum de M. Schoelcher intitulé* La vérité aux ouvriers et cultivateurs de la Martinique (Paris: Imprimerie de Poussielgue, 1850), 113, 122.

19. Cook, "The Literary Contribution of the French West Indian," 524.

20. Bissette, *Réponse au factum de M. Schoelcher*, 10–11.

21. Bissette and Perrinon would fight a duel in 1850.

22. There was some confusion that Dumas's family was from Martinique. At enlistment in 1786, Dumas's father, Thomas-Alexandre, was described incorrectly as being from Martinique rather than St. Domingue. See Robert Landru, *À propos d'Alexandre Dumas: les aïeux, le général, le bailli, premiers amis* (Paris: Landru, 1977), 77–78.

23. "Note sur les élections en Guadeloupe," *L'Avenir*, May 1848, in *Cahiers Alexandre Dumas* 25 (1998), 362.

24. *Cahiers Alexandre Dumas* 27 (2000), 314.

25. Supplément extraordinaire au journal *L'Avenir*, 7 January 1850, in *Cahiers Alexandre Dumas* 27 (2000), 314–315.

26. *L'Avenir*, 9 January 1850, in *Cahiers Alexandre Dumas* 27 (2000), 315–317.

27. For example, *La Presse* reported in February that "Bissette's party and Schoelcher's party ... have chosen their candidates. The first selects Dumas and Charbonneau; the second, the two representatives whose election has been annulled by the Legislative Assembly, Schoelcher and Perrinon." See *La Presse*, 4 February 1850.

28. *L'Avenir*, 12 January 1850, in *Cahiers Alexandre Dumas* 27 (2000), 317; The statement was also reprinted in *La Presse*, 7 February 1850.

29. *L'Avenir*, 10 January 1850, in *Cahiers Alexandre Dumas* 27 (2000), 317–318.

30. *L'Avenir*, 16 January 1850, in *Cahiers Alexandre Dumas* 27 (2000), 318.

31. *Gazette officielle de la Guadeloupe*, 20 January 1850; *Cahiers Alexandre Dumas* 27 (2000), 318.

32. René Maran, "Contribution of the Black Race to European Art," trans. Mercer Cook, *Phylon* 10, no. 3 (1949), 240.

33. *L'Ordre*, 17 February 1850, in *Cahiers Alexandre Dumas* 27 (2000), 318–319.

34. *L'Ordre*, 25 February 1850, in *Cahiers Alexandre Dumas* 27 (2000), 319; *L'Ordre*, 26 February 1850, in *Cahiers Alexandre Dumas* 27 (2000), 319.

35. For example, see Stephen Franzoi, *Psychology: A Discovery Experience* (Mason, OH: South-Western Cengage, 2011), 266–267.

36. Philibert Audebrand, *Alexandre Dumas à la Maison d'or* (Paris: Calman Lévy, 1888), in *Alexandre Dumas en bras de chemise*, 114.

37. Frantz Fanon, *Black Skin, White Masks*, trans. Richard Philcox (New York: Grove, 2008), 168.

38. *Ibid.*, 2.

39. *Ibid.*, 126, 128, 168; Later French Caribbean writer Patrick Chamoiseau articulated a critique of the assimilationist view through his character of Monsieur Alcibiade in the novel *Texaco* (1992). Alcibiade defended colonialism since it "had brought 'Civilization' everywhere" and therefore "definitive progress succeeds any transitional colonial suffering." He argued that through assimilation, "all of the progress of civilization and of the mind, will apply to the colonies, setting straight all those local feudalisms.... The Mother and her children will, from now on, walk in step, in full equality." Yet, Alcibiade believed that "the same laws could not possibly apply to all colonies, because their development ... [and] degree of civilization were not uniform." Thus, the Caribbean, "the work of colonization being nearly complete," had more in common with the metropole than territories in Africa, which "are barely emerging from the barbarian straitjacket!" See Patrick Chamoiseau, *Texaco*, trans. Rose-Myriam Réjouis and Val Vinokurov (New York: Vintage International, 1997), 245, 246, 247–248.

40. Fanon, *Black Skin, White Masks*, 169.

41. *Ibid.*, 202, 80, 200.

42. *Ibid.*, 2; Fanon described this psychological condition the "colonial complex." His mentor, Caribbean intellectual Aimé Césaire, termed this condition the "dependency complex." See Aimé Césaire, *Discourse on Colonialism*, trans. Joan Pinkham (New York: Monthly Review Press, 2000), 59.

43. Édouard Glissant, *Caribbean Dis-*

course: Selected Essays, trans. J.M. Dash (Charlottesville: University of Virginia Press, 1997), 7; Fanon, *Black Skin, White Masks*, 4, 186.

44. Lilyan Kesteloot, *Black Writers in French: A Literary History of Négritude*, trans. Ellen Conroy Kennedy (Washington, D.C.: Howard University Press, 1991), 21–22.

45. René Depestre, *À ma mère: 60 écrivains parlent de leur mère* (1988), quoted in Joan Dayan, "France Reads Haiti: René Depestre's *Hadriana dans tous mes rêves*," *Yale French Studies* 83 (1993), 155.

46. Michel Fabre, *From Harlem to Paris: Black American Writers in France, 1840–1980* (Urbana: University of Illinois Press, 1993); Cook, "The Literary Contribution of the French West Indian," 526.

47. Léon-François Hoffmann has described *Francesca* as "a historical novel in the style of Alexandre Dumas, set in Turkey and Renaissance Italy." See Léon-François Hoffmann, "The Haitian Novel During the Last Ten Years," *Callaloo* 15, no. 3 (1992), 761.

48. "Lettre à Demesvar Delorme," 29 December 1869, in *Cahiers Alexandre Dumas* 29 (2002), 337–339.

49. Alexandre Bonneau, "Les Noirs, les Jaunes et la littérature française en Haïti," *Revue contemporaine*, 1 December 1856, 37–38.

50. For example, in September 1890, the journal covered the marriage of Dumas *fils*'s daughter Jeannine Dumas with Ernest d'Hauterive, an event that received much less attention in the metropolitan press. See *La Fraternité*, 30 September 1890.

51. *La Fraternité*, 9 May 1894.
52. *La Fraternité*, 1 June 1895.
53. *La Fraternité*, 9 May 1894.
54. *La Fraternité*, 26 May 1891.

55. "A propos de l'élection de M. de Hérédia à l'Académie française," *La Fraternité*, 27 March 1894.

56. Blair Niles and Robert Niles, *Black Haiti: A Biography of Africa's Eldest Daughter* (New York: Grosset and Dunlap, 1926), 37, 196.

57. See Baron Jean Louis de Vastey, *The Colonial System Unveiled*, trans. Chris Bongie (Liverpool: Liverpool University Press, 2014).

58. For example, in Latibolière, René Mailloux, a Canadian missionary, founded a college named after Dumas. See Dominique Fernandez, "Visite à Jérémie," *Le Mousquetaire de la Société des amis d'Alexandre Dumas* (2007), 25.

59. The Association of the Trois Dumas at Dumas's birthplace of Villers-Cotterêts even gave a commemorative plaque to be placed there.

Chapter 3

1. Albert Southwick, "Alexandre Dumas père," *The Galaxy* (November 1870), 691, 694.

2. Kenneth Jackson, ed., *Encyclopedia of New York City* (New Haven: Yale University Press, 1995), 325; Jacques Lucas-Dubreton, *The Fourth Musketeer*, trans. Maida Casteltun Darnton (New York: Coward-McCann, 1928), 271.

3. "Works of Alexandre Dumas," *North American Review* (January 1843), 115.

4. "Review of *The Memoirs of a Physician*," *United States Democratic Review* (January 1849), 90.

5. "*Mes Mémoires*," in Frank Wild Reed, *A Bibliography of Alexandre Dumas père* (Pinner Hill, Middlesex, UK: J.A. Neuhuys, 1933). For a review of the full translation, see George Hellman, "The Memoirs of Alexandre Dumas: Lively Reminiscences of the French Novelist whose Life Synchronized with Thrilling Historic Events," *New York Times*, 12 October 1907.

6. James David, *Who Is Black? One Nation's Definition* (University Park: Pennsylvania University Press, 1991); Lawrence Wright, "One Drop of Blood," *New Yorker* (25 July 1994), 46–55; Fabre, *From Harlem to Paris*, 1, 19–20.

7. "Review of the Autobiography of Alexandre Dumas," *Littell's Living Age* (December 1852), 587.

8. Michel Fabre, "International Beacons of African-American Memory: Alexandre Dumas *père*, Henry O. Tanner, and Josephine Baker as Examples of Recognition," in *History and Memory in African-American Culture*, eds. Geneviève Fabre and Robert O'Meally (New York: Oxford University Press, 1994), 125.

9. Entry for 12 October 1878, in Charles Chestnutt, *The Journals of Charles Chestnutt*, ed. Richard Brodhead (Durham: Duke University Press, 1993), 92.

10. Fabre, *From Harlem*, 1, 19–20.

11. See Thomas Hamilton, ed., *The Anglo-African Magazine* (New York: Arno/New York Times, 1968).

12. We can define a *lieu de mémoire* as "any significant entity, whether material or non-material in nature, which by dint of

human will or the work of time has become a symbolic element of the memorial heritage of any community." See Pierre Nora, "Introduction: Between Memory and History," in *Realms of Memory*, I: xvii.

13. For examples of anecdotes on Dumas and the U.S., see Bell, *Alexandre Dumas*, 345–346; Clouard, *Alexandre Dumas*, 394; Hemmings, *Alexandre Dumas*, 203, 204, 205.

14. For example, Fabre mentions Dumas throughout *From Harlem*, but no reference is longer than a few sentences. Fabre's article "International Beacons" in *History and Memory in African-American Culture* rehashes his earlier comments about Dumas in *From Harlem*, but collects them in a few pages to establish that Dumas was an idealized figure among African Americans (see pages 122–126). Tyler Stovall makes a note on Dumas in his study on African Americans in Paris. See Tyler Stovall, *Paris Noir: African Americans in the City of Light* (New York: Mariner, 1996), 56–57.

15. Fabre, "International Beacons," in *History and Memory in African-American Culture*, 122–128.

16. G.W. Gong, *The Standard of "Civilization" in International Society* (Oxford: Clarendon, 1984).

17. Soma Hewa and Darwin Stapleton, "Introduction: Structure and Process of Global Integration," in Soma Hewa and Darwin Stapleton, eds., *Globalization, Philanthropy, and Civil Society: Toward a New Political Culture in the Twenty-First Century* (New York: Springer, 2005), 4.

18. Richard Mansbach, *The Globle Puzzle: Issues and Actors in World Politics*, 2nd ed. (Boston: Houghton Mifflin, 1997), 29.

19. As Du Bois continued, "there has been absolutely no proof that the white race has any larger share of the gifted strains of human heritage than the black race or the yellow race"; the birth of "Dumas from a black beast of burden" was provided as proof. See W.E.B. Du Bois, "The White World," in *Dusk of Dawn: An Essay Toward an Autobiography of a Race Concept* (1940; reprint, New York: Schocken, 1970), 143–145.

20. Cheikh Anta Diop, *The African Origin of Civilization: Myth or Reality* (Chicago: Lawrence Hill, 1974), 26.

21. David Featherstone, "The Spatial Politics of the Past Unbound: Transnational Networks and the Making of Political Identities," *Global Networks* 7, no. 4 (2007), 432, 435–436, 447–449.

22. Jan Aart Scholte, *Globalization: A Critical Introduction*, 2nd ed. (New York: Palgrave Macmillan, 2005), 236–237, 249–250.

23. Featherstone, "Spatial Politics," 435.

24. Scholte, *Globalization*, 226, 252.

25. Featherstone, "Spatial Politics," 448.

26. Paul Gilroy, *The Black Atlantic: Modernity and Double Consciousness* (Cambridge: Harvard University Press, 1993), 30, 120; W.E.B. Du Bois, "Blacks in France," *The Crisis*, March 1922. See also W.F. Feuser, "Afro-American Literature and Negritude," *Comparative Literature* 28, no. 4 (1976), 292.

27. Susan Koshy, "Morphing Race into Ethnicity: Asian Americans and Critical Transformations of Whiteness," *boundary 2* 28, no. 1 (2001), 168.

28. African American intellectuals have maintained the view that "American means white" well into the contemporary era. See Toni Morrison, *Playing in the Dark: Whiteness and the Literary Imagination* (Cambridge: Harvard University Press, 1992), 8.

29. Jennifer Hurstfield, "The Educational Experiences of Mexican Americans: 'Cultural Pluralism' or 'Internal Colonialism'?" *Oxford Review of Education* 1, no. 2 (1975), 138; Andrew Hacker, *Two Nations* (New York: Macmillan, 1992), 4; Lionel Maldonado, "Internal Colonialism and Triangulation: A Research Example," *Social Service Review* 53, no. 3 (1979), 466.

30. Amritjit Singh and Peter Schmidt, eds., *Postcolonial Theory and the United States* (Jackson: University Press of Mississippi, 2000), 5.

31. See Susan Willis, "Memory and Mass Culture," in *History and Memory in African-American Culture*, 178–187.

32. Schomburg, "The Negro Digs up His Past," in *The New Negro*, 237.

33. Ibid.

34. "Pot Pourri," *Opportunity*, December 1923.

35. See *Savannah Tribune*, 23 September 1911.

36. A prime example of this type of chronicle is *Progress of a Race, or, the Remarkable Advancement of the American Negro*, attributed to African American scholar William Crogman and many collaborators during its various editions beginning in the 1890s. Others include P. Thomas Stanford, *The Tragedy of the Negro in America: A Condensed History of the Enslavement, Sufferings, Emancipation, Present Condition and Progress of the Negro Race* (1897); Mary

Helm, *From Darkness to Light: The Story of Negro Progress* (1909); and W.D. Weatherford, *Present Forces in Negro Progress* (1912).

37. *New York Times*, 22 September 1912; *Independent*, 19 September 1912; *New York Times*, 6 February 1910.

38. David Blight, "W.E.B. Du Bois and the Struggle for American Historical Memory," in *History and Memory in African-American Culture*, 46.

39. W.E.B. Du Bois, *Black Reconstruction in America, 1860–1880* (1935; reprint, New York: Free Press, 1998), 725–726; Blight, "W.E.B. Du Bois," in *History and Memory in African-American Culture*, 45–71.

40. As a result, Nathan Huggins has suggested that fully incorporating African American history would change the tone and meaning of American history. See Nathan Huggins, *Black Odyssey: The African-American Ordeal in Slavery* (New York: Vintage, 1990).

41. Rogers, *World's Great Men of Color*, 117.

42. Wilson Moses, "Dark Forests and Barbarian Vigor: Paradox, Conflict, and Africanity in Black Writing before 1914," *American Literary History* 1, no. 3 (1989), 639.

43. Frederick Douglass, "The Life and Times of Frederick Douglass," in *Frederick Douglass: Autobiographies*, ed. Henry Louis Gates, Jr. (New York: Library of America College Editions, 1996), 938.

44. Carter G. Woodson, *The Mis-Education of the Negro*, reprint ed. (Radford, VA: Wilder, 2008), 13.

45. W.E.B. Du Bois, "Negro Art and Literature," in *The Gift of Black Folks* (1924), excerpts in Eric Sundquist, ed., *The Oxford W.E.B. Du Bois Reader* (New York: Oxford University Press, 1996), 319–320.

46. W.E.B. Du Bois, *Darkwater* (1920); reprint, New York: Washington Square Press, 2004), 155.

47. As Schomburg argued: "it is the social damage of slavery that the present ... must repair and offset." See "The Negro Digs up His Past," in *The New Negro*, 231.

48. Dickinson Bruce, *The Origins of African American Literature, 1680–1865* (Charlottesville: University Press of Virginia, 2001), 228.

49. "Mixed Blood Aided White Geniuses: Startling Statement by Colored Atlanta University Professor," *New York Times*, 18 February 1907.

50. Rogers, *World's Great Men*, 117.

51. "About the World," *Scribner's Magazine* (May 1896), 659. See also J. Brander Mathews, "The Dramas of the Elder Dumas," *Atlantic Monthly* (September 1881), 383.

52. Southwick, "Alexandre Dumas," 696, 697.

53. "Mixed Blood."

54. "Editor's Literary Record," *Harper's New Monthly Magazine* (March 1871), 620.

55. "The Mosaic and the Melting Pot," *New York Times*, 23 September 1991.

56. B. Phillips, "A Reminiscence of Alexandre Dumas," *The Galaxy* (October 1871), 508; "Editor's Literary Record," 620.

57. Schomburg, "The Negro Digs up His Past," in *The New Negro*, 231, 232.

58. Alyssa Sepinwall Goldstein, "Abbé Grégoire," in the *Encyclopedia of Blacks in European History and Culture*, ed. Eric Martone (Westport, CT: Greenwood, 2009), 253–254.

59. Such collections include William Wells Brown's mid-nineteenth century work *The Black Man, His Antecedents, His Genius, His Achievements*; Rogers's early twentieth-century study *World's Great Men of Color*; Marion Jackson Pryde and Beatrice Jackson Fleming's *Distinguished Negroes Abroad* (1946); and Russell Adams's *Great Negroes, Past and Present* (1963).

60. "Alexandre Dumas," *The Crisis*, October 1921.

61. Gilroy, *Black Atlantic*, 26.

62. Fabre, *From Harlem*, 12, 17.

63. Dumas may have collaborated with Séjour on the play. On Séjour, see J. John Perret, "Victor Séjour: Black French Playwright from Louisiana," *French Review* 57, no. 2 (1983): 187–193; Charles O'Neill, *Séjour: Parisian Playwright from Louisiana* (Lafayette: University of Southwestern Louisiana, 1995); Fabre, *From Harlem*, 14, 15, 16.

64. The three include the Dumas Company of Louisville, Kentucky (which staged productions of *The Rough Diamond* and *Above the Clouds* in 1886); the Dumas Dramatic Club of St. Louis, Missouri (which staged a production of *Bound by an Oath* in 1902); and the Dumas Players of Cleveland (although the troupe changed its name in 1922 to the Gilpin Players). See Errol Hill and James Hatch, *A History of African American Theatre* (Cambridge: Cambridge University Press, 2003), 86, 226, 228.

65. Tad Bennicoff, "African Americans and Princeton University: A Brief History," 11 March 2005, http://www.princeton.edu/mudd/news/faq/topics/African_Americans.shtml (consulted 1 December 2013).

66. William Wells Brown, *The Black Man*,

His Antecedents, His Genius, His Achievements, 4th ed. (1865; reprint, Miami: Mnemosyne, 1969), 128–131; Du Bois quoted Brown's description of Dumas in his later essays; for an example, see "Phillis Wheatley and African American Culture (1941)," in Sundquist, *Du Bois Reader*, 335.

67. Elizabeth Bethel, *The Roots of African-American Identity: Memory and History in Antebellum Free Communities* (Houndmills, Hampshire, UK: Palgrave Macmillan, 1997), 183.

68. W.E.B. Du Bois, "My Evolving Program for Negro Freedom," excerpts in David Levering Lewis, ed., *W.E.B. Du Bois: A Reader* (New York: Henry Holt, 1995), 615. Du Bois made the same argument in "President Harding and Social Equality," *The Crisis*, December 1921.

69. Mirecourt, *Fabrique de romans* (1845).

70. Brown, *Black Man*, 131.

71. See Emmanuel Nelson, *African American Dramatists: An A to Z Guide* (Westport, CT: Greenwood, 2004), 366. A modern play to tackle the same issue was written by African American writer Charles Smith. See Charles Smith, *Les Trois Dumas* (Woodstock, IL: Dramatic, 2003).

72. Dumas's novel *Georges* (1843), which concerns slavery and race, and has a biracial hero, was largely ignored in the U.S., including by African Americans, even though it was translated into an American English edition in 1849. The reasons why remain unclear.

73. Phillips, "A Reminiscence," 508.

74. Du Bois later rephrased the realization of black consciousness as knowing "the call of the blood when it came and listened and answered." See Du Bois, *Darkwater*, 155.

75. See Waldo Martin, Jr., *The Mind of Frederick Douglass* (Chapel Hill: University of North Carolina Press, 1984), 93.

76. William McFeely, *Frederick Douglass* (New York: W.W. Norton, 1991), 328.

77. *Cahiers Alexandre Dumas* 29 (2002), 308, n. 1. See also Spurr, *The Life and Writings of Alexandre Dumas*, 117.

78. Alexandre Dumas, "Lettre à Abraham Lincoln," 15 June 1864, in *Le Petit Journal*, 30 September 1864, reproduced in *Cahiers Alexandre Dumas* 29 (2002), 307–308. See also Bell, *Alexandre Dumas*, 346. On the French press's perceptions of the American Civil War, see Dominique Laurent, "The American Civil War in the French Press," in *National Stereotypes in Perspective*, 187–208.

79. Rogers, *World's Great Men*, 120.

80. Alexandre Dumas, "À Cyrille Charles Auguste Bissette, directeur de la Revue des colonies," 10 March 1838, reproduced in *Cahiers Alexandre Dumas* 29 (2002), 74–75 (emphasis added).

81. "Frederick Douglass to Friends Hayden and Watson," 19 November 1886, in Philip Foner, *The Life and Writings of Frederick Douglass* (New York: International, 1950–1975), vol. 4, 445–446. On the report being false, see Wilson Moses, *Creative Conflict in African American Thought* (Cambridge: Cambridge University Press, 2004), 56–57.

82. Douglass, "Life and Times," in *Frederick Douglass: Autobiographies*, 995; Dumas's novel made Marseilles and other locations featured in the novel popular tourist attractions. See "In Monte Cristo's Home: Places in Marseilles Made Famous by Dumas's Hero," *New York Times*, 2 January 1898; Bernhard Ragner, "A Visit with Dumas: *The Count of Monte Cristo*'s Château d'If Brings Tourist Cash to French Treasury," *New York Times*, 18 July 1937; "Tourist Haven Planned on Monte Cristo Island," *New York Times*, 24 August 1965.

83. Carter Woodson, "Review of *Five French Negro Authors* by Mercer Cook," *Journal of Negro History* 28, no. 4 (1943), 496. For an analysis of the complicated relationship between African Americans and perceptions of race in France, see Stovall, *Paris Noir*.

84. Frances E.W. Harper, *Iola Leroy, or Shadows Uplifted* (1892; reprint, New York: Oxford University Press, 1990), 84.

85. Rogers, *World's Great Men*, 117, 120.

86. W.E.B. Du Bois, "The Future of the Negro Race in America (1904)," excerpts in Sundquist, *Du Bois Reader*, 372.

87. William Brief, "San Francisco Correspondence," *Appeal* (Carson City), 24 May 1865; Southwick, "Alexandre Dumas," 691.

88. Featherstone, "Spatial Politics," 440.

89. James M'Cune Smith, "Introduction (1855)," to Frederick Douglass, "My Bondage, My Freedom," in *Frederick Douglass: Autobiographies*, 136–137; George Ruffin, "Introduction (1881)," to Douglass, "Life and Times," in *Frederick Douglass: Autobiographies*, 473.

90. Cook, "The Literary Contribution of the French West Indian," 530; Rogers, *World's Great Men*, 120.

91. "A Boston Premier of the Film: *The Three Dumas*," *Boston Central*, 2007, accessed 29 August 2017. http://bostoncentral.com/events/film/p6437.php.

92. See Bethel, *Roots*, 183.
93. In 1856, *Littell's Living Age* even mocked Dumas's claim to nobility through his association with slaves in the colonies: "Who has not heard of ... the *St. Domingan Marquis de la Pailleterie*." See "Literary Leviathan," 87 (emphasis added).
94. Brown, *Black Man*, 129–130.
95. Woodson, "Review," 495 (emphasis added).
96. For an example, see Paul Finkelman, ed., *Encyclopedia of African American History, 1619–1895: From the Colonial Period to the Age of Frederick Douglass* (New York: Oxford University Press, 2006), 429–430.
97. Amistad Research Center, Mary McLeod Bethune, diary, 23 July 1927, Bethune file, box 2, 11–12.
98. Fabre, *From Harlem*, 133.
99. Arna Bontemps was a fan of Dumas since her childhood. See *Ibid.*, 279.
100. Langston Hughes, *The Big Sea: An Autobiography* (1940; reprint, New York: Hill and Wang, 2001), 61–62.
101. Schomburg Collection, Gwendolyn Bennett, journal, 23 August 1925, 31.
102. Gwendolyn Bennett, "Lines Written at the Grave of Alexandre Dumas," *Opportunity*, June 1926.
103. Richard Wright discusses Dumas briefly in some of his work, including *White Man, Listen!* (1957).
104. Chestnutt, *Journals*, 93.
105. W.E.B. Du Bois, *The Souls of Black Folk* (1903; reprint, New York: Penguin, 1989), 90; Du Bois's choice of Dumas and Balzac, however, is ironic based on the personal animosity that existed between them, as discussed in Chapter One.
106. *Ibid.*, 5.
107. Blight, "W.E.B. Du Bois," in *History and Memory in African-American Culture*, 46.
108. Fabre, "International Beacons," in *History and Memory in African-American Culture*, 122.
109. Albert Memmi, *Portrait du colonisé, précédé du portrait du colonisateur* (Paris: Gallimard, 1985), 92.
110. Richard Wright, *White Man, Listen!* (New York: Doubleday, 1957), 109.

Chapter 4

1. Mercer Cook, "The Race Problem in Paris and the French West Indies," *Journal of Negro Education* 8, no. 4 (1939), 673.

2. W.E.B. Du Bois, "The Negro Mind Reaches Out," in *The New Negro*, 393–394.
3. Modern Western authority, like Foucault's notion of disciplinary power, functioned on the principle of difference, regulation, and policing of "unmodern" cultures' progress to keep the categories of people (once defined) in their place. See Michel Foucault, *Discipline and Punish*, trans. Alan Sheridan (New York: Vintage, 1977), 199.
4. Fanon, *The Wretched of the Earth*, 5, 58.
5. *Ibid.*, 96, 6.
6. Robin Blackburn, *The Overthrow of Colonial Slavery, 1776–1848* (London: Verso, 1988), 494–506.
7. It seemed that the divide between black and white Creoles would never be breached. Martinican Salvina (Virgile Savane) invoked Dumas (a "*mulâtre*" and republican) when publishing *Saint-Pierre, la Venise Tropicale*, which focused on color prejudice during the Lota Affair (1881). Salvina concluded that "this colonial malady represents the vicissitudes of racial prejudice." In Martinique, "more than other places, racial prejudice has become tangible ... on the island, the *colon* disembarks as the master; the Black, a slave, a pariah." See Réginald Hamel, "De la créolité américaine," *Le Magazine Littéraire*, September 2002, 60.
8. Initially, French Caribbean intellectual and politician Aimé Césaire hoped that departmentalization would put the overseas departments on an equal footing with those in the metropole. See Gary Wilder, "Race, Reason, Impasse: Césaire, Fanon, and the Legacy of Emancipation," *Radical History Review* 90 (Fall 2004), 38; Ernest Moutoussamy, *Aimé Césaire: Député à l'Assemblée nationale, 1945–1993* (Paris: L'Harmattan, 1993), 9–29; Fred Reno, "Aimé Césaire ou l'ambivalence féconde," *French Politics, Culture and Society* 27, no. 3 (2009): 19–23; Justin Daniel, "Aimé Césaire et les Antilles françaises: une histoire inachevée?" *French Politics, Culture and Society* 27, no. 3 (2009): 24–33; Fred Constant, "Aimé Césaire et la politique: sept leçons de leadership," *French Politics, Culture and Society* 27, no. 3 (2009): 34–43.
9. David Beriss, "Culture-As-Race or Culture-As-Culture: Caribbean Ethnicity and the Ambiguity of Cultural Identity in French Society," in *Race in France: Interdisciplinary Perspectives on the Politics of Difference*, eds. Herrick Chapman and Laura Frader (New York: Berghahn, 2004), 116, 119.

Chapter Notes—4

10. Jules Huret, *De New York à la Nouvelle-Orléans* (Paris: Fasquelle, 1904), 402.

11. Only about 15,000 to 20,000 blacks lived in Paris in 1938 among a total population of about three million. See Cook, "The Race Problem in Paris and the French West Indies," 674.

12. Fanon, *Black Skin, White Masks*, 92, 95.

13. *Ibid.*, 96, 128, 175.

14. *Ibid.*, 14–15.

15. As Aimé Césaire observed, "In France people spoke of a civilized world [in the present] and a barbarian world [stuck in the past]. The barbarian world was Africa, and the civilized world was Europe." The assimilated citizen from the French Caribbean, Fanon argued, was thus traumatized when he heard "Europeans mention 'Negroes'" and realized that "they [were] ...talking about him as well as the Senegalese." See René Depestre, "Interview with Aimé Césaire (1967)," trans. Maro Riofrancos, in Aimé Césaire, *Discourse on Colonialism*, trans. Joan Pinkham (New York: Monthly Review Press, 2000), 88; Fanon, *Black Skin, White Masks*, 126–127.

16. Fanon, *Black Skin, White Masks*, 18, 121; Consequently, as Marie-Sophie Laborieux remarks in Chamoiseau's celebrated novel *Texaco*, their dark skin still bore "slavery's color." See Chamoiseau, *Texaco*, 71.

17. For example, although articles in *La Fraternité* helped solidify Dumas's status as a black and "Caribbean" writer, they nevertheless asserted this ancestry to question its relevance. Benito Sylvan, for one, asked in an 1892 article whether it mattered if Dumas *fils* was "at close inspection" white or black because "one is a man." Consequently, "one's worth cannot be based on the color of his skin." See Benito Sylvan, "A propos des sentiments de Dumas père," *La Fraternité*, 17 October 1892.

18. African Prince Kojo Tovalou Houenou argued in a colonial petition that colonials, crying for "justice," wished for "complete assimilation without frontier—without distinction of race ... since the label of nationality has been attached to us.... We wish that you recognize our rights to citizenship—the elementary rights of man—and that ... we might be called to share your destiny." See "The Problem of Negroes in French Colonial Africa," *Opportunity* (July 1924), 203–206.

19. Bright Molande, "Rewriting Memory: Ideology of Difference in the Desire and Demand for Whiteness," *European Journal of American Culture* 27, no. 3 (2008), 181; Fanon, *Black Skin, White Masks*, 186; As Caribbean intellectual Wilfred Cartey exclaimed, "the mind of the black man was held in bondage; his mind was often whitewashed with a biting corrosive lime which seemed to eat away at the very structure of his life. The serfdom was not only menial, but moral, and black men seemed to be living forms without life, garbed and robed in the skin of Europe.... And the black man's rhythm became the cry of blood and pounding of his oppressed heart." See Wilfred Cartey, "Dark Voices," *Présence Africaine* 28, no. 65 (1963), 97–98.

20. Franzoi, *Psychology*, 266–267.

21. Arthur Schomburg, for example, argued that "a new notion of the cultural attainment and potentialities of the African stocks has recently come about.... [W]ith limited horizons lifting in all directions, the mind of the Negro has *leapt forward* faster than the slow clearings of scholarship will yet safely permit." African American intellectual Alain Locke similarly expressed a view that "liberal minds to-day ... [will not] find a mind and soul bizarre and alien as the mind of a savage.... That was yesterday, and the day before." See "The Negro Digs up His Past," in *The New Negro*, 237; Alain Locke, "Forward," in *The New Negro*, xxvi.

22. As Senghor wrote: "But the great western world holds me in fee/ And I may never hope for full release.../ Something in me is lost, forever lost/ Some vital thing has gone out of my heart/ And I must walk the way of life of a ghost/ Among the sons of earth, a thing apart/ For I was born, far away from my native clime/ Under the white man's menace, *out of time*." Quoted in Colin Legum, *Pan-Africanism: A Short Political Guide* (New York: Praeger, 1962), 15.

23. Patrick Chamoiseau, *Chronicle of the Seven Sorrows*, trans. Linda Coverdale (Lincoln: University of Nebraska Press, 1999), 54 (Emphasis added).

24. Fanon, *Black Skin, White Masks*, 188.

25. André Breton connected *Négritude* with the goals of surrealism, which rebelled against the modern world's values. Surrealists were also developing an anticolonial stance. Breton also associated the black struggle for identity with that of a larger humanity, for "it is a black who is not only a black but *all* of man, who conveys all of man's questionings, all of his anguish, all of his hopes and all of his ecstasies and who will remain more and more for me the pro-

totype of dignity." See André Breton, "A Great Black Poet," in Aimé Césaire, *Notebook of a Return to the Native Land*, trans. and ed. Clayton Eshleman and Annette Smith (Middletown, CT: Wesleyan University Press, 2001), xii, xvii–xviii.

26. K.O.K. Onyioha, *Revival of Culture in Independent Nigeria* (Enugu: Eastern Nigeria Printing, 1962), 6

27. Fanon, *Black Skin, White Masks*, 93–94, 157.

28. Césaire, *Discourse on Colonialism*, 53.

29. Césaire, *Notebook of a Return to the Native Land*, 44.

30. Aimé Césaire, *A Tempest*, trans. Richard Miller (New York: TCG Translations, 2002), 17.

31. Depestre, "Interview with Aimé Césaire (1967)," 89.

32. *Notes de l'Agent Désiré: LDRN et milieux nègres de Paris*, 1 February 1927, quoted and translated in Jennifer Anne Boittin, "Black in France: The Language and Politics of Race in the Late Third Republic," *French Politics, Culture and Society* 27, no. 2 (2009), 33.

33. Boittin, "Black in France," 29, 30.

34. Richard Wright, *Twelve Million Black Voices* (London: Lindsay Drummond, 1947), 30.

35. "Le Mot 'nègre,'" *La Voix des nègres* (1927), quoted and translated in Boittin, "Black in France," 23.

36. Cheikh Anta Diop, "Civilization or Barbarism: An Authentic Anthropology," *Great African Thinkers*, ed. Ivan Van Sertima (Oxford: Transaction, 1986), 162.

37. Césaire, *Notebook of a Return to the Native Land*, 27–28.

38. Depestre, "Interview with Aimé Césaire (1967)," 92.

39. Laurent Dubois, *Avengers of the New World: The Story of the Haitian Revolution* (Cambridge: Belknap/Harvard University Press, 2004), 166, 170; Laurent Dubois, *A Colony of Citizens: Revolution and Slave Emancipation in the French Caribbean, 1787–1804* (Chapel Hill: University of North Carolina Press, 2004), 182; Catherine Reinhardt, *Claims to Memory: Beyond Slavery and Emancipation in the French Caribbean* (New York: Berghahn, 2006), 87–105.

40. Quoted in Martin Munro, "Can't Stand Up for Falling Down: Haiti, Its Revolutions, and Twentieth-Century Negritudes," *Research in African Literatures* 35, no. 2 (2004), 3.

41. Césaire, for one, redefined "universal" in 1956 in a way that expressed burgeoning notions of a global civilization comprised of many local cultures, "a universal rich with all that is particular, rich with all the particulars there are, the deepening of each particular, the coexistence of them all." See Aimé Césaire, *Letter to Maurice Thorez* (Paris: Présence Africaine, 1957), 14–15.

42. Charles Rowell, "It Is Through Poetry That One Copes with Solitude: An Interview with Aimé Césaire," *Callaloo* 38 (Winter 1989), 65; Fanon expressed a similar view: "Since I realize that the black man is the symbol of sin, I start hating the black man. But I realize that I am a black man. I have two ways of escaping the problem. Either I ask people not to pay attention to the color of my skin; or else ... I want people to notice it. I then try to esteem what is bad.... In order to put an end to this neurotic situation where I am forced to choose an unhealthy, conflicted solution, nurtured fantasies, that is antagonistic—inhuman, in short—there is but one answer: skim over this absurd drama that others have staged around me; rule out these two elements that are equally unacceptable; and through the particular, reach out for the universal." See Fanon, *Black Skin, White Masks*, 174.

43. Césaire, *Discourse on Colonialism*, 77–78.

44. Césaire, *A Tempest*, 27.

45. As Césaire exclaimed in interview, "I am a man who loves ... cultures, all cultures ... everything human beings—in whatever part of the world—have undertaken to cope with life.... That is what it is all about. And you will see that this can be found in a Chinese poem as well as in a Bantu poem." See Rowell, "It Is Through Poetry," 55.

46. Chamoiseau, *Texaco*, 249.

47. "Awakening of Race Consciousness," *The Review of the Black World*, April 1932, 25; see also Shireen Lewis, *Race, Culture, and Identity: Francophone West African and Caribbean Literature from Négritude to Créolité* (Lanham, MD: Lexington, 2006), 55–69; In *Texaco*, Caribbean writer Patrick Chamoiseau described Césaire as so dark in appearance "that he could have been taken for one of these just-off-the boat half-dumb congos," but he "knew French better than a thick French dictionary ... [and] everything about poetry, Greece, Rome, Latin humanities, [and] philosophers." Nevertheless, he "declared himself *nègre* and seemed proud of it. The worst was that he was ungrateful, denouncing colonialism. He whom France had taught to read, write, called himself an

Chapter Notes—4

African and claimed this identity as his own." See Chamoiseau, *Texaco*, 248–249.

48. Léopold Senghor, *Anthologie de la nouvelle poésie nègre et malgache* (Paris: Presses Universitaires de France, 1948), xv; Alfred Guillaume, "Conversation with Léopold Sédar Senghor on His Poetry and Baudelaire's," *The French Review* 52, no. 6 (1979): 839–847; David Murphy, "Birth of a Nation? The Origins of Senegalese Literature in French," *Research in African Literatures* 39, no. 1 (2008): 48–69.

49. Quoted in Bongie, *Island and Exiles*, 19.

50. Austin Shelton, "The Black Mystique: Reactionary Extremes in 'Negritude,'" *African Affairs* 63 (April 1964), 115, 120–121; Feuser, "Afro-American Literature and Negritude," 297.

51. Rowell, "It Is Through Poetry," 55.

52. Ndabaningi Sithole, *African Nationalism* (Cape Town: Oxford University Press, 1959), 74.

53. As an African American scholar noted in 1920, "this world-wide reaction of the darker races to their common as well as local grievances is one of the most significant facts of recent development. Exchange of views and sympathy ... and cooperation ... are bound to develop on a considerable scale in the near future." See W.A. Domingo, "Gift of the Black tropics," in *The New Negro*, 348.

54. For example, African American writer Gwendolyn Bennet expressed her fondness for Maran's salon, recalling a conversation in which Maran expressed indignation at lynching in the United States. She noted that "it was a beautiful thing to note that such kindredship existed in his heart because of the irradicable black of our skins." See Gwendolyn Bennet, *Opportunity* (August 1927), 234; Michel Fabre, "René Maran, the New Negro, and Negritude," *Phylon* 36, no. 3 (1975), 340–351.

55. *Les Continents*, 1 September 1924.

56. René Maran to Alain Locke, 23 February 1928, Howard University Library, quoted in Fabre, "René Maran: The New Negro and Negritude," 346.

57. Léopold Senghor, *Hommage à René Maran* (Paris: Présence Africaine, 1965), 9–15.

58. Feuser, "Afro-American Literature and Negritude," 293.

59. Rowell, "It Is Through Poetry," 51, 65; Depestre, "Interview with Aimé Césaire (1967)," 87.

60. Léopold Senghor, "La Poésie négro-américaine," *Liberté I: Négritude et Humanisme* (Paris: Seuil, 1964), 116.

61. Léopold Senghor, 1966 address at Howard University, excerpts in Mercer Cook, "President Senghor's Visit: A Tale of Five Cities," *African Forum* 2, no. 3 (1967), 78–79.

62. Stovall, *Paris Noir*, 105–106.

63. Césaire, *A Tempest*, 61–62.

64. Jean-Paul Sartre, "*Orphée noir*," preface to *Anthologie de la nouvelle poésie nègre et malgache*, xii.

65. James Ivy, a critic for the African American paper the *Crisis*, noted this paradox in his review of Senghor's *Négritude et Humanisme*: "Senghor ... is like a man placed between two mirrors, one French and the other African; but the French mirror is the larger, and the light that enters his eyes is more often reflected from the French mirror. Yet there is this paradox: His subject is eternally the African." See James Ivy, "Review of Senghor's *Négritude et Humanisme*," *African Forum* 1, no. 1 (1965), 139.

66. Manthia Diawara, "Reading Africa through Foucault: V.Y.l Mudimbe's Reaffirmation of the Subject," *October* 55 (Winter 1990), 82.

67. Depestre, "Interview with Aimé Césaire (1967)," 83.

68. Léopold Senghor, "Vues sur l'Afrique noire, ou assimiler, non être assimilés," in *La communauté impériale française*, eds. Robert Lemagnen, Léopold Senghor, and Sisowath Youtévong (Paris: Alsatia, 1945), 95.

69. Diawara, "Reading Africa Through Foucault," 84.

70. Lewis, *Race, Culture, and Identity*, 23–54.

71. See *Revue Mondiale*, 1 April 1925; *Revue Mondiale*, 15 April 1925; Roland Lebel, *Études de littérature coloniale* (Paris: J. Peyronnet, 1928), 215; Cook, "The Literary Contribution of the French West Indian," 520–521.

72. VèVè Clark, for example, has counted 63 plays about the Haitian revolution from 1796 to 1975. See "Haiti's Tragic Overture: (Mis)Representations of the Haitian Revolution in World Drama (1796–1975)," in *Representing the French Revolution: Literature, Historiography, and Art*, ed. James Heffernan (Hanover, NH: University Press of New England, 1992), 240, 249–256.

73. Quoted in Léon-François Hoffmann, *Haïti: lettres et l'être* (Toronto: GREF, 1992), 133.

74. Depestre, "Interview with Aimé Césaire (1967)," 89.
75. Ibid., 88–89.
76. Munro, "Can't Stand Up for Falling Down," 4–5; Léon Damas, "Price-Mars, le père du haïtianisme," *Présence Africaine* 32–33 (1960), 168, 178.
77. Depestre, "Interview with Aimé Césaire (1967)," 90; See Aimé Césaire, *Toussaint Louverture: La révolution française et le problème colonial* (Paris: Présence Africaine, 1961); Aimé Césaire, *La tragédie du roi Christophe* (Paris: Présence Africaine, 1963).
78. Munro, "Can't Stand Up for Falling Down," 7–9.
79. Césaire, *La tragédie du roi Christophe*, 49.
80. Mercer Cook, "The Negro in French Literature: An Appraisal," *French Review* 23, no. 5 (1950), 383.
81. Munro, "Can't Stand Up for Falling Down," 4.
82. Césaire, *Notebook of a Return to the Native Land*, 15.
83. Intellectuals in other parts of the Caribbean, particularly the British Caribbean, seemed to share the view of their African American counterparts. For example, British Caribbean intellectual C.L.R. James praised the black actor Paul Robeson's impact on Britain and concluded with "a few words about similar activities in France," discussing Dumas collectively with Maran, Césaíre, and Fanon. See C.L.R. James, "Black Intellectuals in Britain," in *Colour, Culture, and Consciousness: Immigrant Intellectuals in Britain*, ed. Bhikhu Parekh (London: Allen and Unwin, 1974), 154, 162–163.
84. Schäfer, "Global History and the Present Time," in *Wiring Prometheus*, 118.
85. Césaire, *Discourse on Colonialism*, 35–36, 37, 41, 42.
86. Schäfer, "Global History and the Present Time," in *Wiring Prometheus*, 118; Abiola Irele, "Négritude: Literature and Ideology," *The Journal of Modern African Studies* 3, no. 4 (1965), 522.
87. Mircea Eliade, quoted in Robin D.G. Kelly, "A Poetics of Anticolonialism," in Césaire, *Discourse on Colonialism*, n15, 102; Fanon, *Black Skin, White Masks*, 119, 206.

Chapter 5

1. Alain Decaux, "Le Curieux centenaire d'Alexandre Dumas," *Le Figaro*, 4 December 1970.
2. In 1992, for example, the Society stated as its mission: "To gather French and international friends devoted to the personality and works of Dumas *père*; To restore Monte-Cristo, a creation characteristic of French Romanticism, through cultural and artistic demonstrations; To devote itself to the study of the life and work of the writer and to diffuse such knowledge through publications and conferences; and to enrich its collection of objects and documents pertaining to Dumas." See *Cahiers Alexandre Dumas* 19 (1992).
3. Neave and Charron, *Monte-Cristo*, 29–31; *Une Visite au Château de Monte-Cristo* (Le Port-Marly, France: Le Syndicat Intercommunal de Monte-Cristo, 2004), 26–29; Georges Poisson, *Combats pour le patrimoine: souvenirs, 1948–2008* (Paris: Pygmalion, 2009), 243–252.
4. Twenty years later, Decaux, then a member of the French Academy and Delegate Minister of Francophonie and International Cultural Relations, remained the Dumas Society's honorary president and its Honorary Committee included Morocco's king, members connected to traditional (and elite) French cultural institutions (like the presidents of the *Société des Gens de Lettres* and *Société des Auteurs et Compositeurs dramatiques*) and dignitaries like Jean Béranger, Counselor of State; Ambassador Pierre de Boisdeffre; historian André Castelot; André Frossard of the French Academy; Armand Salacrou of the Goncourt Academy; Édouard Bonnefous, Chancellor of the Institute of France; and chief curators of the National Library. See *Cahiers Alexandre Dumas* 17 (1990–1991).
5. Lahlou, *Alexandre Dumas*, 131–132.
6. Augé, *An Anthropology for Contemporaneous Worlds*, 70.
7. Claude Schopp, "Le Testament perdu," in Alexandre Dumas, *Le Chevalier de Sainte-Hermine* (Paris: Phébus, 2005), 47–66; Youjun Peng, *La nation chez Alexandre Dumas* (Paris: L'Harmattan, 2003).
8. Hippolyte Parigot, *Alexandre Dumas père* (Paris: Librairie Hachette, 1902), 140–141. For a larger discussion on Dumas's musketeers as a symbol of French identity, see Brigitte Krulic, "Le Mousquetaire, figure exemplaire de l'imaginaire national," in *Mousquetaires! (Cahiers Alexandre Dumas 43)*, eds. Matthieu Letourneux and Isabelle Safa (Paris: Classiques Garnier, 2017), 29–38.
9. Todd Ruthven, *The Laughing Mulatto: The Story of Alexandre Dumas* (London: Rich and Cowan, 1939).

10. Koshy, "Morphing Race into Ethnicity," 168.
11. Bell, *Alexandre Dumas*, ix–x.
12. André Maurois, *Les Trois Dumas* (Paris: Librairie Hachette, 1957), 11–12.
13. Eric Martone, "All for One, One for All: Recasting Alexandre Dumas as Popular Educator in France during the New Imperialism," *Global Education Review* (forthcoming).
14. Taguieff, *The Force of Prejudice*.
15. Oruno Lara, "Les réflexions d'un historien guadeloupéen," *France-Antilles*, 13 May 1998; Philippe-Jean Catinchi, "Penser l'abolition: Réponse à la mondialisation," *Le Monde*, 24 April 1998; "La dette de l'esclavage," *Le Monde*, 27 April 1998; Jean-Louis Saux, "Une proposition de loi qualifie l'esclavage de crime contre l'humanité," *Le Monde*, 19 February 1999; Amadou Lamine Sall, "Pardonner sans jamais oublier," *Courrier international*, 18 March 1999; Véziane de Vezins, "Les brûlots de l'abbé Raynal, " *Le Figaro*, 25 April 1998.
16. Caribbean intellectuals like Annick Cojean noted, "Commemorate ... Reveal the ... 'triangular trade,' which enriched France and her slave-trading ports. Reveal two centuries of barbarism covered up by ... humanists, the Enlightenment, the Church.... And not to forget that the celebrated abolition was ... the second one, since the first ... in 1794 was revoked amid a bloodbath. Finally reveal the uprooting, the traumatism, the search for an identity." See "En Guadeloupe, des voix demandent à la France de reconnaître son passé esclavagiste," *Le Monde*, 26–7 April 1998, quoted and translated in Reinhardt, *Claims to Memory*, 3.
17. Jean-Yves Camus, "The Commemoration of Slavery in France and the Emergence of a Black Political Consciousness," *European Legacy* 11, no. 6 (2006), 647–655; As politician Alfred Marie-Jean argued, "we do not celebrate the abolition of slavery! We commemorate the antislavery insurrection.... The Negroes did not wait for a divine liberator from metropolitan France.... The slaves conquered their freedom on their own." See "En Martinique, la commémoration de l'abolition est d'abord celle de la révolte des esclaves," *Le Monde*, 26–27 April 1998, quoted and translated in Reinhardt, *Claims to Memory*, 6–7.
18. Doris Garraway, "Memory as Reparation? The Politics of Remembering Slavery in France from Abolition to the Loi Taubira," *International Journal of Francophone Studies* 11, no. 3 (2008): 365–386. In 2005, however, the state passed a controversial measure including a clause encouraging the teaching of colonialism's "positive" aspects to promote social cohesion. See Robert Aldrich, "Colonial Past, Post-Colonial Present: History Wars French-Style," *History Australia* 3 (2006): 14.1–14.10; Évelyne Héry, "L'histoire dans les textes officiels de l'enseignement secondaire," in *Politiques du passé*, 95–104.
19. *Le Monde*, 30 January 2006; Jacques Chirac, "Discours du 10 mai 2006," 10 May 2006, accessed 12 October 2017. http://discours.vie-publique.fr/notices/067001675.html; Eric Martone, "May 10 Holiday," in *Encyclopedia of Blacks in European History and Culture*, 344–345.
20. S. Binet, 'Les revendications des noirs en France,' *Libération*, 22 February 2005; Camus, "The Commemoration of Slavery," 647–655.
21. Philippe Moreau Defarges, *Repentance et réconciliation* (Paris: Presses de Sciences Po, 1999); Fanon, *The Wretched of the Earth*, 238; Philippe Bernard, "Réparer les crimes du passé," *Le Monde*, 10 April 2002.
22. Pierre Martin, "L'élection présidentielle et les élections législatives françaises de 2002," *French Politics, Culture, and Society* 21 (Spring 2003): 1–19; James Shields, "The Far Right Vote in France: From Consolidation to Collapse?" *French Politics, Culture, and Society* 28, no. 1 (2010), 27–36; Nonna Mayer, *Ces Français qui votent Le Pen* (Paris: Flammarion, 2002), 378.
23. Struggles over collective memory thus force a rewriting of history, causing the past to be in flux. While the past cannot be changed, new events and figures are added, omitted or modified, to create a narrative that alters who and what compose the nation. Thus, "historians do not discover a past as much as they create it." See Martha Howell and Walter Prevenier, *From Reliable Sources: An Introduction to Historical Methods* (Ithaca: Cornell University Press, 2001), 1.
24. Troyat, *Alexandre Dumas*, 388.
25. The review was published in *Le Voleur* and *Le Cabinet de lecture*, 20 August 1843, reprinted in Léon-François Hoffmann, "Dossier," in Alexandre Dumas, *Georges* (Paris: Gallimard, 1974), 476–477.
26. See Eric Martone, "Creating a Local Black Identity in a Global Context: The French Writer Alexandre Dumas as an African American *Lieu de Mémoire*," *Journal of Global History* 5, no. 3 (2010), 395–422.
27. Werner Sollors, "Introduction," in

Alexandre Dumas, *Georges*, trans. Tina Kover (New York: Modern Library, 2007), xxiii.

28. Alexandre Dumas, *Georges*, eds. W.N. Rivers and John Matheus (Washington, DC: Associated Publishers, 1936).

29. I.W. Brock, "Review of *Georges*," *Modern Language Journal* 22, no. 4 (1938), 314; V.B. Spratlin, "Review of *Georges* by Dumas (ed. W. N. Rivers and J. F. Matheus)," *Journal of Negro Education* 6, no. 2 (1937), 202.

30. Spratlin, "Review of *Georges*," 202, 203.

31. Brock, "Review of *Georges*," 314.

32. Spratlin, "Review of *Georges*," 202.

33. Alexandre Dumas, *Georges*, eds. W.N. Rivers, John F. Matheus, and Messaoud Belateche (Washington, DC: Associated Publishers, 1970).

34. Renée Fulton, "Review of *Georges*," *French Review* 46, no. 4 (1973), 884–885.

35. Léon-François Hoffmann, "Dumas et les noirs," in *Georges* (1974), 7–8.

36. *Ibid.*, 9, 23.

37. *Ibid.*, 9.

38. *Ibid.*, 9–10, Jacques-Henry Bornecque, "Introduction," in Alexandre Dumas, *Le Comte de Monte-Cristo* (Paris: Garnier, 1956), xlvi, li; "Introduction," in Alexandre Dumas, *Georges; or, the Isle of France*, trans. Alfred Allinson (London: Methuen, 1903).

39. Hoffmann, "Dumas et les noirs," in *Georges* (1974), 11–13.

40. *Ibid.*, 13–14.

41. *Ibid.*, 16–17, 477, 479–480.

42. *Ibid.*, 17–23.

43. *Ibid.*, 22, 23.

44. However, at around the same time, historian William Cohen argued that in *Georges*, "color is not an issue." See Cohen, *The French Encounter with Africans*, 247.

45. Henry, *Monte-Cristo*; Henry, *Les Dumas*; Henry, *Dans les pas des ... Dumas*; Anne-Marie Romero, "Une exposition permanente mêle la réalité et le roman d'Alexandre Dumas," *Le Figaro*, 19 October 2002; Marie Colmant, "Dumas pour tous, tous pour Dumas," *Télérama*, 10 July 2002, 14–16; *Revue de la Bibliothèque nationale de France: Alexandre Dumas* 11 (2002), 76–77; Lahlou, *Alexandre Dumas*, 9–10; Tom Reiss, *The Black Count: Glory, Revolution, Betrayal, and the Real Count of Monte Cristo* (New York: Broadway Paperbacks, 2012).

46. See Grivel, *Alexandre Dumas, l'homme 100 têtes*.

47. Fernandez, *Les Douze muses d'Alexandre Dumas*, 13, 235–258; Fernandez also wrote a novel about a student passionate about Dumas who travels to Haiti and learns of the hybrid Caribbean heritage and memory that was a part of the writer (and of contemporary France). The novel implied that Dumas's work had not received the merits it warranted because of the writer's origins. See Dominique Fernandez, *Jérémie! Jérémie!* (Paris: Grasset, 2005).

48. Charles Grivel, "Alexandre Dumas: mal écrire, bien écrire," in *Cent-Cinquante ans après*; 190; Didier Decoin, "Préface," in *Alexandre Dumas: Deux siècles de gloire, 1802–2002*, eds. Irène Gintzburger and Frédérique Lurol (Le Port-Marly, France: Musée du Château de Monte-Cristo, 2002), 7.

49. Glissant, *Caribbean Discourse*, 8; For an overview of his *Antillanité*, see Lewis, *Race, Culture, and Identity*, 70–88.

50. Glissant, *Caribbean Discourse*, 140; Maryse Condé, "The Stealers of Fire: The French-Speaking Writers of the Caribbean and Their Strategies of Liberation," *Journal of Black Studies* 35, no. 2 (2004), 157; Bongie, *Islands and Exiles*, 347.

51. Many black intellectuals argued that essentialization involved a fabricated homogenization of cultures to conform to Western conceptions since what was viewed as culturally homogenous nation-states were actually culturally heterogeneous entities. See Michel Giraud, "De la négritude à la créolité: Une évolution paradoxale à l'ère départementale," in *1946–1996: Cinquante ans de départementalisation outre-mer*, eds. Fred Constant and Justin Daniel (Paris: L'Harmattan, 1997), 373–403.

52. Ousmane Socé, *Mirages de Paris* (Paris: Nouvelles Éditions Latines, 1937), 183.

53. Glissant, *Caribbean Discourse*, xii, 97–109; Édouard Glissant, *L'Intention poétique* (Paris: Seuil, 1969), 158; Édouard Glissant, *Traité du Tout-Monde* (Paris: Gallimard, 1997), 22; Édouard Glissant, "A Word Scratcher," in *Chronicle of the Seven Sorrows*, vii.

54. Glissant, *Caribbean Discourse*, xii.

55. Barnabé, Chamoiseau, and Confiant, *In Praise of Creoleness*, 92, 88–89, 114–115.

56. Édouard Glissant, "The French Language in the Face of Creolization," trans. Georges Van Den Abbeele, in *French Civilization and Its Discontents: Nationalism, Colonialism, Race*, eds. Tyler Stovall and George van den Abbeele (Lanham, MD: Lexington, 2003), 109, 112.

57. Glissant, *Caribbean Discourse*, 61–62.

58. *Ibid.*, xviii–xix, 88–92.

Chapter Notes—5

59. Barnabé, Chamoiseau, and Confiant, *In Praise of Creoleness*, 76, 104–110, 111.

60. Such intellectuals thought that acquiring the "civilizing" language made one a stranger in his or her own land, resulting in a loss of identity. As African writer Albert Tevoedjre exclaimed, "I ... regret the fact of having been obliged to learn French first; to think in French while being ignorant in my own mother tongue. I ... deplore the fact that anyone should have wanted to make me a foreigner in my own country." See *L'Afrique révoltée* (Paris: Présence Africaine, 1958), 114–115; Richard Wright noted that the black artist "brought up in France ... finds it more convenient to use French ... but in doing so he finds himself ... confined to Western themes and ... way of seeing things, even though he is describing ... a life that is on a plane and a level of existence that is completely different." See Jean Jose Marchand, "Black Culture" (1958), in *Conversations with Richard Wright*, eds. Keneth Kinnamon and Michel Fabre (Jackson: University Press of Mississippi, 1993), 182.

61. Glissant, *Caribbean Discourse*, 187.

62. Trench-Bonett, "Alexandre Dumas: Black French Author," in *Charles VII*, 23, 24; American academic attention toward *Georges* increased during the 1990s and early 2000s in the form of doctoral dissertations and some articles. See Scott Russell's "*Héroïsme et Bâtardise:* Alexandre Dumas's *Georges*" (PhD dissertation, Brown University, 1992); Molly Krueger Enz, "The Mulatto as Island and the Island as Mulatto in Alexandre Dumas's *Georges*," *The French Review* 80, no. 2 (2006), 383–394.

63. Anténor Firmin, *The Equality of the Human Races*, trans. Asselin Charles (New York: Garland, 2000), 207–208.

64. Dominic Thomas, *Black France: Colonialism, Immigration, and Transnationalism* (Bloomington: Indiana University Press, 2006), 41–81.

65. Chamoiseau, *Texaco*, 280.

66. As Condé remarked, "I followed the rules for that type of novel: coincidences, sensational developments, dramatic turns of events, and unexpected encounters. Like everyone else, I had read ... Dumas's works." See Françoise Pfaff, *Conversations with Maryse Condé* (Lincoln: University of Nebraska Press, 1996), 49.

67. For example, in 1968, Adrien Martin, a professor at the French Institute of Haiti, established a school renamed after Dumas in 1972 to "symbolize the close bond between Haiti and France." Another Lycée Alexandre-Dumas opened in Algeria. See *Lycée Alexandre Dumas*, accessed 12 October 2017. http://lyceefrancaishaiti.org/index.php; "Alger de ma fenêtre," *Le Monde*, 23 December 2004.

68. Nicki Hitchcott, "Calixthe Beyala: Prizes, Plagiarism, and 'Authenticity,'" *Research in African Literatures* 37, no. 1 (2006): 100–109.

69. Calixthe Beyala, *La petite fille du réverbère* (Paris: Albin Michel, 1998), 233.

70. Calixthe Beyala, "Préface," in Alexandre Dumas, *Georges* (Paris: Éditions 1, 1998), 7–15.

71. *Ibid.*, 7, 8.

72. Dumas, *Georges* (1998), back cover.

73. Beyala, "Préface," in *Georges* (1998) 7.

74. *Ibid.*, 14–15, 7.

75. *Ibid.*, 7, 8.

76. *Ibid.*, 13.

77. *Ibid.*, 7, 10.

78. *Ibid.*, 14, 18.

79. *Ibid.*, 16.

80. *Ibid.*, 9, 10.

81. *Ibid.*, 10, 11.

82. *Ibid.*, 17; Dumas, *Georges* (1998), back cover.

83. Beyala, "Préface," in *Georges* (1998), 7.

84. *Ibid.*, 15, 18.

85. Lacouture, *Alexandre Dumas*, 29–30.

86. *Ibid.*, 30.

87. Gilles Henry has conceded that while Dumas's depiction of blacks often depicted them in stereotype, he nevertheless provided all people of black descent a hero in the character of Georges. See Henry, *Les Dumas*, 191.

88. Mirecourt, in his 1840s pamphlet attacking Dumas, maintained that Mallefille was the novel's sole writer. This accusation retained credibility in Europe and America into the early twentieth century. For example, American literary historian Ferdinand Masse suggested as late as 1933 that he doubted Dumas's authorship. Consequently, early twentieth century biographers often defended Dumas as the author, or co-author, of *Georges*. In 1902, for example, Harry Spurr argued that in *Georges*, "the hero, who suffers social ostracism for the black blood in his veins; the hero, who allows nothing to stand between himself and his desires—in short, 'Dumas-Antony,'—betrays his origin" unmistakably as Dumas's pen. French literary scholar Léon-François Hoffmann, as late as the 1970s, also felt the need to defend Dumas as the author. See Fernand Masse, "The Negro Race in French Literature," *Journal of Negro History* 18, no. 3 (1933), 228; Spurr,

The Life and Writings of Alexandre Dumas, 197; Hoffmann, "Dossier," in *Georges* (1974), 466–468.

89. For examples of articles on Dumas's global popularity (or universality), see Pierre Marcabru, "Alexandre Dumas, l'écrivain universel," *Le Figaro*, 24 August 2000; François Cérésa, "Alexandre le toujours grand," *Le Figaro Littéraire*, 2 March 2006, 3; Yves-Marie Lucot, "Du Bois dont on fait les Mousquetaires," *La Tribune*, 23 August 2002, 17; Thierry Grillet, "Éditorial," *Revue de la Bibliothèque nationale de France: Alexandre Dumas* 11 (2002), 18; Gérard de Cortanze, "Un auteur compris et aimé dans le monde entier," *Le Figaro*, 30 November 2002.

90. "Lettre de Didier Decoin au Président de la République," 20 March 2001, *Alexandre Dumas: Deux siècles de littérature*, accessed 12 October 2017. http://www.dumaspere.com/pages/pantheon/lettre.html.

91. Martine Silber, "Les cendres d'Alexandre Dumas pourraient être bientôt transférées au Panthéon," *Le Monde*, 21 April 2001; Anne Fulda, "Comment Decaux et Decoin ont plaidé la 'panthéonisation' auprès de Jacques Chirac," *Le Figaro*, 30 November 2002; Yves-Marie Lucot, "Première approche vers le Panthéon," *Le Magazine Littéraire*, September 2002, 26; Patrick de Jacquelot, "La consécration du bicentenaire," 2002, *Alexandre Dumas: Deux siècles de littérature*, accessed 12 October 2017. http://www.dumaspere.com/pages/pantheon/consecration.html.

92. Fulda, "Comment Decaux et Decoin"; *Le Mousquetaire* 3 (2003), 8–9; "La Signature du décret," *Alexandre Dumas: Deux siècles de littérature*, March 2002, accessed 12 October 2017. http://www.dumaspere.com/pages/pantheon/signature.html; Patrick de Jacquelot, "Encretien avec le Président de la République," *Alexandre Dumas: Deux siècles de littérature*, 2002, accessed 12 October 2017. http://www.dumaspere.com/pages/pantheon/chirac.html.

93. Chantal Chemla, ed., *Aramis* (July 2003), 1; Isabelle Martin, "Dumas le grand: Plus qu'un simple amuseur, un auteur lu et bien relu," *Le Temps*, 3 August 2002; *Catalogue Dallay des timbres de France. Édition 2005–2006* (Paris: Dallay, 2007); Rebecca Thomas, "France Remembers 'Forgotten' Dumas," *BBC News*, 28 November 2002, accessed 12 October 2017. http://news.bbc.co.uk/2/hi/entertainment/2519563.stm.

94. Monte Cristo ran an exhibit entitled "Alexandre Dumas, Two Centuries of Glory."

The *Société de Villers-Cotterêts* organized a colloquium on "Alexandre Dumas's Childhood and Adolescence" in October, the University of Paris III—La Sorbonne organized a colloquium entitled "Dumas: A Reading of History" the same month, and the University of Paris IV—Sorbonne Nouvelle organized a colloquium on "Dumas and the Theater" in December. The Comédie-Française honored Dumas with an uncensored performance of his play, *Christine*. See Chantal Chemla, ed., *Aramis* (2002), 2, 4.

95. In 2002, membership swelled to about 340 members. Such numbers dwindled to 283 in 2003 and 213 in 2007. See Chemla, *Aramis* (July 2003), 2; Chantal Chemla, ed., *Aramis* (May 2004), 2; Jean Hournan, ed., *Compte-rendu de l'Assemblée générale de la Société des Amis d'Alexandre Dumas*, 19 May 2007, 1; The site reported 264,000 visits in 2005 and 361,000 in 2006; about 40 percent of these visits came from users outside France. See Chemla, *Aramis* (July 2003), 2; Hournan, *Compte-rendu*, 2.

96. The committee included Decaux; Decoin; Sophie Guichard, president of the Inter-Communal Syndicate of the Château de Monte-Cristo; François Goven, assistant director of historic monuments; Jean-Marc Boyer, head of the national public works service; Bernard Jeannot, administrator of the Panthéon; Hervé Baptiste, head architect of historic monuments, Panthéon; and Sibylle Madelin-Beau, curator of the Panthéon. See Chemla, *Aramis* (2002), 1–4; Jacquelot, "La consécration du bicentenaire"; Lucot, "Première approche vers le Panthéon," 26; *Le Mousquetaire* (2003), 13–14; "Dumas: en route vers le Panthéon," *Le Figaro*, 29 November 2002.

97. "Vengeance populaire," *Libération*, 30 November 2002; Silber, "Les cendres d'Alexandre Dumas"; Some press members did express "a bit of a surprise" over the choice. See Lahlou, *Alexandre Dumas*, 131.

98. In Dumas's hometown of Villers-Cotterêts, "Alexandre Dumas Weekend" emerged as an annual celebration. See the official website for tourism in Aisne. http://www.aisne-tourisme.com.

99. "La controverse du Panthéon (Interview with Didier Decoin and Geneviève Dormann)," *Le Figaro (hors-série)*: *Alexandre Dumas*, 2002, 106–107.

100. Invading German forces removed and smelted the Dumas statue. All that remained was the pen from Dumas's hand, pre-

served in the local museum, and the pedestal, stored in a neighboring quarry. The Minister of Culture selected sculptor Jean-Loup Bouvier to create a replica. Since no mold of the original existed, Bouvier used the original sculptor's models (which were different from the statue produced) and old photographs. In 2005, the statue was "returned." The event was marked with local festivities. In a speech, Mayor Renaud Bellière expressed the town's "great sadness" at Dumas's removal, but thanked the state for offering compensation. The Minister of Culture, Renaud Donnedieu de Vabre, described how the state "had chosen to restore this statue," rather than commission a new one, to repair an injustice. Continuing with the bicentennial's themes, he praised Dumas's accomplishments, especially since he was "the grandson of a slave, when slavery had yet to be abolished." See Lucot, "Première approche vers le Panthéon," 26; Elizabeth Campbell Karlsgodt, "Recycling French Heroes: The Destruction of Bronze Statues under the Vichy Regime," *French Historical Studies* 29, no. 1 (2006): 143–181; Chantal Chemla, ed., *Aramis* (Dec. 2005), 1; "Alexandre Dumas en statue à Villers-Cotterêts," *Le Figaro*, 14 December 2005.

101. Dumas was linked to France's broader immigration history. Dominique Fernandez, for one, noted metaphorically that "we are all mulattoes, all *métis*." See Sylvie Chalaye, "La face cachée d'Alexandre Dumas," Africultures.com, 1 September 2005, accessed 12 October 2017. http://www.africultures.com/php/index.php?nav=article&no=3903; Michel De Jaeghere, "Éditorial," *Le Figaro (hors-série)*, 2002, 3; Fernandez, *Les douze muses*, 258; Elisabeth Levy, "La France, une chance pour les immigrés?" *Le Figaro Magazine*, 7 May 2004, 60.

102. Bernard Fillaire, *Alexandre Dumas et associés* (Paris: Bartillat, 2002), 118.

103. Lévy, "La France, une chance pour les immigrés?" 60.

104. Claude Schopp argued that Dumas represented "in his person the *diverse France* of this post-revolutionary period," thereby pushing the origins of a multiethnic France further into the past to create greater continuity with the present. See Claude Schopp, "Le fil de l'Histoire," *Le Figaro (hors-série)*: *Alexandre Dumas*, 2002, 66.

105. The press observed Chirac's government as supporting "the *métissage* of [French] ... culture," united through an attachment to the Republic and its values.

Consequently, *Le Figaro* observed that "for Chirac, Dumas was the ideal *panthéonisé*." See Fulda, "Comment Decaux et Decoin"; "Le choix du 'grand homme,'" *Les Echos*, 29 November 2002 ; "La France métisse," *Le Monde*, 1 December 2002.

106. "La France métisse."

107. "Jacques Chirac: La République répare une injustice," *Le Monde*, 3 December 2002; "La France métisse"; Lahlou, *Alexandre Dumas*, 137; De Jaeghere, "Editorial," 3; Lévy, "La France, une chance pour les immigrés?"60.

108. "Daniel Picouly a répondu à vos questions," LaProvence.com, October 2008, accessed 12 October 2017. http://www2.laprovence.com/tchat/daniel-picouly-a-repondu-a-vos-questions.

109. "La France métisse"; Levy, "La France, une chance pour les immigrés?" 60.

110. Michèle Gazier, "Populaire, donc suspect," *Télérama*, 10 July 2002, 20.

111. Dumas had "his Caribbean atavism ... as the grandson of Marie-Cessette Dumas, an indigenous slave." See Christian Biet, Jean-Paul Brighelli, and Jean-Luc Rispail, *Alexandre Dumas ou les aventures d'un romancier* (Paris: Découvertes Gallimard, 1986), 59.

112. Claude Schopp, in an interview, noted that Dumas "took a sweet revenge on the ostracization that his contemporary society reserved for his Caribbean origins." See Yves-Marie Lucot, "Claude Schopp: Dumas au-delà de sa légende," *Le Magazine Littéraire*, September 2002, 22.

113. "Dumas ... is a Haitian writer." See Dominique Fernandez, "Visite à Jérémie," *Le Mousquetaire* 7 (2007): 24–26.

114. Dumas was perceived as regarding himself as "Franco-Haitian," despite this improbability. See Claude Ribbe, "Inauguration officielle du monument général Dumas. Même Obama est invité!" Communiqué de l'association des Amis du général Dumas, *Sangonet: Connaissance de l'Afrique, Information, Culture, Histoire, Africonomie,* 24 March 2009. Accessed 12 October 2017. http://www.sangonet.com/hist/FiguresMDA/a-dumas/inaugurer-monu-gl-A-Dumas.html.

115. Claude Imbert, "Hercule au Panthéon," *Le Point*, 29 November 2002; Lahlou, *Alexandre Dumas*, 11; Biet, Brighelli, and Rispail, *Alexandre Dumas*, 59.

116. Lahlou, *Alexandre Dumas*, 12.

117. Fernandez, *Les douze muses*, 13, 245.

118. Thomas, *Black France*, 82–113; Con-

sequently, Ricki Stevenson, an African American journalist, included Dumas in her "Black Paris Tours." See Jamey Keaten, "Paris Tours Look at City's Ties with Black Americans," *The Bay State Banner,* 10 January 2008, accessed 12 October 2017. http://www.baystate-banner.com/issues/2008/01/10/news/world01100822.htm; See also the Black Paris Tours website: http://www.blackparistour.com/. Other tour companies offer such tours. For examples, see https://discoverparis.net/entree-to-black-paris; http://www.walkthespirit.com.

119. "La France métisse." For more on French "*sans-papiers*," see Laurent Dubois, "*La République métissée*: Citizenship, Colonialism, and the Borders of French History," *Cultural Studies* 14, 1 (2000): 15–34.

120. Decaux made reference to Dumas's "dark complexion." Chirac noted that Dumas had both "blue" and "black" blood because of his noble and racial ancestry. See "Le discours d'Alain Decaux, de l'Académie française," 30 November 2002, *Alexandre Dumas: Deux siècles de littérature,* accessed 12 October 2017. http://www.dumaspere.com/pages/pantheon/reportages/30decaux.html; Jacques Chirac, French President, Speech at the Panthéon, 30 November 2002, in *Le Mousquetaire* (2003), 29–33 or "Le discours du Président de la République," 30 November 2002, *Alexandre Dumas: Deux siècles de littérature,* accessed 12 October 2017. http://www.dumaspere.com/pages/pantheon/reportages/30chirac.html.

121. David Beriss, "Culture-As-Race or Culture-As-Culture: Caribbean Ethnicity and the Ambiguity of Cultural Identity in French Society," in *Race in France,* 124.

122. "The Body of a Legendary Black Novelist Is Laid to Rest in the French Panthéon," *Journal of Blacks in Higher Education* 38 (Winter 2002–2003), 43.

123. Chalaye, "La face cachée d'Alexandre Dumas."

124. *Une Visite au Château de Monte-Cristo,* 5.

125. Colmant, "Dumas pour tous, tous pour Dumas," 14.

126. *Ibid.,* 17, 18.

127. "The Body of a Legendary Black Novelist," 43.

128. Didier Decoin, "Éditorial: Alexandre Dumas au Panthéon," *Le Mousquetaire* 2 (2001), 6–7.

129. Colmant, "Dumas pour tous, tous pour Dumas," 19; "Le discours d'Alain Gournac, Sénateur-maire du Pecq," 29 November 2002, *Alexandre Dumas: Deux siècles de littérature,* accessed 12 October 2017. http://www.dumaspere.com/pages/pantheon/reportages/29gournac.html; Sébastien Lapaque, "Serait favorable au transfert des cendres au Panthéon de l'auteur des *Trois Mousquetaires*; Dumas canonisé par la République?" *Le Figaro,* 20 April 2001.

130. Pierre Georges, *Le Monde,* 21 April 2001; *Libération,* 20 April 2001; *Télérama,* 10 July 2002, front cover; Alain Salles, "Dumas prend sa revanche au Panthéon," *Le Monde,* 2 December 2002; Fernandez, *Les douze muses,* 256.

131. "Le discours de Didier Decoin, Président de la Société des Amis d'Alexandre Dumas," 29 November 2002, *Alexandre Dumas: Deux siècles de littérature,* accessed 12 October 2017. http://www.dumaspere.com/pages/pantheon/reportages/29decoin.html.

132. Olivier Barlet, "Droits de l'homme, droit des peuples: Rencontre Edwy Plenel/Edouard Glissant," Africultures.com, 30 July 2005, accessed 12 October 2017. http://www.africultures.com/php/index.php?nav=article&no=3915.

133. "Jacques Chirac: La République répare une injustice"; "Le discours du Président de la République," 30 November 2002.

134. In 2008, for example, upon the initiative of Parisian official Pascal Joseph, the memory of the three Dumas was celebrated on May 10. See Gaël Octavia, "Le Dumas noir: Vers la réhabilitation de sa mémoire," Afrik.com, accessed 12 October 2017. http://www.afrik.com/article16897.html.

135. In 2005, Dumas had over 220 titles in print with seventy-five publishers. *Livre de poche* recorded that only Zola and Hugo could compare in terms of sales, but they had the benefit of being assigned in schools while Dumas did not. That year, Dumas's unfinished novel, the serialized *Le Chevalier de Sainte-Hermine,* was released in book form for the first time. It made the top 10 bestsellers list. See Mohamed Aissaoui, "Au panthéon de l'édition," *Le Figaro Littéraire,* 2 March 2006, 3; Xavier Houssin, "Alexandre Dumas ultime," *Le Monde: Des Livres,* 17 June 2005; Hugh Schofield, "Hats Off to France's Literary Star," *BBC News,* 9 August 2008, accessed 12 October 2017. http://news.bbc.co.uk/2/hi/programmes/from_our_own_correspondent/7549210.stm; Sophie Nicholson, "Missing Dumas Novel in Print," *The Guardian,* 3 June 2005, accessed 12 October 2017. https://www.theguardian.com/world/

2005/jun/04/france.books; John Crace, "Claude Schopp: The Man Who Gave Dumas 40 Mistresses," *The Guardian* (UK), 6 May 2008, accessed 12 October 2017. https://www.theguardian.com/education/2008/may/06/highereducationprofile.academicexperts.

136. Pierre Thivolet, "L'Académie française doit accueillir Aimé Césaire," *Le Monde*, 25 October 2006, 21; "La France métisse."

137. Salles, "Dumas prend sa revanche au Panthéon"; Christophe Mercier, "Alexandre Dumas: Le génie du récit," *Le Magazine Littéraire*, February 2010, 50, 51.

138. Lyonel Trouillot, "Ces forcenés du vice ou de l'idéal," *Le Magazine Littéraire*, February 2010, 81.

139. Claude Allègre, former minister of education, noted that when he became minister, Dumas "was not taught in secondary schools." Efforts from academics to include him became more noticeable. See Sophie Coignard, "Le français: Interview avec Claude Allègre," *Le Point*, 24 March 2005; "Vengeance populaire"; To encourage the teaching of Dumas's works, Daniel Compère published a guide providing "an historical and thematic approach to the ... reading or rereading of this great classic text." See *Le Monte-Cristo d'Alexandre Dumas: Lecture des textes* (Amiens, France: Encrage, 1998).

140. Mariana Net, *Alexandre Dumas, écrivain du XXIe siècle: L'Impatience du lendemain* (Paris: L'Harmattan, 20008), 11, 303; *Le Magazine Littéraire*, September 2002, 309–310.

141. Crace, "Claude Schopp"; Lucot, "Claude Schopp: Dumas au-delà de sa légende," 22.

142. Christophe Mercier, "Dumas, deux siècles après; Les sept ciels d'Alexandre Dumas," *Le Point*, 12 July 2002 ; Troyat, *Alexandre Dumas*, 7; Biet, Brighelli, and Rispail, *Alexandre Dumas*, 93; Tulard, *Alexandre Dumas*, 74–76; Lahlou, *Alexandre Dumas*, 91, 95, 135; "Le discours du Président de la République," 30 November 2002.

143. Tallandier, "Introduction," in *Le Comte de Monte-Cristo*, I:17; Schopp, "Le fil de l'Histoire," 66.

144. Jean-Yves Mollier, "Multimédia avant l'heure," *Le Magazine Littéraire*, February 2010) 68–69; Net, *Alexandre Dumas*, 11, 303; *Le Magazine Littéraire*, September 2002, 20.

145. Net, *Alexandre Dumas*, 15; Mercier, "Alexandre Dumas: Le génie du récit," 50–53; In particular, he was credited with inventing the French historical novel and influencing the adventure novel in Western literature. See Colmant, "Dumas pour tous, tous pour Dumas," 14; "Jacques Chirac: La République répare une injustice"; "Le discours du Président de la République," 30 November 2002; Matthieu Letourneux, "Cape et épée, un feuilleton sans fin," *Le Magazine Littéraire*, February 2010, 76–77.

146. He was credited with writing "the first Romantic melodrama" and "the first modern drama of Romantic theater." See Fernande Bassan, "L'invention du drame moderne," *Le Magazine Littéraire*, September 2002, 46–48; Pierre Marcabru, "Les planchers de la gloire," *Le Figaro (hors-série)*: *Alexandre Dumas*, 2002, 62. His works, like *Antony*, were cited as influencing later literary works and styles, like Flaubert's *Madame Bovary*, and twentieth-century avant-gardes. See Stéphane Denis, "12 journées de la vie d'un titan: À nous deux, Paris! 5 avril 1823," *Le Figaro (hors-série)*: *Alexandre Dumas*, 2002, 28–29; Net, *Alexandre Dumas*, 15; Serge Moussa, "Un écrivain voyageur," *Le Magazine Littéraire*, September 2002, 50–53.

147. "Le discours du Président de la République," 30 November 2002; "Le discours d'Alain Decaux, de l'Académie française," 30 November 2002 ; Jean-Jacques Mourreau, "A.D. Productions," *Le Figaro (hors-série)*: *Alexandre Dumas*, 2002, 72–73; Mercier, "Dumas, deux siècles après"; Net, *Alexandre Dumas*, 11; Troyat, *Alexandre Dumas*, 336.

148. Lucot, "Première approche vers le Panthéon," 26.

149. Réginald Hamel, "De la créolité américaine," *Le Magazine Littéraire*, September 2002, 58–59, 60.

150. Pierre Thivolet, "L'Académie française doit accueillir Aimé Césaire," *Le Monde*, 25 October 2006, 21.

151. Lahlou, *Alexandre Dumas*, 131–132.

152. Chalaye, "La face cachée d'Alexandre Dumas"; "Jacques Chirac: La République répare une injustice," *Le Monde*, 3 December 2002; "Le discours du Président de la République," 30 November 2002.

153. Chalaye, "La face cachée d'Alexandre Dumas"; "The Body of a Legendary Black Novelist," 43.

154. Alain Decaux, "Les mille et une nuits d'Alexandre le Grand," *Le Figaro (hors-série)*: *Alexandre Dumas*, 2002, 52.

155. Martin, "Dumas le grand"; Chalaye, "La face cachée d'Alexandre Dumas."

156. Events included a tree planting in the Forest of Retz, familiar to the young Dumas, renaming a school in his honor, and the placing of a new inscription on his former grave. See *Le Mousquetaire* (2003), 10–12; Elizabeth Mismes-Thomas, "Le 30 novembre, les cendres d'Alexandre Dumas seront transférées au Panthéon," *Le Figaro*, 22 November 2002.

157. "Dumas: en route vers le Panthéon"; Chemla, *Aramis* (2002), 3; *Le Mousquetaire* (2003), 15–16.

158. *Le Mousquetaire* (2003), 6, 17–18.

159. *Le Mousquetaire* (2003), 19; "Dumas: en route vers le Panthéon"; "Musketeers Carry Dumas to Panthéon," *BBC News*, 30 November 2002, accessed 12 October 2017. http://news.bbc.co.uk/2/hi/europe/2531617.stm.

160. Claude Ribbe and Christian Poncelet, Speeches at the Senate, 30 November 2002, *Alexandre Dumas: Deux siècles de littérature*, accessed 12 October 2017. http://www.dumaspere.com/pages/pantheon/sommaire.html.

161. *Le Mousquetaire* (2003), 19; "Dumas: en route vers le Panthéon"; "Musketeers Carry Dumas to Panthéon"; Ribbe and Poncelet, Speeches at the Senate, 30 November 2002.

162. *Richard Darlington* (1831), *La Tour de Nesle* (1832), *Henri III et sa cour* (1829), *Charles VII* (1831), *Christine* (1830), *Don Juan de Marana* (1836) and *Antony* (1831).

163. Pierre Georges, "Alexandre le randonneur," *Le Monde*, 14 June 2002; "Dumas: en route vers le Panthéon."

164. *Le Mousquetaire* (2003), 22–23; Schofield, "Hats Off to France's Literary Star."

165. Roxane Petit-Rasselle makes such arguments in "From the Literary Myth to the *Lieu de Mémoire*: Alexandre Dumas and French National Identity(ies)," in *The Black Musketeer: Reevaluating Alexandre Dumas within the Francophone World*, ed. Eric Martone (Newcastle upon Tyne: Cambridge Scholars, 2011), 163–191.

166. Ernest Renan, *Discours et Conférences* (1887), in Kohn, *Nationalism*, 136–139.

167. "Le discours du Président de la République," 30 November 2002.

168. *Ibid.*; "Jacques Chirac: La République répare une injustice."

169. "Jacques Chirac: La République répare une injustice."

170. Tulard, *Alexandre Dumas*, 18.

171. "Jacques Chirac: La République répare une injustice."

172. Havelock Ellis, "The Genius of France," *The Atlantic Monthly*, March 1893, 72.

173. A struggle emerged over Aimé Césaire's remains in 2008. President Nicolas Sarkozy and his government sought to put him in the Panthéon. Martinicans objected, arguing that such an honor reinforced metropolitan supremacy over the overseas departments. Césaire was ultimately buried in Martinique. Only three other writers, including Hugo, had received state funeral honors. Césaire's was the first held beyond the metropole. The discussion of the panthéonization of Franco-Algerian writer Albert Camus continues this expansion. See A. James Arnold, "Césaire Is Dead: Long Live Césaire! Recuperations and Reparations," *French Politics, Culture and Society* 27, no. 3 (2009), 9, 10.

174. Schäfer, "Global History and the Present Time," in *Wiring Prometheus*, 109, 113, 115; Wolf Schäfer, *Ungleichzeitigkeit als Ideologie: Beiträge zur Historischen Aufklärung* (Frankfurt am Main, Germany: Fischer Sozialwissenschaft, 1994); Augé, *An Anthropology for Contemporaneous Worlds*; Bruce Mazlish, *The Idea of Humanity in a Global Era* (New York: Palgrave Macmillan, 2008); Roland Robertson, *Globalization: Social Theory and Global Culture* (Thousand Oaks, CA: Sage, 1992), 58–59; Bernard McGrane, who has examined "the history of the different conceptions of difference" in the modern age, traces ways that maintained "the alienness of the non-European Other," such as the use of time as "lodged ... between the European and non-European Other." See Bernard McGrane, *Beyond Anthropology* (New York: Columbia University Press, 1989).

175. Glissant, *Caribbean Discourse*, 2, 196.

176. *Ibid.*, xxx, 64, 199.

177. V.Y. Mudimbe, *The Invention of Africa* (Bloomington: Indiana University Press, 1998), 2.

178. Barnabé, Chamoiseau, and Confiant, *In Praise of Creoleness*, 98.

179. Michel Foucault, *Language, Counter-Memory, Practice: Selected Essays and Interviews*, ed. Donald Bouchard (Ithaca: Cornell University Press, 1977), 144, 148, 150–151.

Bibliography

Archives/Private Collections

Amistad Research Center, New Orleans, Louisiana
Archives départementales de l'Aisne, Laon, France
Bibliothèque nationale de France, Paris
Schomburg Center for Research in Black Culture, New York, New York
La Société des Amis d'Alexandre Dumas, Le Port-Marly, France

English-Language News Sources and Periodicals

Alt Film Guide
The Anglo-African Magazine
Appeal (Carson City)
The Atlantic Monthly
The Australian
Bay Star Banner
BBC News
Blackwood's Magazine
Boston Central
CBC News
The Crisis
Daily Mail (UK)
Every Saturday
Le Figaro
The Galaxy
The Guardian (UK)
Harper's New Monthly Magazine
History News Network
The Illustrated London News
Independent
Littell's Living Age
The Living Age
New York Times
New Yorker
North American Review
North County Times (CA)
Opportunity
Redorbit News
The Review of the Black World
Savannah Tribune
Scribner's Magazine
Scribner's Monthly
The Smithsonian
Star Tribune (Minneapolis)
United States Democratic Review

French-Language News Sources and Periodicals

Africultures.com
Afrik.com
Aramis: 'Le Mousquetaire' par intérim de la Société des Amis d'Alexandre Dumas
Le Blog de Claude Ribbe
Le Blog de diversiteé
Bulletin de la Société Historique Régionale de Villers-Cotterêts
Cahiers de la Société des Amis d'Alexandre Dumas
Le Constitutionnel
Les Continents
Courrier international

Bibliography

La Dépêche du Midi
Les Échos
Le Figaro
Le Figaro (hors-série)
Le Figaro Littéraire
Le Figaro Magazine
France-Antilles
La Fraternité
Gazette officielle de la Guadeloupe
JeuneAfrique.com
LaProvence.com
L'Avenir
L'Express
L'Humanité
Libération
L'Illustration
L'Ordre
Le Magazine Littéraire
Médiatropiques
Le Monde
Le Monde: Des Livres
Le Moniteur universel
Le Mousquetaire de la Société des Amis d'Alexandre Dumas
La Nouvelle Revue
Le Parisien
Le Petit Journal
Le Point
La Presse
Revue contemporaine
Revue de la Bibliothèque nationale de France
Revue des deux mondes
Revue Mondiale
Sangonet: Connaissance de l'Afrique, Information, Culture, Histoire, Africonomie
Télérama
Le Temps
La Tribune

Books and Articles

Abenon, Lucien-René. *Petite histoire de la Guadeloupe*. Paris: L'Harmattan, 1992.
Adams, Russell. *Great Negroes, Past and Present*. Chicago: Afro-Am, 1963.
Alalou, Ali. "Language and Ideology in the Maghreb: Francophonie and Other Languages." *The French Review* 80, no. 2 (2006): 408–421.
Aldrich, Robert. "Colonial Past, Post-Colonial Present: History Wars French-Style." *History Australia* 3 (2006): 14.1–14.10.
Alexander, Martin, ed. *French History Since Napoleon*. New York: Arnold/Oxford University Press, 1999.
Alexandre Dumas: Deux siècles de littérature. Website of the Société des Amis d'Alexandre Dumas. Accessed 29 September 2017. http://www.dumaspere.com/pages/pantheon/lettre.html.
Alger, Dennis. *"Francophonie" in the 1990s: Problems and Opportunities*. Philadelphia: Multilingual Matters, 1996.
Aliano, David. "Revisiting Saint-Domingue: Toussaint L'Ouverture and the Haitian Revolution in the French Colonial Debates of the Late Nineteenth Century (1870–1900)." *French Colonial History* 9 (2008): 15–35.
Allin, Michael. *Zarafa: A Giraffe's True Story from Deep in Africa to the Heart of Paris*. 2nd ed. New York: Delta, 1999.
Alter, Peter. *Nationalism*. 2nd ed. New York: Edward Arnold, 1994.
Altink, Henrice, and Sharif Gemie, eds. *At the Border: Margins and Peripheries in Modern France*. Cardiff: University of Wales Press, 2008.
Amselle, Jean-Loup. *Affirmative Exclusion: Cultural Pluralism and the Rule of Custom in France*. Ithaca: Cornell University Press, 2003.
Anderson, Benedict. *Imagined Communities: Reflections on the Origin and Spread of Nationalism*. Rev. ed. New York: Verso, 2006.
Andrieu, Claire, Marie-Claire Lavabre, and Danielle Tartakowsky, eds. *Politiques du passé: Usages politiques du passé dans la France contemporaine*. Provence, France: Publications de l'Université de Provence, 2006.

Bibliography

Arnold, A. James. "Césaire Is Dead: Long Live Césaire! Recuperations and Reparations." *French Politics, Culture and Society* 27, no. 3 (2009): 9–18.
Arnold, John. *History: A Short Introduction*. New York: Oxford University Press, 2000.
Arnold, Kathleen. *Homelessness, Citizenship, and Identity: The Uncanniness of Late Modernity*. Albany: SUNY Press, 2004.
Arrous, Michel, ed. *Dumas, une lecture de l'Histoire*. Paris: Maisonneuve & Larose, 2003.
Audebrand, Philibert. *Alexandre Dumas à la Maison d'or: souvenirs de la vie littéraire*. Paris: Calmann Lévy, 1888.
Augé, Marc. *An Anthropology for Contemporaneous Worlds*. Trans. Amy Jacobs. Stanford: Stanford University Press, 1999.
Babb, Valerie. *Whiteness Visible: The Meaning of Whiteness in American Literature and Culture*. New York: New York University Press, 1998.
Baldwin, James. *The Pride of the Ticket: Collected Non-fiction, 1948–1985*. London: Michael Joseph, 1985.
Baldwin, James. *Tell Me How Long the Train's Been Gone*. London: Corgi, 1970.
Balibar, Étienne, and Immanuel Wallerstein, eds. *Race, Nation, Class: Ambiguous Identities*. New York: Verso, 1991.
Balzac, Honoré de. *Lettres à Madame Hanska*. Ed. Roger Pierrot. 4 vols. Paris: Du Delta, 1967–1971.
Bancel, Nicolas, Pascal Blanchard, and Françoise Vergès. *La République coloniale: Essai sur une utopie*. Paris: Albin Michel, 2003.
Banville, Théodore de. *Poésies complètes*. Paris: E. Fasquelle, 1909.
Barkan, Elazar. *Guilt of Nations: Restitution and Negotiating Historical Injustices*. New York: W.W. Norton, 2000.
Barnabé, Jean, Patrick Chamoiseau, and Raphaël Confiant. *Éloge de la Créolité/In Praise of Creoleness*. Trans. M.B. Taleb-Khyar. Paris: Gallimard, 1993.
Barzun, Jacques. *The French Race: Theories of Its Origins and Their Social and Political Implications Prior to the Revolution*. New York: Columbia University Press, 1932.
Bassan, Fernande. "Alexandre Dumas père et le théâtre romantique." *The French Review* 47, no. 4 (1974): 767–772.
Bassan, Fernande. "Histoire de La Tour de Nesle de Dumas père et Gaillardet." *Nineteenth-Century French Studies* 3, no. 1–2 (1974–1975): 40–57.
Bassan, Fernande. "Le Roman-feuilleton et Alexandre Dumas père (1802–1870)." *Nineteenth-Century French Studies* 22, no. 1–2 (1993–1994): 100–111.
Begag, Azouz. *Ethnicity and Equality: France in the Balance*. Trans. Alec Hargreaves. Lincoln: University of Nebraska Press, 2007.
Bell, A. Craig. *Alexandre Dumas: A Biography and Study*. London: Cassell, 1950.
Bellegarde, Dantès. *Haïti et son peuple*. Paris: Nouvelles Éditions Latines, 1953.
Benbassa, Esther, ed. *Dictionnaire des racismes, de l'exclusion et des discriminations*. Paris: Larousse, 2010.
Benhabib, Seyla. *The Claims of Culture: Equality and Diversity in the Global Era*. Princeton: Princeton University Press, 2002.
Benitez-Rojo, Antonio. *The Repeating Island: The Caribbean and the Postmodern Perspective*. Trans. James Maraniss. Durham: Duke University Press, 1996.
Bénot, Yves. *La Révolution française et la fin des colonies*. Paris: La Découverte, 1987.
Berenson, Edward, and Eva Giloi, eds. *Constructing Charisma: Celebrity, Fame, and Power in Nineteenth-Century Europe*. New York: Berghahn, 2010.
Berger, Peter, Bridgette Berger, and Hansfried Kellner. *The Homeless Mind: Modernization and Consciousness*. New York: Random House, 1973.
Beriss, David. *Black Skins, French Voices: Caribbean Ethnicity and Activism in Urban France*. Boulder: Westview, 2004.

Bibliography

Berliner, Brett. *Ambivalent Desire: The Exotic Black Other in Jazz-Age France.* Amherst: University of Massachusetts Press, 2002.
Berthier, Patrick. "Dumas, l'immoral: quelques images du dramaturge dans la presse des années 1830." *Dix-neuf Vingt: Revue de littérature moderne* 5 (March 1998): 55–65.
Bertière, Simone. *Dumas et les Mousquetaires: Histoire d'un chef-d'œuvre.* Paris: Fallois, 2009.
Bethel, Elizabeth. *The Roots of African-American Identity: Memory and History in Antebellum Free Communities.* Houndmills: Palgrave Macmillan, 1997.
Betts, Raymond. *Assimilation and Association in French Colonial Theory, 1890–1914.* Lincoln: University of Nebraska Press, 2005.
Beyala, Calixthe. *La petite fille du réverbère.* Paris: Albin Michel, 1998.
Biet, Christian, Jean-Paul Brighelli, and Jean-Luc Rispail. *Alexandre Dumas ou les aventures d'un romancier.* Paris: Découvertes Gallimard, 1986.
Bissette, Cyrille. *Examen rapide des deux projets de loi relatifs aux colonies.* Paris: De l'imprimerie d'Éverat, 1833.
Bissette, Cyrille. *Réfutation du livre de M. V. Schoelcher sur Haïti.* Paris: Ébrard, 1844.
Bissette, Cyrille. *Réfutation du livre de M. Victor Schoelcher, intitulé 'Des colonies françaises'.* Paris: Imprimerie Breton, 1843.
Bissette, Cyrille. *Réponse au factum de M. Schoelcher intitulé* La vérité aux ouvriers et cultivateurs de la Martinique. Paris: Imprimerie de Poussielgue, 1850.
Bissette, Cyrille. *De la situation des gens de couleur libres aux Antilles françaises.* Paris: J. MacCarthy, 1823.
Blackburn, Robin. *The Overthrow of Colonial Slavery, 1776–1848.* London: Verso, 1988.
Blanchard, Pascal, Nicolas Bancel, and Sandrine Lemaire, eds. *La Fracture coloniale.* Paris: La Découverte, 2006.
Blanchard, Pascal, Sandrine Lemaire, and Nicolas Bancel. *Culture coloniale en France: De la Révolution française à nos jours.* Paris: Centre Nationale de la Recherche Scientifique, 2008.
Bleich, Erik. *Race Politics in France and Britain: Ideas and Policymaking since the 1960s.* New York: Cambridge University Press, 2003.
Bloch, Ernst. *Heritage of Our Times.* Trans. and ed. Neville Plaice and Stephen Plaice. Berkeley: University of California Press, 1991.
Blowen, Sarah, Marion Demoisier, and Jeanne Picard, eds. *Recollections of France: Memories, Identities and Heritage in Contemporary France.* New York: Berghahn, 2000.
Bodin, Jean. *La Méthode de l'histoire.* Ed. Pierre Mesnard. Paris: Société d'Édition Les Belles Lettres, 1941.
"The Body of a Legendary Black Novelist Is Laid to Rest in the French Panthéon." *Journal of Blacks in Higher Education* 38 (Winter 2002–2003): 43.
Boittin, Jennifer Anne. "Black in France: The Language and Politics of Race in the Late Third Republic." *French Politics, Culture and Society* 27, no. 2 (2009): 23–46.
Bongie, Chris. "'C'est du papier ou de l'Histoire en marche?': The Revolutionary Compromises of a Martiniquan *Homme de Couleur*, Cyrille-Charles-Auguste Bissette." *Nineteenth-Century Contexts* 23, no. 4 (2001): 439–473.
Bongie, Chris. *Islands and Exiles: The Creole Identities of Post/Colonial Literature.* Stanford: Stanford University Press, 1998.
Bongie, Chris. "A Street Named Bissette: Nostalgia, Memory, and the *Cent-Cinquantenaire* of the Abolition of Slavery in Martinique (1848–1998)." *The South Atlantic Quarterly* 100, no. 1 (2001): 215–257.
Boubeker, Ahmed, and Abdellali Hajjat, eds. *Histoire politique des immigrations (post) coloniales: France, 1920–2008.* Paris: Amsterdam, 2008.
Boulle, Pierre. *Race et esclavage dans la France de l'Ancien Régime.* Paris: Perrin, 2007.

Bibliography

Brakke, David. "Ethiopian Demons: Male Sexuality, the Black-Skinned Other, and the Monastic Self." *Journal of the History of Sexuality* 10, no. 3–4 (2001): 501–535.
Brock, Colin. *The Caribbean in Europe: Aspects of the West Indies Experience in Britain, France, and the Netherlands*. London: Routledge, 1986.
Brock, I.W. "Review of *Georges*." *Modern Language Journal* 22, no. 4 (1938): 314.
Brooks, Peter. *The Melodramatic Imagination: Balzac, Henry James, Melodrama, and the Mode of Excess*. New Haven: Yale University Press, 1976.
Brown, William Wells. *The Black Man, His Antecedents, His Genius, His Achievements*. 4th ed. Reprint. Miami: Mnemosyne, 1969.
Brubaker, Rogers. *Citizenship and Nationhood in France and Germany*. Cambridge: Harvard University Press, 1992.
Bruce, Dickinson. *The Origins of African American Literature, 1680–1865*. Charlottesville: University Press of Virginia, 2001.
Bryant, Kelly Duke. "Black but Not African: Francophone Black Diaspora and the *Revue des Colonies*, 1834–1842." *International Journal of African Historical Studies* 40, no. 2 (2007): 251–282.
Bury, Henri Blaze de. *A. Dumas, sa vie, son temps, son œuvre*. Reprint. Montreal: Joyeux Roger, 2008.
Callahan, Kevin, and Sarah Curtis, eds. *Views from the Margins: Creating Identities in Modern France*. Lincoln: University of Nebraska Press, 2008.
Calmettes, Fernand, ed. *Mémoires du général Baron Thiébault*. 5 vols. Paris: E. Plon, 1893–1895.
Camus, Jean-Yves. "The Commemoration of Slavery in France and the Emergence of a Black Political Consciousness." *European Legacy* 11, no. 6 (2006), 647–655.
Carrier, Peter. *Holocaust Monuments and National Memory Cultures in France and Germany Since 1989*. New York: Berghahn, 2006.
Cartey, Wildred. "Dark Voices." *Présence Africaine* 28, no. 65 (1963): 97–98.
Catalogue Dallay de timbres de France. Edition 2005–2006. Paris: Dallay, 2007.
Césaire, Aimé. *Discourse on Colonialism*. Trans. Joan Pinkham. New York: Monthly Review Press, 2000.
Césaire, Aimé. *Letter to Maurice Thorez*. Paris: Présence Africaine, 1957.
Césaire, Aimé. *Notebook of a Return to the Native Land*. Trans. and ed. Clayton Eshleman and Annette Smith. Middletown, CT: Wesleyan University Press, 2001.
Césaire, Aimé. *A Tempest*. Trans. Richard Miller. New York: TCG Translations, 2002.
Césaire, Aimé. *Toussaint Louverture: La révolution française et le problème colonial*. Paris: Présence Africaine, 1961.
Césaire, Aimé. *La Tragédie du roi Christophe*. Paris: Présence Africaine, 1963.
Chamoiseau, Patrick. *Chronicle of the Seven Sorrows*. Trans. Linda Coverdale. Lincoln: University of Nebraska Press, 1999.
Chamoiseau, Patrick. *Texaco*. Trans. Rose-Myriam Réjouis and Val Vinokurov. New York: Vintage International, 1997.
Chamoiseau, Patrick, and Raphaël Confiant. *Lettres créoles: Tracées antillaises et continentales de la littérature—Haïti, Guadeloupe, Martinique, Guyane, 1635–1975*. Paris: Hatier, 1991.
Chapman, Herrick, and Laura L. Frader, eds. *Race in France: Interdisciplinary Perspectives on the Politics of Difference*. New York: Berghahn, 2004.
Charavay, Étienne. *Lettres autographes composant la collection Alfred Bovet*. Paris: Librairie Charavay frères, 1885.
Chateaubriand, François-René. *Génie du christianisme*. 2 vols. Paris: Garnier, 1926.
Chatman, Samuel. "'There are no Slaves in France': A Re-Examination of Slave Laws in Eighteenth Century France." *Journal of Negro History* 85, no. 3 (2000): 144–153.

Bibliography

Chestnutt, Charles. *The Journals of Charles Chestnutt*. Ed. Richard Brodhead. Durham: Duke University Press, 1993.
Chew, William. Ed. *National Stereotypes in Perspective: Americans in France, Frenchmen in America*. Amsterdam: Rodopi, 2001.
Children's Literature Review: Volume 205—Alexandre Dumas and Neil Gaiman. Farmington Hills, MI: Gale/Cengage Learning, 2016.
Clouard, Henri. *Alexandre Dumas*. Paris: Albin Michel, 1955.
Cohen, Henry. "Lamartine's *Toussaint Louverture* (1848) and Glissant's *Monsieur Toussaint* (1961): A Comparison." *Studia Africana* 1, no. 3 (1979): 255–269.
Cohen, William. "The Algerian War and French Memory." *Contemporary European History* 9, no. 3 (2000): 489–500.
Cohen, William. "The Algerian War, the French State and Official Memory." *Historical Reflections* 28, no. 2 (2002): 219–239.
Cohen, William. *The French Encounter with Africans: White Response to Blacks, 1530–1880*. Reprint. Bloomington: Indiana University Press, 2003.
Coller, Ian. *Arab France: Islam and the Making of Modern Europe, 1798–1831*. Berkeley: University of California Press, 2011.
Compère, Daniel. *Le Monte-Cristo d'Alexandre Dumas: Lecture des textes*. Amiens, France: Encrage, 1998.
Condé, Maryse. "The Stealers of Fire: The French-Speaking Writers of the Caribbean and Their Strategies of Liberation." *Journal of Black Studies* 35, no. 2 (2004): 154–164.
Conklin, Alice, Sarah Fishman, and Robert Zaretsky. *France and Its Empire Since 1870*. Cambridge: Cambridge University Press, 2011.
Connor, Walker. "A Nation is a Nation, is a State, is an Ethnic Group, is a..." *Ethnic and Racial Studies* 1 (October 1978): 377–400.
Constant, Fred. "Aimé Césaire et la politique: sept leçons de leadership." *French Politics, Culture and Society* 27, no. 3 (2009): 34–43.
Constant, Fred. "Pour une lecture sociale des revendications mémorielles 'victimaires.'" *Esprit* (February 2007): 105–116.
Constant, Fred, and Justin Daniel, eds. *1946–1996: Cinquante ans de départementalisation outre-mer*. Paris: L'Harmattan, 1997.
Cook, Mercer. "The Haitian Novel." *The French Review* 19, no. 6 (1946): 406–412.
Cook, Mercer. "The Literary Contribution of the French West Indian." *Journal of Negro History* 25, no. 4 (1940): 520–530.
Cook, Mercer. "The Negro in French Literature: An Appraisal." *French Review* 23, no. 5 (1950): 378–388.
Cook, Mercer. "President Senghor's Visit: A Tale of Five Cities." *African Forum* 2, no. 3 (1967), 78–79.
Cook, Mercer. "The Race Problem in Paris and the French West Indies." *Journal of Negro Education* 8, no. 4 (1939): 673–680.
Costantini, Dino. *Mission civilisatrice: Le rôle de l'histoire coloniale dans la construction de l'identité politique française*. Paris: Découverte, 2008.
Crogman, William, and Henry Kletzing. *Progress of a Race, or, the Remarkable Advancement of the American Negro*. Atlanta: J.L. Nichols, 1898.
Crouche, Sheila. *Globalization and Belonging: The Politics of Identity in a Changing World*. Lanham, MD: Rowman & Littlefield, 2003.
Cunard, Nancy, ed. *Negro: An Anthology*. New York: Continuum, 1996.
D'Alméras, Henri. *Alexandre Dumas et les Trois Mousquetaires*. Paris: Edgar Malfère, 1929.
Damas, Léon. "Price-Mars, le père du haïtianisme." *Présence Africaine* 32–33 (1960): 166–178.

Bibliography

Daniel, Justin. "Aimé Césaire et les Antilles françaises: une histoire inachevée?" *French Politics, Culture and Society* 27, no. 3 (2009): 24–33.
Dantzig, Charles, ed. *Le Grand Livre de Dumas*. New York: Belles Lettres/toExcel, 1999.
Dash, Comtesse (Vicomtesse de Saint-Mars). *Mémoires des autres*. Paris: Librairie Illustrée, 1896–1898.
Dash, J. Michael. *Literature and Ideology in Haiti: 1915–1961*. London: Macmillan, 1981.
Daut, Marlene. "Haiti and the Black Romantics: Enlightenment and Color Prejudice After the Haitian Revolution in Alexandre Dumas's *Georges* (1843)." *Studies in Romanticism* 56 (Spring 2017): 73–91.
David, James. *Who Is Black? One Nation's Definition*. University Park: Pennsylvania University Press, 1991.
Davidson, Arthur. *Alexandre Dumas: His Life and Works*. Westminster, UK: Archibald Constable, 1902.
Dayan, Joan. "France Reads Haiti: René Depestre's *Hadriana dans tous mes rêves*." *Yale French Studies* 83 (1993): 154–175.
Daykin, Jeffer. "'They Themselves Contribute to Their Misery': The Justification of Slavery in Eighteenth-Century French Travel Narratives." *European Legacy* 11, no. 6 (2006): 623–632.
Defarges, Philippe Moreau. *Repentance et réconciliation*. Paris: Les Presses de Sciences Po, 1999.
Delacampagne, Christian. "Torturante Mémoire." *French Politics, Culture, and Society* 19, no. 3 (2001): 95–107.
Demangeon, Albert. *L'Union française: France et outre-mer*. Paris: Hachette, 1942.
Derrida, Jacques. *Margins of Philosophy*. Trans. Allan Bass. Chicago: University of Chicago Press, 1982.
Desormeaux, Daniel. *Alexandre Dumas, fabrique d'immortalité*. Paris: Classiques Garnier, 2014.
Dewitte, Philippe. *Les mouvements nègres en France, 1919–1939*. Paris: L'Harmattan, 1985.
Diawara, Manthia. "Reading Africa through Foucault: V.Y. Mudimbe's Reaffirmation of the Subject." *October* 55 (Winter 1990): 79–92.
Dictionnaire de L'Académie française. 5th ed. Paris: J.J. Smits, 1798.
Dictionnaire de L'Académie française. 6th ed. Paris: Firmin-Didot frères, 1835.
Dine, Philip. "Decolonizing the Republic." *Contemporary French and Francophone Studies* 12, no. 2 (2008): 173–181.
Diop, Cheikh Anta. *The African Origin of Civilization: Myth or Reality*. Chicago: Lawrence Hill, 1974.
Dirks, Nicholas, ed. *Colonialism and Culture*. Ann Arbor: University of Michigan Press, 1992.
Donnelly, Jack. *International Human Rights*. 2nd ed. Boulder: Westview, 1998.
Douglass, Frederick. *Frederick Douglass: Autobiographies*. Ed. Henry Louis Gates, Jr. New York: Library of America College Editions, 1996.
Du Bois, W.E.B. *Black Reconstruction in America, 1860–1880*. Reprint. New York: Free Press, 1998.
Du Bois, W.E.B. *Darkwater*. Reprint. New York: Washington Square, 2004.
Du Bois, W.E.B. *Dusk of Dawn: An Essay Toward an Autobiography of a Race Concept*. Reprint. New York: Schocken, 1970.
Du Bois, W.E.B. *The Souls of Black Folk*. Reprint. New York: Penguin, 1989.
Dubois, Laurent. *Avengers of the New World: The Story of the Haitian Revolution*. Cambridge: Belknap/Harvard University Press, 2004.
Dubois, Laurent. *A Colony of Citizens: Revolution and Slave Emancipation in the French Caribbean, 1787–1804*. Chapel Hill: University of North Carolina Press, 2004.

Bibliography

Dubois, Laurent. "*La République métissée*: Citizenship, Colonialism, and the Borders of French History." *Cultural Studies* 14, no. 1 (2000): 15–34.
Duclert, Vincent. "L'État et les historiens." *Regards sur l'actualité* 325 (November 2006): 5–15.
Dumas, Alexandre. *Adventures in Algeria*. Trans. and ed. Alma Elizabeth Murch. Philadelphia: Chilton, 1959.
Dumas, Alexandre. *Adventures in Spain*. Trans. and ed. Alma Elizabeth Murch. Philadelphia: Chilton, 1959.
Dumas, Alexandre. *Adventures in Switzerland*. Trans. and ed. R.W. Plummer and A. Craig Bell. Philadelphia: Chilton, 1960.
Dumas, Alexandre. *Adventures with My Pets*. Trans. and ed. A. Craig Bell. Philadelphia: Chilton, 1960.
Dumas, Alexandre. *Le Caucase*. 3 vols. Paris: Calmann-Lévy, 1889.
Dumas, Alexandre. *Charles VII at the Homes of his Great Vassals*. Trans. and ed. Dorothy Trench-Bonett. Chicago: Noble, 1991.
Dumas, Alexandre. *Le Chevalier de Sainte-Hermine*. Ed. Claude Schopp. Paris: Phébus, 2005.
Dumas, Alexandre. *Le Comte de Monte-Cristo*. Ed. Jacques-Henry Bornecque. Paris: Garnier, 1956.
Dumas, Alexandre. *Le Comte de Monte-Cristo*. Ed. François Tallandier. 2 vols. Paris: Le Livre de Poche, 1995.
Dumas, Alexandre. *Georges*. Eds. W.N. Rivers and John Matheus. Washington, D.C.: Associated Publishers, 1936.
Dumas, Alexandre. *Georges*. Eds. W.N. Rivers, John F. Matheus, and Messaoud Belateche. Washington, D.C.: Associated Publishers, 1970.
Dumas, Alexandre. *Georges*. Ed. Léon-François Hoffmann. Paris: Gallimard, 1974.
Dumas, Alexandre. *Georges*. Ed. Calixthe Beyala. Paris: Éditions 1, 1998.
Dumas, Alexandre. *Georges*. Trans. Tina Kover. New York: Modern Library, 2007.
Dumas, Alexandre. *Georges; or, the Isle of France*. Trans. Alfred Allinson. London: Methuen, 1903.
Dumas, Alexandre. *Histoire de mes bêtes*. 2nd ed. Paris: Michel Lévy, 1868.
Dumas, Alexandre. *The Last Vendée; or, The She-Wolves of Machecoul*. Trans. Katherine Prescott Wormeley. 2 vols. Boston: Colonial Press, n.d. [1894?].
Dumas, Alexandre. *Lettres à mon fils*. Ed. Claude Schopp. Paris: Mercure de France, 2008.
Dumas, Alexandre. *My Memoirs*. Trans. E.M. Waller. 6 vols. New York: Macmillan, 1907–1909.
Dumas, Alexandre. *The Progress of Democracy; Illustrated in the History of Gaul and France*. Trans. anonymous. Reprint. Honolulu: University Press of the Pacific, 2002.
Dumas, Alexandre. *The Three Musketeers*. Trans. anonymous. Norwalk, CT: Easton, 1978.
Dumas, Alexandre. *The Wolf-Leader*. Trans. Alfred Allinson. London: Methuen, 1904.
Dumas, Alexandre. *The Woman with the Velvet Necklace*. Trans. anonymous. Reprint. Amsterdam: Fredonia, 2002.
Dunbar, Paul Laurence. *The Collected Poetry of Paul Laurence Dunbar*. Ed. Joanne M. Braxton. Charlottesville: University Press of Virginia, 1993.
Durand, Pascal, and Sarah Mombert, eds. *Entre presse et littérature:* Le Mousquetaire, *journal de M. Alexandre Dumas*. Liège, Belgium: Bibliothèque de la Faculté de Philosophie et Lettres/Diffusion Droz, 2009.
Edwards, Brent Hayes. "Pebbles of Consonance: A Reply to Critics." *Small Axe* 17 (March 2005): 134–149.
Elias, Norbert, and John Scotson. *The Established and the Outsiders: A Sociological Enquiry into Community Problems*. 2nd ed. London: Sage, 1994.

Bibliography

Enz, Molly Krueger. "The Mulatto as Island and the Island as Mulatto in Alexandre Dumas's *Georges*." *The French Review* 80, no. 2 (2006): 383–394.
Evans, Martin, and Emmanuel Godin. *France: 1815–2003*. London: Arnold, 2004.
Fabian, Johannes. *Time and the Other: How Anthropology Makes Its Object*. New York: Columbia University Press, 1983.
Fabre, Geneviève, and Robert O'Meally, eds. *History and Memory in African-American Culture*. New York: Oxford University Press, 1994.
Fabre, Michel. *From Harlem to Paris: Black American Writers in France, 1840–1980*. Urbana: University of Illinois Press, 1993.
Fabre, Michel. "René Maran, the New Negro, and Negritude." *Phylon* 36, no. 3 (1975): 340–351.
Falk, Bernard. *The Naked Lady*. London: Hutchinson, 1952.
Fanon, Frantz. *Black Skin, White Masks*. Trans. Richard Philcox. New York: Grove, 2008.
Fanon, Frantz. *Toward the African Revolution*. New York: Grove, 1967.
Fanon, Frantz. *The Wretched of the Earth*. Trans. Richard Philcox. New York: Grove, 2004.
Featherstone, David. "The Spatial Politics of the Past Unbound: Transnational Networks and the Making of Political Identities." *Global Networks* 7, no. 4 (2007): 430–452.
Featherstone, Mike. *Undoing Culture: Globalization, Postmodernism, and Identity*. London: Sage, 1995.
Febvre, Lucien, and François Crouzet. *Nous sommes tous des sang-mêlés: Manuel d'histoire de la civilisation française*. Eds. Denis and Élisabeth Crouzet. Paris: A. Michel, 2012.
Feldblum, Miriam. *Reconstructing Citizenship: The Politics of Nationality Reform and Immigration in Contemporary France*. Albany: State University of New York Press, 1999.
Feldman, Hanna. *From a Nation Torn: Decolonizing Art and Representation in France, 1945–1962*. Durham: Duke University Press, 2014.
Féraud, Jean-François. *Dictionnaire critique de la langue française*. Paris: France-expansion, 1787.
Fernandes, Dominique. *Les douze muses d'Alexandre Dumas*. Paris: Grasset, 1999.
Fernandes, Dominique. *Jérémie! Jérémie!* Paris: Grasset, 2005.
Ferry, Gabriel. *Les Dernières années d'Alexandre Dumas, 1864–1870*. Paris: Calmann Lévy, 1883.
Feuser, W.F. "Afro-American Literature and Negritude." *Comparative Literature* 28, no. 4 (1976): 289–308.
Fillaire, Bernard. *Alexandre Dumas et associés*. Paris: Bartillat, 2002.
Finkelman, Paul, ed. *Encyclopedia of African American History, 1619–1895: From the Colonial Period to the Age of Frederick Douglass*. New York: Oxford University Press, 2006.
Fiorentino, Pier Angelo. *Comédies et comédiens*. 2 vols. Paris: Michel Lévy, 1866.
Firmin, Anténor. *The Equality of the Human Races*. Trans. Asselin Charles. New York: Garland, 2000.
Fischer, Sibylle. *Modernity Disavowed: Haiti and the Cultures of Slavery in the Age of Revolution*. Durham: Duke University Press, 2004.
Fitzgerald, Percy. *Life and Adventures of Alexandre Dumas*. 2 vols. London: Tinsley, 1873.
Foner, Philip, ed. *The Life and Writings of Frederick Douglass*. New York: International, 1950–1975.
Fontaney, Antoine. *Journal intime*. Ed. René Jasinski. Paris: Presses Françaises, 1925.
Forsdick, Charles. "Situating Haiti: On Some Early Nineteenth-Century Representations of Toussaint Louverture." *International Journal of Francophone Studies* 10, no. 1–2 (2007): 17–34.

Bibliography

Foucault, Michel. *History of Sexuality, Volume One: An Introduction*. Trans. R. Hurley. New York: Vintage, 1990.
Foucault, Michel. *Language, Counter-Memory, Practice: Selected Essays and Interviews*. Ed. Donald Bouchard. Ithaca: Cornell University Press, 1977.
Foucault, Michel. *"Society Must be Defended": Lectures at the Collège de France, 1975–1976*. Trans. David Macey. New York: Picador, 1997.
Foucher, Paul. *Les Coulisses du passé*. Paris: E. Dentu, 1873.
Franzoi, Stephen. *Psychology: A Discovery Experience*. Mason, OH: South-Western Cengage, 2011.
Frémeaux, Jacques. *Les empires coloniaux dans le processus de mondialisation*. Paris: Maisonneuve and Larose, 2002.
Fritzsche, Peter. *Stranded in the Present: Modern Time and the Melancholy of History*. Cambridge: Harvard University Press, 2004.
Fulton, Renée. "Review of *Georges*." *French Review* 46, no. 4 (1973): 884–885.
Gafaiti, Hafid, Patricia Lorchin, and David Troyansky, eds. *Transnational Spaces and Identities in the Francophone World*. Lincoln: University of Nebraska Press, 2009.
Gallaher, John. *General Alexandre Dumas: Soldier of the French Revolution*. Carbondale: Southern Illinois University Press, 1997.
Garraway, Doris. *The Libertine Colony: Creolization in the Early French Caribbean*. Durham: Duke University Press, 2005.
Garraway, Doris. "Memory as Reparation? The Politics of Remembering Slavery in France from Abolition to the Loi Taubira." *International Journal of Francophone Studies* 11, no. 3 (2008): 365–386.
Garraway, Doris, ed. *Tree of Liberty: Cultural Legacies of the Haitian Revolution in the Atlantic World*. Charlottesville: University of Virginia Press, 2008.
Garrigus, John. *Before Haiti: Race and Citizenship in French Saint-Domingue*. New York: Palgrave Macmillan, 2006.
Gauthier, Florence. *L'Aristocratie de l'épiderme: Le combat de la Société des Citoyens de Couleur, 1789–1791*. Paris: CNRS, 2007.
Gautier, Théophile. *Histoire du romantisme*. Paris: Charpentier, 1874.
Gellner, Ernest. *Nations and Nationalism*. Ithaca: Cornell University Press, 1983.
Gely, Cyril, and Eric Rouquette. *Signé Dumas*. Paris: Les Impressions Nouvelles, 2003.
Gengembre, Gérard. *Le Romantisme*. Paris: Ellipses, 1995.
Gensburger, Sarah. "From Jerusalem to Paris: The Institutionalization of the Category of 'Righteous of France.'" *French Politics, Culture and Society* 30, no. 2 (2012): 150–171.
Gibney, Mark, and Erik Roxstrom. "The Status of State Apologies." *Human Rights Quarterly* 23 (2001): 929–934.
Gilroy, Paul. *The Black Atlantic: Modernity and Double Consciousness*. Cambridge: Harvard University Press, 1993.
Gintzburger, Irène, and Frédérique Lurol, eds. *Alexandre Dumas: Deux siècles de gloire, 1802–2002*. Le Port-Marly, France: Musée de Château de Monte-Cristo, 2002.
Glinel, Charles. *Alexandre Dumas et son Œuvre*. Rheims, France: F. Michaud, 1884.
Glinel, Charles. *Le théâtre inconnu d'Alexandre Dumas père*. Paris: Revue Biblio-Iconographique, 1899.
Glissant, Édouard. *Caribbean Discourse: Selected Essays*. Trans. J.M. Dash. Charlottesville: University of Virginia Press, 1997.
Glissant, Édouard. *L'Intention poétique*. Paris: Seuil, 1969.
Glissant, Édouard. *Traité du Tout-Monde*. Paris: Gallimard, 1997.
Goncourt, Edmond de, and Jules de Goncourt. *Journal des Goncourt: mémoires de la vie littéraire*. Ed. Jean-Louis Cabanès. 2 vols. Paris: H. Champion, 2005–2008.
Goncourt, Edmond de, and Jules de Goncourt. *Pages from the Goncourt Journals*. Trans. and ed. Robert Baldick. Reprint. New York: New York Review of Books, 2007.

Bibliography

Gong, G.W. *The Standard of "Civilization" in International Society.* Oxford: Clarendon, 1984.
Gooch, G.P. *History and Historians in the Nineteenth Century.* 2nd ed. Boston: Beacon, 1959.
Gordon, Philip, and Sophie Meunier. "Globalization and French Cultural Identity." *French Politics, Culture, and Society* 19, no. 1 (2001): 22–41.
Grégoire, Abbé. *Considérations sur le mariage et sur le divorce adressées aux citoyens d'Haïti.* Paris: Badouin Frères, 1823.
Grivel, Charles. *Alexandre Dumas, l'homme 100 têtes.* Villeneuve d'Ascq, France: Presses Universitaires du Septentrion, 2008.
Grivel, Charles, ed. *Les Vies parallèles d'Alexandre Dumas.* Villeneuve d'Ascq, France: Presses Universitaires du Septentrion/Revue des Sciences humaines, 2008.
Guillaume, Alfred. "Conversation with Léopold Sédar Senghor on His Poetry and Baudelaire's." *The French Review* 52, no. 6 (1979): 839–847.
Haberland, E., ed. *Leo Frobinus: An Anthology.* Wiesdaden, Germany: Franz Steiner, 1973.
Hacker, Andrew. *Two Nations.* New York: Macmillan, 1992.
Hale, Grace. *Making Whiteness: The Culture of Segregation in the South, 1890–1940.* New York: Pantheon, 1998.
Hamilton, Thomas, ed. *The Anglo-African Magazine.* New York: Arno/New York Times, 1968.
Harbi, Mohammed, and Benjamin Stora, eds. *La Guerre d'Algérie: 1954–2004, la fin de l'amnésie.* Paris: Laffont, 2004.
Hargreaves, Alec. *Immigration, Race and Ethnicity in Contemporary France.* New York: Routledge, 1995.
Hargeaves, Alec, and Mark McKinney, eds. *Post-Colonial Culture in France.* London: Routledge, 1997.
Harper, Frances E.W. *Iola Leroy, or Shadows Uplifted.* Reprint. New York: Oxford University Press, 1990.
Harvey, David. *The Condition of Postmodernity: An Enquiry into the Origins of Cultural Change.* Cambridge, MA: Basil Blackwell, 1989.
Hefferman, James. Ed. *Representing the French Revolution: Literature, Historiography, and Art.* Hanover, NH: University Press of New England, 1992.
Helm, Mary. *From Darkness to Light: The Story of Negro Progress.* Chicago: F.H. Revell, 1909.
Hemmings, F.J.W. *Alexandre Dumas: The King of Romance.* New York: Charles Scribner's, 1979.
Henry, Gilles. *Dans les pas des ... Dumas. Les mousquetaires de l'aventure: Normandie, Haïti, Paris.* France: OREP, 2010.
Henry, Gilles. *Les Dumas: Le secret de Monte Cristo.* Paris: France-Empire, 1999.
Henry, Gilles. *Monte-Cristo ou l'extraordinaire aventure des ancêtres d'Alexandre Dumas.* Paris: Perrin, 1976.
Heuer, Jennifer. "The One-Drop Rule in Reverse? Interracial Marriages in Napoleonic and Restoration France." *Law and History Review* 27, no. 3 (2009): 515–548.
Hewa, Soma, and Darwin Stapleton, eds. *Globalization, Philanthropy, and Civil Society: Toward a New Political Culture in the Twenty-First Century.* New York: Springer, 2005.
Hill, Errol, and James Hatch. *A History of African American Theatre.* Cambridge: Cambridge University Press, 2003.
Hitchcott, Nicki. "Calixthe Beyala: Prizes, Plagiarism, and 'Authenticity.'" *Research in African Literatures* 37, no. 1 (2006): 100–109.
Hoffmann, Léon-François. *Haïti: lettres et l'être.* Toronto: GREF, 1992.

Bibliography

Hoffmann, Léon-François. "The Haitian Novel During the Last Ten Years." *Callaloo* 15, no. 3 (1992): 761–769.
Hoffmann, Léon-François. *Le Nègre romantique: Personnage littéraire et obsession collective*. Paris: Payot, 1973.
Hoffmann, Léon-François. "Les personnages noirs et mulâtres, la traite et l'esclavage dans l'œuvre d'Alexandre Dumas." *Cahiers de l'Association internationale des études françaises* (2012): 171–186.
Holland, Barbara. *Gentleman's Blood: A History of Dueling from Swords at Dawn to Pistols at Dusk*. New York: Bloomsbury, 2003.
Houssaye, Arsène. *Les Confessions: souvenirs d'un demi-siècle 1830–1880*. 6 vols. Paris: E. Dentu, 1885–1891.
Hovelacque, Abel. *Les nègres de l'Afrique sous équatoriale*. Paris: Lecrosnier et Babé, 1889.
Howell, Martha, and Walter Prevenier. *From Reliable Sources: An Introduction to Historical Methods*. Ithaca: Cornell University Press, 2001.
Huggins, Nathan. *Black Odyssey: The African-American Ordeal in Slavery*. New York: Vintage, 1990.
Hughes, Langston. *The Big Sea: An Autobiography*. Reprint. New York: Hill and Wang, 2001.
Hugo, Charles. *Les Hommes de l'exil*. Paris: Alphonse Lemerre, 1875.
Hunt, Lynn. *Inventing Human Rights: A History*. New York: W.W. Norton, 2007.
Hunt, Lynn. *Measuring Time, Making History*. New York: Central European University Press, 2008.
Hunt, Lynn. *Politics, Culture, and Class in the French Revolution*. Berkeley: University of California Press, 2004.
Huret, Jules. *De New York à la Nouvelle-Orléans*. Paris: Fasquelle, 1904.
Hurley, E. Anthony, ed. *Through a Black Veil: Readings in French Caribbean Poetry*. Trenton, NJ: Africa World Press, 2000.
Hurstfield, Jennifer. "The Educational Experiences of Mexican Americans: 'Cultural Pluralism' or 'Internal Colonialism'?" *Oxford Review of Education* 1, no. 2 (1975): 137–149.
Irele, Abiola. "Négritude: Literature and Ideology." *The Journal of Modern African Studies* 3, no. 4 (1965): 499–526.
Ivy, James. "Review of Senghor's *Négritude et Humanisme*," *African Forum* 1, no. 1 (1965): 139.
Jackson, Kenneth, ed. *Encyclopedia of New York City*. New Haven: Yale University Press, 1995.
Jennings, Lawrence. *French Anti-Slavery: The Movement for the Abolition of Slavery in France, 1802–1848*. New York: Cambridge University Press, 2000.
Jules-Rosette, Bennetta. *Black Paris: The African Writer's Landscape*. Urbana: University of Illinois Press, 1998.
Karlsgodt, Elizabeth Campbell. "Recycling French Heroes: The Destruction of Bronze Statues under the Vichy Regime." *French Historical Studies* 29, no. 1 (2006): 143–181.
Karr, Alphonse. *Le livre de bord: souvenirs, portraits, notes au crayon*. Paris: Calmann-Lévy, 1880.
Kesteloot, Lilyan. *Black Writers in French: A Literary History of Negritude*. Trans. Ellen Conroy Kennedy. Washington, D.C.: Howard University Press, 1991.
King, Stewart. *Blue Coat or Powdered Wig: Free People of Color in Pre-Revolutionary Saint-Domingue*. Athens: University of Georgia Press, 2001.
Kinnamon, Keneth, and Michel Fabre, eds. *Conversations with Richard Wright*. Jackson: University Press of Mississippi, 1993.

Bibliography

Kohn, Hans, ed. *Nationalism: Its Meaning and History*. Malabar, FL: Krieger, 1982.
Koshy, Susan. "Morphing Race into Ethnicity: Asian Americans and Critical Transformations of Whiteness." *boundary 2* 28, no. 1 (2001): 153–194.
Kramer, Steven. *Does France Still Count? The French Role in the New Europe*. Westport, CT: Praeger, 1994.
Lacouture, Jean. *Alexandre Dumas à la conquête de Paris, 1822–1831*. Brussels: Complexe, 2005.
Lahlou, Raphaël. *Alexandre Dumas ou le don de l'enthousiasme*. Paris: Bernard Giovanangeli, 2006.
Lambert, Michael. "From Citizenship to Negritude: 'Making a Difference' in Elite Ideologies of Colonized Francophone West Africa." *Comparative Studies in Society and History* 35, no. 2 (1993): 239–262.
Landru, Robert. *À propos d'Alexandre Dumas: les aïeux, le général, le bailli, premiers amis*. Paris: Landru, 1977.
Latour, Bruno. *We Have Never Been Modern*. Trans. Catherine Porter. Cambridge: Harvard University Press, 1993.
Launay, Vicomte de (Delphine de Girardin). *Lettres parisiennes*. Vol. 4. Paris: Michel Lévy, 1857.
Lawrence, Jonathan. "The New French Minority Politics." The Brookings Institution. U.S.-France Analysis Series, March 2003.
Lebel, Roland. *Études de littérature coloniale*. Paris: J. Peyronnet, 1928.
Lebovics, Herman. *Bringing the Empire Back Home: France in the Global Age*. Durham: Duke University Press, 2004.
Lebovics, Herman. *True France: The Wars over Cultural Identity, 1900–1945*. Ithaca: Cornell University Press, 1992.
Lecomte, Jules. *Lettres de Van Engelgom*. Reprint. Paris: Boissard, 1925.
Lecomte, L. Henry. *Alexandre Dumas*. Paris: Tallandier, 1902.
Legum, Colin. *Pan-Africanism: A Short Political Guide*. New York: Praeger, 1962.
Lemaignen, Robert, Léopold Senghor, and Sisowath Youtévong, eds. *La communauté impériale française*. Paris: Alsatia, 1945.
Letourneux, Matthieu, and Isabelle Safa, eds. *Mousquetaires! (Cahiers Alexandre Dumas 43)*. Paris: Classiques Garnier, 2017.
Lequin, Yves, ed. *La Mosaïque France: histoire des étrangers et de l'immigration en France*. Paris: Larousse, 1988.
Lewis, David, ed. *W.E.B. Du Bois: A Reader*. New York: Henry Holt, 1995.
Lewis, Shireen. *Race, Culture, and Identity: Francophone West African and Caribbean Literature from Négritude to Créolité*. Lanham, MD: Lexington, 2006.
Liauzu, Claude. *La société française face au racisme*. Brussels: Complexe, 1999.
Locke, Alain, ed. *The New Negro: Voices of the Harlem Renaissance*. New York: Touchstone, 1997.
López, Ian Haney. *White by Law: The Legal Construction of Race*. New York: New York University Press, 1996.
Lucas-Dubreton, Jacques. *The Fourth Musketeer*. Trans. Maida Casteltun Darnton. New York: Coward-McCann, 1928.
Lynch, Kevin. *The Image of a City*. Cambridge: MIT Press, 1960.
Lyth, Peter, and Helmuth Trischler, eds. *Wiring Prometheus: Globalisation, History, and Technology*. Aarhus, Denmark: Aarhus University Press, 2004.
McFeely, William. *Frederick Douglass*. New York: W.W. Norton, 1991.
Maldonado, Lionel. "Internal Colonialism and Triangulation: A Research Example." *Social Service Review* 53, no. 3 (1979): 464–473.
Manning, Patrick. *Francophone Sub-Saharan Africa, 1880–1985*. Cambridge: Cambridge University Press, 1998.

Bibliography

Mansbach, Richard. *The Globle Puzzle: Issues and Actors in World Politics*. 2nd ed. Boston: Houghton Mifflin, 1997.
Maran, René. "Contribution of the Black Race to European Art." Trans. Mercer Cook. *Phylon* 10, no. 3 (1949): 240–241.
Martin, Pierre. "L'élection présidentielle et les élections législatives françaises de 2002." *French Politics, Culture, and Society* 21 (Spring 2003): 1–19.
Martin, Waldo, Jr. *The Mind of Frederick Douglass*. Chapel Hill: University of North Carolina Press, 1984.
Martone, Eric. "All for One, One for All: Recasting Alexandre Dumas as Popular Educator in France during the New Imperialism." *Global Education Review*. Forthcoming.
Martone, Eric. "Creating a Local Black Identity in a Global Context: The French Writer Alexandre Dumas as an African American *Lieu de Mémoire*." *Journal of Global History* 5, no. 3 (2010): 395–422.
Martone, Eric, ed. *The Black Musketeer: Reevaluating Alexandre Dumas in the Francophone World*. Newcastle upon Tyne: Cambridge Scholars, 2011.
Martone, Eric, ed. *Encyclopedia of Blacks in European History and Culture*. 2 vols. Westport, CT: Greenwood, 2009.
Masse, Fernand. "The Negro Race in French Literature." *Journal of Negro History* 18, no. 3 (1933): 225–245.
Massol, Chantal, ed. *Stendhal, Balzac, Dumas: Un récit romantique?* Toulouse: Presses Universitaires du Mirail, 2006.
Mauco, Georges. *Les Étrangers en France et le problème du racisme*. Paris: La Pensée Universelle, 1977.
Maurice, Charles. *Histoire anecdotique du théâtre, de la littérature et de diverses impressions contemporaines*. 2 vols. Paris: H. Plon, 1856.
Maurois, André. *Les Trois Dumas*. Paris: Librairie Hachette, 1957.
Maurois, André. *The Titans: A Three-Generation Biography of the Dumas*. Trans. Gerard Hopkins. New York: Harper and Brothers, 1957.
Mayer, Nonna. *Ces Français qui votent Le Pen*. Paris: Flammarion, 2002.
Mazlish, Bruce. *The Idea of Humanity in a Global Era*. New York: Palgrave Macmillan, 2008.
Mazlish, Bruce, and Leo Marx, eds. *Progress: Fact or Illusion?* Ann Arbor: University of Michigan Press, 1998.
Mazzeo, Tilar. *Plagiarism and Literary Property in the Romantic Period*. Philadelphia: University of Pennsylvania Press, 2007.
McGrane, Bernard. *Beyond Anthropology*. New York: Columbia University Press, 1989.
Memmi, Albert. *Portrait du colonisé, précédé du portrait du colonisateur*. Paris: Gallimard, 1985.
Metternich, Pauline de. *Souvenirs de la princesse Pauline de Metternich, 1859–1871*. Paris: H. Plon, 1922.
Miller, Christopher. *The French Atlantic Triangle: Literature and Culture of the Slave Trade*. Durham: Duke University Press, 2008.
Mirecourt, Eugène de. *Alexandre Dumas*. Paris: Gustave Havard, 1856.
Mirecourt, Eugène de. *Fabrique de Romans, Maison Alexandre Dumas et compagnie*. Paris: Hauquelin et Bautruche, 1845.
Mitchell, Timothy. *Colonising Egypt*. Berkeley: University of California Press, 1991.
Molande, Bright. "Rewriting Memory: Ideology of Difference in the Desire and Demand for Whiteness." *European Journal of American Culture* 27, no. 3 (2008): 178–190.
Morrison, Toni. *Playing in the Dark: Whiteness and the Literary Imagination*. Cambridge: Harvard University Press, 1992.
Moses, Wilson. *Creative Conflict in African American Thought*. Cambridge: Cambridge University Press, 2004.

Bibliography

Moses, Wilson. "Dark Forests and Barbarian Vigor: Paradox, Conflict, and Africanity in Black Writing before 1914." *American Literary History* 1, no. 3 (1989): 637–655.

Motte, Dean de la, and Jeannene Pryzblyski, eds. *Making the News: Modernity and the Mass Press in Nineteenth-Century France*. Amherst: University of Massachusetts Press, 1999.

Moutoussamy, Ernest. *Aimé Césaire: Député à l'Assemblée nationale, 1945–1993*. Paris: L'Harmattan, 1993.

Mudimbe, V.Y. *The Invention of Africa*. Bloomington: Indiana University Press, 1998.

Mudimbe-Boyi, Elisabeth, ed. *Empire Lost: France and Its Other Worlds*. Lanham, MD: Lexington, 2009.

Munro, Martin. "Can't Stand Up for Falling Down: Haiti, Its Revolutions, and Twentieth-Century Negritudes." *Research in African Literatures* 35, no. 2 (2004): 1–17.

Murdoch, H. Adlai, and Anne Donadey, eds. *Postcolonial Theory and Francophone Literary Studies*. Gainesville: University Press of Florida, 2005.

Murkoff, Heidi, and Sharon Mazel. *What to Expect When You're Expecting*. 4th ed. New York: Workman, 2008.

Murphy, David. "Birth of a Nation? The Origins of Senegalese Literature in French." *Research in African Literatures* 39, no. 1 (2008): 48–69.

Nadar. *Quand j'étais photographe*. Reprint. Le Plan-de-la-Tour, France: Éditions d'Aujourd'hui, 1979.

Nagapen, Amédée. *Esclavage et marronnage dans le roman Georges d'Alexandre Dumas: l'apport des chroniques de J.G. Milbert*. Mauritius: University of Mauritius, 2005.

Neave, Christine, and Hubert Charron. *Monte-Cristo: Château de Rêve*. Marly-le-Roi, France: Champflour/Syndicat Intercommunal de Monte-Cristo/ Société des Amis d'Alexandre Dumas, 1994.

Neave, Christine, and Digby Neave, eds. *Iconographie d'Alexandre Dumas père*. Marly-le-Roi, France: Champflour/Société des Amis d'Alexandre Dumas, 1991.

Necheles, Ruth. *The Abbé Grégoire, 1787–1831: The Odyssey of an Egalitarian*. Westport, CT: Greenwood, 1971.

Nelson, Charmaine. "Hiram Power's America: Shackles, Slaves, and the Racial Limits of Nineteenth-Century National Identity." *Canadian Review of American Studies* 34, no. 2 (2004): 167–183.

Nelson, Emmanuel. *African American Dramatists: An A to Z Guide*. Westport, CT: Greenwood, 2004.

Nelson, William. "Making Men: Enlightenment Ideas of Racial Engineering." *American Historical Review* 115, no. 5 (2010): 1364–1394.

Nesbitt, Nick. *Universal Emancipation: The Haitian Revolution and the Radical Enlightenment*. Charlottesville: University of Virginia Press, 2008.

Net, Mariana. *Alexandre Dumas, écrivain du XXIe siècle: L'Impatience du lendemain*. Paris: L'Harmattan, 2008.

Nicolas, Armand. *Histoire de la Martinique: de 1848 à 1939*. Paris: L'Harmattan, 1996.

Niles, Blair, and Robert Niles. *Black Haiti: A Biography of Africa's Eldest Daughter*. New York: Grosset and Dunlap, 1926.

Noiriel, Gérard. *The French Melting Pot: Immigration, Citizenship, and National Identity*. Trans. Geoffroy de Laforcade. Minneapolis: University of Minnesota Press, 1996.

Nora, Pierre, and Lawrence Kritzman, eds. *Realms of Memory: The Construction of the French Past*. Trans. Arthur Goldhammer. Vol. I. New York: Columbia University Press, 1996.

O'Brien, Laura. *The Republican Line: Caricature and French Republican Identity, 1830–1852*. Manchester: Manchester University Press, 2015.

O'Neill, Charles. *Séjour: Parisian Playwright from Louisiana*. Lafayette: University of Southwestern Louisiana, 1995.

Bibliography

Onyioha, K.O.K. *Revival of Culture in Independent Nigeria.* Enugu: Eastern Nigeria Printing, 1962.
Oulmont, Charles. "Un portrait d'Alexandre Dumas par Daumier." *Les Arts* 186 (1920): 23.
Palaiseau, Mlle de. *Histoire des Mesdemoiselles de Saint-Janvier: Les deux seules blanches conservées à Saint-Domingue.* 2nd ed. Paris: J.J. Blaise, 1812.
Paldiel, Mordecai. "Righteous Gentiles and Courageous Jews: Acknowledging and Honoring Rescuers of Jews." *French Politics, Culture, and Society* 30, no. 2 (2012): 134–149.
Parigot, Hippolyte. *Alexandre Dumas père.* Paris: Librairie Hachette, 1902.
Pastoureau, Michel. *Black: The History of a Color.* Princeton: Princeton University Press, 2008.
Peabody, Sue, and Tyler Stovall, eds. *The Color of Liberty: Histories of Race in France.* Durham: Duke University Press, 2003.
Pâme, Stella. *Cyrille Bissette: Un martyr de la liberté.* Fort-de-France, Martinique: Desormeaux, 1999.
Parekh, Bhikku, ed. *Colour, Culture, and Consciousness: Immigrant Intellectuals in Britain.* London: Allen and Unwin, 1974.
Peabody, Sue. *"There Are No Slaves in France": The Political Culture of Race and Slavery in the Ancien Régime.* New York: Oxford University Press, 1996.
Peng, Youjun. *La nation chez Alexandre Dumas.* Paris: L'Harmattan, 2003.
Perret, J. John. "Victor Séjour: Black French Playwright from Louisiana." *French Review* 57, no. 2 (1983): 187–193.
Pfaff, Françoise. *Conversations with Maryse Condé.* Lincoln: University of Nebraska Press, 1996.
Philips, Peggy. *Republican France, Divided Loyalties.* Westport, CT: Greenwood, 1993.
Pifteau, Benjamin. *Alexandre Dumas en manches de chemise.* Reprint. Montreal: Joyeux Roger, 2009.
Pilbeam, Pamela. *Republicanism in Nineteenth-Century France, 1814–1871.* New York: St. Martin's Press, 1995.
Poirrier, Philippe. *L'État et la culture en France au XXe siècle.* 2nd ed. Paris: Librairie Générale Française, 2006.
Poisson, Georges. *Combats pour le patrimoine: souvenirs, 1948–2008.* Paris: Pygmalion, 2009.
Poisson, Georges. *Monte-Cristo, un château de roman.* Marly-le-Roi, France: Champflour, 1987.
Pooser, C.L. "Creole in the Public Eye: Written Instances of Creole in Public Spaces in Guadeloupe." *French Cultural Studies* 22, no. 4 (2011): 289–302.
Popkin, Jeremy. *Facing Racial Revolution: Eyewitness Accounts of the Haitian Insurrection.* Chicago: University of Chicago Press, 2007.
Popkin, Jeremy, and Richard Popkin, eds. *The Abbé Grégoire and His World.* Dordrecht, Netherlands: Kluwer, 2000.
Prévost, Christine. "D'un rôle convenu à la promotion d'un personnage original: le maure de *Fiesque* à *Charles VII*." *Le Rocambole: Bulletin des Amis du Roman populaire* 36 (Fall 2006): 33–42.
Pryde, Marion Jackson, and Beatrice Jackson Fleming. *Distinguished Negroes Abroad.* Washington, D.C.: Associated, 1946.
Reed, Frank Wild. *A Bibliography of Alexandre Dumas père.* Pinner Hill, Middlesex, UK: J.A. Neuhuys, 1933.
Régent, Frédéric. *La France et ses esclaves: De la colonisation aux abolitions, 1620–1848.* Paris: Grasset et Fasquelle, 2007.
Reinhardt, Catherine. *Claims to Memory: Beyond Slavery and Emancipation in the French Caribbean.* New York: Berghahn, 2006.

Bibliography

Reiss, Tom. *The Black Count: Glory, Revolution, Betrayal, and the Real Count of Monte Cristo*. New York: Broadway Paperbacks, 2012.
Remond, René. "Pourquoi abroger les lois mémorielles?" *Regards sur l'actualité* 325 (November 2006): 17–25.
Reno, Fred. "Aimé Césaire ou l'ambivalence féconde." *French Politics, Culture and Society* 27, no. 3 (2009): 19–23.
Resnick, Daniel. "The Society of the Friends of the Blacks and the Abolition of Slavery." *French Historical Studies* 7, no. 4 (1972): 558–569.
Reynaud, Jacques (Vicomtesse de Saint-Mars). *Portraits contemporains*. Paris: Amyot, 1859.
Ribbe, Claude. *Le Diable Noir: Biographie du général Alexandre Dumas, père de l'écrivain*. Monaco: Alphée, 2009.
Rioux, Jean-Pierre. "Perte de mémoire et déni du temps." *Regards sur l'actualité* 325 (2006): 37–45.
Robertson, Roland. *Globalization: Social Theory and Global Culture*. Thousand Oaks, CA: Sage, 1992.
Robin, Charles. *Galerie des Gens de lettres au XIXe siècle*. Paris: V. Lecou, 1848.
Rogers, J.A. *World's Great Men of Color, Volume II: Europe, South and Central America, the West Indies, and the United States*. Reprint. New York: Touchstone, 1996.
Rowell, Charles. "It Is Through Poetry That One Copes with Solitude: An Interview with Aimé Césaire." *Callaloo* 38 (Winter 1989): 49–67.
Russell, Scott. "Héroïsme et Bâtardise: Alexandre Dumas's *Georges*." PhD dissertation. Brown University, 1992.
Ruthven, Todd. *The Laughing Mulatto: The Story of Alexandre Dumas*. London: Rich and Cowan, 1939.
Sahlins, Peter. *Unnaturally French: Foreign Citizens in the Old Regime and After*. Ithaca: Cornell University Press, 2004.
Said, Edward. *Orientalism*. New York: Vintage, 2003.
Sala-Molins, Louis. *Dark Side of the Light: Slavery and the French Enlightenment*. Trans. John Conteh-Morgan. Minneapolis: University of Minnesota Press, 2006.
Santa, Ángels, and Francisco Lafarga, eds. *Alexandre Dumas y Victor Hugo: Viaje de los textos y textos de viaje*. Lleida, Spain: Pagès, 2006.
Santa, Ángels, ed. *Honoré de Balzac: Camins creuats*. Lleida, Spain: Pagès, 1997.
Sarton, George. *Six Wings: Men of Science in the Renaissance*. Bloomington: Indiana University Press, 1957.
Sartre, Jean-Paul. *Being and Nothingness: An Essay on Phenomenological Ontology*. Trans. Hazel Barnes. London: Routledge, 2003.
Sautman, Francesca. "Hip-Hop/scotch: 'Sounding Francophone' in French and United States Cultures." *Yale French Studies* 100 (2002): 95–112.
Savarèse, Eric. *Histoire coloniale et immigration: une invention de l'étranger*. Brussels: Séguier, 2000.
Saxton, Alexander. *The Rise and Fall of the White Republic: Class Politics and Mass Culture in Nineteenth-Century America*. New York: Verso, 1990.
Schäfer, Wolf. "Global Civilization and Local Cultures: A Crude Look at the Whole." *International Sociology* 16, no. 3 (2001): 301–319.
Schäfer, Wolf. "The New Global History: Toward a Narrative for Pangaea Two." *Erwägen Ethik* 14 (April 2003): 75–88.
Schäfer, Wolf. *Ungleichzeitigkeit als Ideologie: Beiträge zur Historischen Aufklärung*. Frankfurt am Main, Germany: Fischer Sozialwissenschaft, 1994.
Schlossman, Beryl. "Balzac's Art of Excess." *Modern Language Notes* 109, no. 5 (1994): 872–896.
Scholte, Jan Aart. *Globalization: A Critical Introduction*. 2nd ed. New York: Palgrave Macmillan, 2005.

Bibliography

Schopp, Claude. *Alexandre Dumas: Genius of Life*. Trans. A.J. Koch. New York: Franklin Watts, 1988.
Schopp, Claude, ed. *Alexandre Dumas en bras de chemise*. Paris: Maisonneuve et Larose, 2002.
Schopp, Claude, ed. *Frères d'armes de la révolution romantique: Lettres d'Alexandre Dumas au Baron Taylor et à Adrien Dauzats*. Paris: Fondation Taylor, 1993.
Schopp, Claude, and Fernande Bassan, eds. *Cent-Cinquante Ans après*: Les Trois Mousquetaires *et* Le Comte de Monte Cristo. Marly-le-Roi, France: Champflour/Société des Amis d'Alexandre Dumas, 1995.
Senghor, Léopold. *Hommage à René Maran*. Paris: Présence Africaine, 1965.
Senghor, Léopold. *Liberté I: Négritude et Humanisme*. Paris: Seuil, 1964.
Senghor, Léopold, ed. *Anthologie de la nouvelle poésie nègre et malgache de langue française*. Paris: Presses Universitaires de France, 1948.
Shelton, Austin. "The Black Mystique: Reactionary Extremes in 'Negritude.'" *African Affairs* 63 (April 1964): 115–128.
Shields, James. "The Far Right Vote in France: From Consolidation to Collapse?" *French Politics, Culture, and Society* 28, no. 1 (2010): 27–36.
Silverman, Max. *Deconstructing the Nation: Immigration, Racism and Citizenship in Modern France*. London: Routledge, 1992.
Silverstein, Paul. *Algeria in France: Transpolitics, Race, and Nation*. Bloomington: Indiana University Press, 2004.
Silvestre, Charles, ed. *La Torture aux aveux: Guerre d'Algérie, l'appel à la reconnaissance du crime d'État*. Vauvert, France: Au diable Vauvert, 2004.
Simon, Gustave. *Histoire d'une collaboration: Alexandre Dumas et Auguste Maquet*. Paris: G. Crès, 1919.
Singh, Amritjit, and Peter Schmidt, eds. *Postcolonial Theory and the United States*. Jackson: University Press of Mississippi, 2000.
Sithole, Ndabaningi. *African Nationalism*. Cape Town: Oxford University Press, 1959.
Smith, Charles. *Les Trois Dumas*. Woodstock, IL: Dramatic, 2003.
Socé, Ousmane. *Mirages de Paris*. Paris: Nouvelles Éditions Latines, 1937.
Spratlin, V.B. "Review of *Georges* by Dumas (ed. W. N. Rivers and J. F. Matheus)." *Journal of Negro Education* 6, no. 2 (1937): 202–203.
Spurr, Harry. *The Life and Writings of Alexandre Dumas, 1802–1870*. Reprint. Honolulu: University Press of the Pacific, 2003.
Stanford, P. Thomas. *The Tragedy of the Negro in America*. Boston: C.A. Wasto, 1897.
Stein, Robert. *The French Sugar Business in the Eighteenth Century*. Baton Rouge: Louisiana State University Press, 1988.
Stoler, Ann. *Race and the Education of Desire: Foucault's History of Sexuality and the Colonial Order of Things*. Durham: Duke University Press, 1995.
Storey, William. *Writing History: A Guide for Students*. 2nd ed. New York: Oxford University Press, 2004.
Stovall, Tyler. *Paris Noir: African Americans in the City of Light*. New York: Mariner, 1996.
Stovall, Tyler, and George van den Abbeele, eds. *French Civilization and Its Discontents: Nationalism, Colonialism, Race*. Lanham, MD: Lexington, 2003.
Striker, Ardell. "Spectacle in the Service of Humanity: The Negrophile Play in France from 1789 to 1850." *Black American Literature Forum* 19, no. 2 (1985): 76–82.
Sundquist, Eric, ed. *The Oxford W.E.B. Du Bois Reader*. New York: Oxford University Press, 1996.
Taguieff, Pierre-André. *The Force of Prejudice: On Racism and Its Doubles*. Trans. and ed. Hassan Melehy. Minneapolis: University of Minnesota Press, 2001.
Tevoedjre, Albert. *L'Afrique révoltée*. Paris: Présence Africaine, 1958.

Bibliography

Thibau, Jacques. *Le Temps de Saint-Domingue: L'Esclavage et la Revolution francaise.* Paris: J.C. Lattès, 1989.

Thilmans, Guy, ed. "La Relation de François de Paris (1682–1683)." *Bulletin de l'Institut Fondamental d'Afrique Noir* 38 (1976): 1–51.

Thomas, Dominic. *Black France: Colonialism, Immigration, and Transnationalism.* Bloomington: Indiana University Press, 2006.

Tin, Louis-Georges. "Who Is Afraid of Blacks in France? The Black Question: The Name Taboo, the Number Taboo." *French Politics, Culture, and Society* 26, no. 1 (2008): 32–44.

Tishkov, Valery. "Forget the 'Nation': Post-Nationalist Understanding of Nationalism." *Ethnic and Racial Studies* 23, no. 4 (2000): 625–650.

Todorov, Tzvetan. *On Human Diversity: Nationalism, Racism, and Exoticism in French Thought.* Trans. Catherine Porter. Cambridge: Harvard University Press, 1993.

Toesca, Catherine. *Les 7 Monte-Cristo d'Alexandre Dumas.* Paris: Maisonneuve and Larose, 2002.

Tomlinson, John. *Cultural Imperialism: A Critical Introduction.* Baltimore: Johns Hopkins University Press, 1991.

Torpey, John. "'Making Whole What Has Been Smashed': Reflections on Reparations." *The Journal of Modern History* 73, no. 2 (2001): 333–358.

Toussenel, Alphonse. *L'Esprit des bêtes: Vénerie française et zoologie passionnelle.* Paris: Librairie Sociétaire, 1847.

Trouillot, Michel-Rolph. *Silencing the Past: Power and the Production of History.* Boston: Beacon, 1997.

Troyat, Henri. *Alexandre Dumas: Le cinquième mousquetaire.* Paris: Grasset et Fasquelle, 2005.

Tulard, Jean. *Alexandre Dumas, 1802–1870.* Paris: Figures et plumes, 2008.

Valenti, Suzanne. "The Black Diaspora: Negritude in the Poetry of West Africans and Black Americans." *Phylon* 34, no. 4 (1973): 390–398.

Van Sertima, Ivan, ed. *Great African Thinkers.* Oxford: Transaction, 1986.

Vastey, Baron Jean Louis de. *The Colonial System Unveiled.* Trans. Chris Bongie. Liverpool: Liverpool University Press, 2014.

Védrine, Hubert, with Dominique Moïsi. *France in an Age of Globalization.* Trans. Philip Gordon. Washington, D.C.: Brookings Institution, 2001.

Vergès, Françoise. *La Mémoire enchaînée: questions sur l'esclavage.* Paris: Albin Michel, 2006.

Vichniac, Judith. "French Socialists and *Droit à la Différence*: A Changing Dynamic." *French Politics, Culture, and Society* 9, no. 1 (1991): 40–56.

Vidal, Cécile, and François-Joseph Ruggiu, eds. *Sociétés, colonisations et esclavages dans le monde atlantique.* Bécherel, France: Perséides, 2009.

Villemessant, Hippolyte de. *Mémoires d'un journaliste: Les Hommes de mon temps.* Paris: E. Dentu, 1872.

Virey, Julien Joseph. *Histoire naturelle du genre humain.* Paris: Crochard, 1824.

Une Visite au Château de Monte-Cristo. Le Port-Marly, France: Syndicat Intercommunal de Monte-Cristo, 2004.

Waberi, Abdourahman. "Les enfants de la postcolonie: Esquisse d'une nouvelle génération d'écrivains francophones d'Afrique noire." *Notre librairie* 135 (September–December 1998): 8–15.

Waters, Sarah. "French Intellectuals and Globalisation: A War of Worlds." *French Cultural Studies* 22, no. 4 (2011): 303–320.

Waters, Sarah. "Globalization, the Confédération Paysanne, and Symbolic Power." *French Politics, Culture and Society* 28, no. 2 (2010): 96–117.

Weatherford, W.D. *Present Forces in Negro Progress.* New York: Association Press, 1912.

Bibliography

Weil, Patrick. *How to be French: Nationality in the Making since 1789*. Trans. Catherine Porter. Durham: Duke University Press, 2008.
Weil, Patrick. *Liberté, égalité, discriminations: L'identité nationale au regard de l'histoire*. Paris: Grasset, 2008.
Weil, Patrick, ed. *L'Esclavage, la colonisation, et après...* Paris: Presses Universitaires de France, 2005.
Wilder, Gary. *The French Imperial Nation-State: Negritude and Colonial Humanism between the Two World Wars*. Chicago: University of Chicago Press, 2005.
Wilder, Gary. "Race, Reason, Impasse: Césaire, Fanon, and the Legacy of Emancipation." *Radical History Review* 90 (Fall 2004): 31–61.
Wilson, Victor. *Le Général Alexandre Dumas: Soldat de la Liberté*. Quebec: Quisqueya-Québec, 1977.
Woodson, Carter G. *The Mis-Education of the Negro*. Reprint. Radford, VA: Wilder, 2008.
Woodson, Carter G. "Review of *Five French Negro Authors* by Mercer Cook." *Journal of Negro History* 28, no. 4 (1943): 494–497.
Wright, Gordon. *France in Modern Times*. 5th ed. New York: W.W. Norton, 1995.
Wright, Richard. *The Outsider*. New York: Harper and Row, 1965.
Wright, Richard. *Twelve Million Black Voices*. London: Lindsay Drummond, 1947.
Wright, Richard. *White Man, Listen!* New York: Doubleday, 1957.
Wryeneth, Robert. "The Power of Apology and the Process of Historical Reconciliation." *The Public Historian* 23, no. 3 (2001): 9–38.
Zimmerman, Daniel. *Alexandre Dumas le Grand*. Paris: Phébus, 2002.

Index

Numbers in **_bold italics_** indicate pages with illustrations.
AD stands for Alexandre Dumas.

abolition: citizenship after 51, 95; commemorating 119–20; rivalry between abolitionists 51–55
Acté (AD) 133
Adventures with My Pets (AD) 28, 43–44
African Americans and New Negro Movement: counter-global identity formation 71–73, 74–77, 91–93; influence on *Négritude* 97, 102–3; view of AD as American 87–91, 103–4; view of AD as black 81–87; view of AD as white 77–80
Aldridge, Ira 86
Alexis (servant of AD) 41–44, **_42_**, 45
Anderson, Ester 88–89
Antony (AD) 23
assimilation 21–22, 60–61, 96–97, 105–8, 117–18
Audebrand, Philibert 59–60
L'Avenir (journal) 55–56, 57, 58

Balibar, Étienne 6
Balzac, Honoré de 13, 24, 33, 139
Barnabé, Jean 10, 127
Bell, A. Craig 116
Benitez-Rojo, Antonio 9–10
Bennett, Gwendolyn 90–91
Berlick (AD's nickname) 35–36
Bethel, Elizabeth 82
Bethune, Mary McLeod 90
Beyala, Calixthe 128–31
Bissette, Cyrille 41, 51–55
black Africans *see* African Americans and New Negro Movement; *Négritude* Movement; race
The Black Man, His Antecedents, His Genius, His Achievements (Brown) 89
Bloch, Ernst 18
Bodin, Jean 19
Bongie, Chris 9

Bontemps, Arna 90
Bornecque, Jacques-Henry 124
Broca, Paul 29
Brown, William Wells 82, 83, 89

Captain Pamphile (AD) 133
Césaire, Aimé 98, 99, 100, 101, 102, 104, 105, 106, 108
Chaffault, Monsieur du 50–51
Chamoiseau, Patrick 10, 97, 127, 128
Charbonneau, Abbé 56
Charles VII at the Homes of His Great Vassals (AD) 55, 132–33
Château de Monte Cristo 13–17, **_16_**, **_17_**, 20–21, 111–12, **_112_**
Chestnutt, Charles W. 69–70, 91, 122–23
Chirac, Jacques 120, 133–34, 138, 142
Cohen, William 29
Coleridge-Taylor, Samuel 76
collaborators, AD's use of 30–31, 83–84, 132, 139
colonial complex 60–61
colonialism: as dehumanizing 108; and European/Western superiority 18–19, 28–29, 70–71, 94–96; inclusion in national identity 6–10, 21–22, 33–34, 56–58, 59–61, 92–93, 114–15, 119; internal 74; *see also* francophone cultural movement; French Caribbean; *Négritude* Movement; race; slavery
Colonies étrangères et Haïti: Résultats de l'Émancipation anglaise (Schoelcher) 53
Des colonies françaises: Abolition immédiate de l'esclavage (Schoelcher) 53
Condé, Maryse 128
Confiant, Raphaël 10, 127
Cook, Mercer 88, 90, 94, 105, 107
The Count of Monte Cristo (AD) 14, 41, 69–70, 124, 125, 133

Index

Creole: identity 126–27; language 42–43, 127–28
culture *see* African Americans and New Negro Movement; francophone cultural movement; national identity and culture; *Négritude* Movement

Dalcour, Pierre 81
Damas, Léon 98, 100, 106
Dantan 27
Daumier, Honoré 26
De la littérature des nègres (Grégoire) 80
Decaux, Alain 111, 142
Decoin, Didier 11, 126, 133–34, 137
Defarges, Philippe Moreau 120
Delany, Martin Robinson 81
Delorme, Demesvar 62–63
Depardieu, Gérard 4
Depestre, René 62, 105
Diop, Cheikh Anta 99
Dormann, Geneviève 134
Dorval, Marie 36
Douglass, Frederick 76, 84, 85, 88
Du Bois, W.E.B. 71, 73, 75–76, 78, 83, 87, 91–92, 94
Dumas, Alexandre: depictions of 4–6, **15**, **25**, 25–26, **26**, 27, **27**, **33**, **42**, **64**, 68, **68**, **69**, **79**, 79–80, 115–16, **116**, **117**, 121, **121**, **135**; reception among African Americans (as Atlantic/American symbol 87–91, 103–4; as "black" symbol of modernity 81–87; compared to African American writers 76–77; evaluations of *Georges* 122–24; as symbolically white 77–80); reception and self-presentation in French metropole (as abolitionist 41, 84–85; ambiguity toward race 41–46, 59–60, 131–32; as celebrity figure 23; château as exotic 13–17, **16**, **17**, 20–21; contempt for and criticism of 24, 29–33, 78, 83–86; election efforts in French metropole 50–51; as exotic outsider 20–21, 23–29, 34; negative self-perception 34–40; as sentimental about ancestry 40–41; as supporter of racial mixing 46–48; as symbolically white 115–17); reception in francophone cultural movement (campaign to save château of 111–12; discourse on, during bicentennial 133–40; as francophone writer 118–19, 120–21, 126, 128–31; interment in Panthéon 133–36, 140–43); reception in French colonial world (candidature in Guadeloupe 51, 55–59, 61; as French Caribbean role model 41, 62–65; as too assimilated 105–8); writings (*Acté* 133; *Adventures with My Pets* 28, 43–44; *Antony* 23; *Captain Pamphile* 133; *Charles VII at the Homes of His Great Vassals* 55, 132–33; *The Count of Monte Cristo* 14, 41, 69–70, 124, 125, 133; *Gaul and France* 48; *Joseph Balsamo* 133; *The Last Vendée; or, The She-Wolves of Machecoul* 47–48; memoirs 35–36, 68–69; *The Woman with the Velvet Necklace* 47; see also *Georges*)
Dumas, Alexandre (son of AD) 63, 64
Dumas, Thomas-Alexandre (father of AD) 34, 35, 89
"Dumas and Blacks" (Hoffmann) 124
Dumas Society 111, 133–34
Dunbar, Paul Laurence 37
Durand, Hippolyte 13

Eau-de-Benjoin/Pierre/Paul (servant of AD) 44–46
The Elder Dumas (Richardson) 83–84
Ellis, Havelock 144
ethnic identity *see* francophone cultural movement; *Négritude* Movement

Fabre, Michel 69, 70
Fanon, Frantz 7, 60, 94, 96, 108–9, 120
Fernandez, Dominique 126, 137
Firmin, Anténor 128
Fitzgerald, Bertram 92
Five French Negro Authors (Cook) 90
Fontenay, Antoine 31
Foucault, Michel 29, 147
francophone cultural movement: and AD's interment in Panthéon 133–36, 140–43; context for emergence of 114–21; discourse on AD during bicentennial 133–40; "francophone" term 118; *Georges* as representative of 128–31; objectives 113–14, 118–19, 126–28
La Fraternité (journal) 63–64
French Academy 39
French Caribbean: AD as role model in 41, 62–65; candidacy elections in Guadeloupe 51, 55–59, 61; revolutions in 26, 43, 99–100, 119–20; rivalry for representation of 51–55; *see also* colonialism; francophone cultural movement; *Négritude* Movement
French Revolution 26, 99–100
Frobenius, Leo 98

Gaillardet, Frédéric 30–31
Gaul and France (AD) 48
Gautier, Théophile 23, 27
Georges (AD): ambiguity in 131–32; compared to broader literary output 132–33; initial commercial failure 122–23; praised as colonial race novel 123–26, 128–31; use of Creole in 43
Gérando, Joseph Marie de 18
Gilroy, Paul 73
Girardin, Delphine de 39–40
Girardin, Émile de 29

202

Index

Glissant, Édouard 10, 126, 127–28, 147
globalization: and cultural flux 127; impact on European worldview 18–19; and Western hegemony 70–73, 112–13
Godoy, Gian 88–89
Golden Legacy (Fitzgerald) 92
Goncourt brothers 37, 39
Gozlan, Léon 13–14
Grégoire, Abbé 3, 46–47
Grégoire, Abbé Henri 54, 58, 80
Grivel, Charles 125–26
Guadeloupe 51, 55–59, 61

L'Habitation Latiboliére 65, **66**
Haiti: AD as role model in 41, 62–65; cultural independence in 105–6; Haitian Revolution 26, 43, 99–100; as symbol 107
Hamel, Réginald 139
Harel, Félix 30
Hassan II, King of Morocco 111
Henry, Gilles 8, 125
An Historical Account of the Black Empire in Hayti (Rainsford) 89
Hoffmann, Léon-François 124, 125
Hughes, Langston 90
Hugo, Victor 24, 29, 39, 133, 138, 142, 143–44
Huret, Jules 95–96

identity *see* African Americans and New Negro Movement; francophone cultural movement; national identity and culture; *Négritude* Movement
internal colonialism 74

Joseph Balsamo (AD) 133

Kesteloot, Lilyan 62

Lacouture, Jean 40, 131–32
The Last Vendée; or, The She-Wolves of Machecoul (AD) 47–48
Lecomte, Jules 24
Le Pen, Jean-Marie 120
lieu de mémoire, as concept 10, 147
Lincoln, Abraham 84–85
Locke, Alain 102
Lozès, Patrick 4–5
Lucas-Dubreton, Jacques 67

Macarthy, Eugene Victor 81
Mallefille, Félicien 122, 132
Mansbach, Richard 70
Maquet, Auguste 4, 31, 33
Maran, René 102
Matheus, John 90, 123
Maurois, André 116
McKay, Claude 102
Memmi, Albert 93

Menken, Adah 24
Mérimée, Prosper 43
métissage (mixing): AD as symbol of 135–36; AD's praise of 46–48; and cultural assimilation 117–18; as universal 127; *see also* francophone cultural movement
Meurice, Paul 31
Michelet, Jules 3, 22
Mirecourt, Eugène de 30, 32–33
Mundimbe, V.Y. 147
Musset, Alfred de 27

Napoleon Bonaparte 20, 100
Nardal, Paulette 101
nation-state, as term 21
national identity and culture: AD's attitude toward 46–48; colonial inclusion in 6–10, 21–22, 33–34, 56–58, 59–61, 92–93, 114–15, 119; and counter-global identity formation 71–73, 74–77, 91–93, 97–101; *see also* francophone cultural movement
nègre, as term 30, 31, 99
Négritude Movement: AD associated with 125, 130, 133, 139–40, 141; connection to French culture 104–5; counter-global identity formation 97–101; criticism of 126–27; incorporation of New Negro Movement 102–3; view of AD as too assimilated 105–8
New Negro Movement *see* African Americans and New Negro Movement
Niles, Blair 64
Nodier, Charles 24, 39
Notebook of a Return to the Native Land (Césaire) 98, 99

Other/Othering: AD as exotic outsider 20–21, 23–29, 34; as concept 9, 18, 20–21; and French Caribbean self-perception 59–61, 96–97; *see also* colonialism; national identity and culture; race

Panthéon 133–36, 140–43
Parigot, Hippolyte 115
Paris, François de 19
Pavie, Victor 32, 34
Perrinon, François-Auguste 55, 56, 58
Petit-Rasselle, Roxane 141–42
Phillips, B. 80, 84
Picouly, Daniel 136
Pierre/Paul/Eau-de-Benjoin (servant of AD) 44–46
Pifteau, Benjamin 24
La Place des trois Dumas 64–65, **65**
politics: AD's election efforts in French metropole 50–51; candidacy elections in Guadeloupe 51, 55–59, 61; rivalry of Bissette and Schoelcher 51–55

Index

Poncelet, Christian 140–41
Portal, Frédéric de 19
Price, Hugh B. 79
Price-Mars, Jean 106

race: AD as exotic outsider 20–21, 23–29, 34; AD's ambiguity toward 41–46, 59–60, 131–32; AD's negative self-perception 34–40; AD's praise for racial mixing 46–48; and European/Western superiority 18–19, 28–29, 70–71, 94–96; experiencing prejudice 54; and inclusion in national identity 6–10, 21–22, 33–34, 56–58, 59–61, 92–93, 114–15, 119; racial attacks against AD 31–33; *see also* African Americans and New Negro Movement; francophone cultural movement; *Négritude* Movement; slavery
Rainsford, Marcus 89
Ranhofer, Charles 67
Renan, Ernst 142
La Revue des Colonies (periodical) 52–53
Ribbe, Claude 5, 141
Richard, Mondésir 56
Richardson, Willis 82–83
Rivers, W.N. 123
Robin, Charles 30
Rogers, J.A. 76, 77, 86–87, 88
Rolland, Sonia 5
Romand, Hippolyte 22
Romantic Movement 20, 28–29
Ruffin, George 88

Saint-Mar, Vicomtesse de 29, 38
Sainte-Beuve, Charles Augustin 29
Sartre, Jean-Paul 104
Schoelcher, Victor 51–55, 56, 58, 84, 85, 138
Schomburg, Arthur 7, 75, 80
Schopp, Claude 20, 138
Second Republic (1848–1852) 95
Séjour, Victor 81
Senghor, Léopold 97, 98, 101, 102, 104–5

slavery: citizenship after abolishment of 51, 95; commemorating abolishment 119–20; depictions 26; as exotic literary backdrop 20; impact on cultural acclivity 71–72, 76–77; and rivalry between abolitionists 51–55; separation from French metropole 19–20
Smith, James M'Cune 88
Socé, Ousmane 127
Société des Amis d'Alexandre Dumas (Dumas Society) 111, 133–34
Sonthonax, Léger-Félicité 100
Southwick, Albert 67, 78, 87

Taguieff, Pierre-André 6–7, 119
Thiébault, General 23–24
Third Republic (1871–1940) 95, 115
The Three Dumas (Anderson and Godoy) 88–89
Trouillot, Lyonel 138
Troyat, Henri 122
Tulard, Jean 143

usable past, as concept 72–73

Vastey, Baron de 64, 105
Verlaine, Paul 24
Vigny, Alfred de 36
Villemessant, Hippolyte de 14, 24, 34

Watkins, Alexandre Dumas 81–82
"We Wear the Mask" (Dunbar) 37
Wheatley, Phillis 76
white gaze 96
The Woman with the Velvet Necklace (AD) 47
Woodson, Carter G. 76, 90
Wright, Richard 99

Zimmerman, Daniel 36
Zola, Émile 139, 142, 143–44

www.ingramcontent.com/pod-product-compliance
Lightning Source LLC
Chambersburg PA
CBHW032057300426
44116CB00007B/776